CONTENTS

INTRODUCTION

Since its first publication in 1908, *The Wind in the Willows* has achieved over a hundred editions, and an average annual sale of about 80,000 copies. In its various editions today the annual figure runs into hundreds of thousands. *The Golden Age* and *Dream Days* have established themselves as minor classics of childhood. Yet their author remains a shadowy figure to the general public. This ignorance is mainly due to the curious fact that hardly anything has been written about him. The biography by Patrick Chalmers, produced a year after Grahame's death in 1932, has been long out of print, and is far from being a satisfactory account. The only other book about Grahame is a Sorbonne thesis by Mlle D. M. Fyrth, which appeared in 1937 and is virtually unobtainable in this country. My first aim in writing the present work, therefore, was simply to fill an inexplicable gap, and, incidentally, to pay tribute to an author who has always occupied a special place in my affections.

It became clear to me that, far from being simple, he was extremely subtle and complex; that he was not, in the normal sense of the word, a children's writer at all; and that he crystallized, in his life and writing, many profoundly important changes which affected English society towards the close of the nineteenth century.

Grahame described himself as a 'mid-Victorian'. This indicates, as it were, his natural centre of gravity. We are inclined to forget that he was a young man before 1880, and middle-aged by the turn of the century. He was, therefore, caught up emotionally in the events connected with Mid-Victorianism—the Industrial Revolution and its by-products, middle-class mercantilism and the collapse of agricultural society, scientific evolution and religious doubt. Like many other sensitive young men, he watched the decay of rural England with bleak horror, having been born early enough to understand just precisely what was being lost as railways and factories multiplied over the ravished countryside. He felt the tyrannous emptiness of a society which was rapidly losing all spontaneity, and which combined the pursuit of money with a rigid and authoritarian moral code.

Despite this, however, he (like many others in similar cases) not only continued to honour the obligations imposed by the hierarchy of family and society, but in some sense actively needed them; and thus two powerful elements were

BEYOND THE WILD WOOD

KENNETH GRAHAME
by John Sargent RA.

BEYOND THE WILD WOOD

THE WORLD OF KENNETH GRAHAME

AUTHOR OF

The Wind in the Willows

PETER GREEN

First published in Great Britain 1982 by
Webb & Bower (Publishers) Limited
9 Colleton Crescent, Exeter, Devon EX2 4BY
in association with
Signatures Limited
24a Gandy Street, Exeter, Devon EX4 3LS

Edited and designed by Peter Wrigley

Kenneth Grahame: A Biography
was first published in 1959
This redesigned, edited and abridged volume
with illustrations

British Library Cataloguing in Publication Data

Green, Peter
Beyond the wild wood.
1. Grahame, Kenneth
2. Authors, English—19th century—Biography
I. Title
823'.8 PR4727

ISBN 0-906671-44-2

Typeset by Busby's Typesetting and Design,
Exeter, Devon
Printed and bound by A. Wheaton and Company Limited,
Exeter, Devon

permanently at conflict in him. He compromised: outwardly he conformed with his society. But his inner self took revenge in satire and fantasy: at first openly, then by more oblique and subtle methods. Like Lear and Carroll, he found relief in the world of childhood, the animal fable, the potent symbols of fantasy. It was a compromise which many of his contemporaries had to make.

Partly through the lack of personal documents such as diaries, partly because Grahame was an essentially autobiographical writer, I have frequently (though with great caution) used his published work to explain or illuminate some aspect of his personality and to place Grahame against that background of social change which so profoundly affected him. His life, his writing, the ideas he absorbed, the code against which he rebelled, his private Hesperidean myth, all are interwoven and interdependent; it is impossible to separate them without distorting the total picture. My intention has been twofold: to illuminate certain aspects of the late nineteenth century through the example which Kenneth Grahame affords and, conversely, to explain Grahame himself in terms of the society which produced him. If I have succeeded even partially in either of these aims, I shall be well satisfied.

Kenneth Grahame
aged 60.

I

DRAGONS AND PTERODACTYLS

1859–67

> Vitality—that is the test; and, whatever its components, mere truth is not necessarily one of them. A dragon, for instance, is a more enduring animal than a pterodactyl. I have never yet met anyone who really believed in a pterodactyl; but every honest person believes in dragons—down in the back-kitchen of his consciousness.
>
> KENNETH GRAHAME: *Introduction to A Hundred Fables of Æsop*

We are so apt to associate Kenneth Grahame in our minds with everything that is rural and English—the Berkshire Downs, Oxford, the lazy reaches of the Thames round Cookham and Pangbourne—that we sometimes forget he was a thoroughbred Scot by birth. This provides one key to his character; like his compatriot Robert Louis Stevenson, he observed England essentially from the outside, and loved her more because he could never take her quite for granted. There was always for him in England, as in Italy, an element of that romance which is bred from unfamiliarity, the lure of the alien tradition.

During the nineteenth century the name of Grahame was a synonym, north of the Border, for solid respectability. Holders of it were liable, as like as not, to be advocates or accountants, though there was an occasional minister among them. When they broke into print, which was seldom, their books tended to be severely functional. In 1817 we find James Grahame, Advocate, penning his *Defence of Usury Laws.* In 1867 a namesake of his (an accountant this time) published *Financial Fenianism and the Caledonian Railway.* Yet a third James Grahame, also an accountant, produced in 1890 *Tables of Silver Exchanges,* and two years later *Mr Goschen's One Pound Note.* These books at least suggest a traditional background for the career in the Bank of England which Kenneth Grahame grudgingly undertook: he was very much in the position of the eldest son in an Army family who is compelled to swallow his pacifist convictions.

Such, temperamentally, were the Grahames: devout Calvinists, with a disposition towards the legal and financial professions. Yet there is always a hint, however conscientiously repressed, of artistic interests. A contemporary of

ELIZABETH GRAHAME.
Kenneth's mother died of scarlet fever when he was only five.

JAMES CUNNINGHAM GRAHAME
with his children. Kenneth is seated. Cunningham Grahame was shattered by his wife's death and he made arrangements for his children to live with their grandmother.

Kenneth's, a distant connection named George Grahame, actually became an art critic, and in 1895, the year *The Golden Age* was published, produced a book on Claude Lorraine; while Kenneth's own father, James Cunningham Grahame, gives every sign of having been a poet *manqué.*

Cunningham Grahame was born on 20 July 1830. He became an advocate, and apparently a popular one: a witty speaker whose *bons mots* were cherished in Parliament House. But he lacked the drive and ambition which then, as now, were essential to an Edinburgh lawyer. He was something of a hedonist; an easy-going *bon vivant,* and already, before tragedy overtook him, a heavy drinker. On 13 March 1855 he married Bessie Ingles, the beautiful daughter of David Ingles of Hilton, Lasswade, and brought her to his home at 32 Castle Street, opposite the site of Sir Walter Scott's former house. Here, during the next five years, she bore him three children: Helen in 1856, Thomas William ('Willie') in 1858, and Kenneth in 1859. Their early married life was extremely happy. They entertained a good deal, and moved in the best Edinburgh society: Cunningham Grahame could claim and substantiate a double line of descent from Robert the Bruce. His branch was 'presumed to be a Cadet of the Earls of Montrose', and his ancestors included Earls of Strathearn and Menteith. His dinner menus had a strong Nationalist flavour about them; yet, like the Lord of Abbotsford, when it came to drink his preference was not for whisky, but claret, of which he was a well-known connoisseur.

Kenneth was born on the morning of 8 March, and Dr James Simpson—Queen Victoria's 'Beloved Professor of chloroform fame'—attended the birth. When we have surveyed the adult Grahame's life and opinions, we shall be able to see how symbolically appropriate it was that his life should have begun in the year that it did. 1859 was a time of change, a watershed dividing the old era from the new. During those twelve months there appeared not only Darwin's *Origin of Species* but also John Stuart Mill's *On Liberty*: what Trevelyan described as the 'revolt against the tame acceptance of conventional opinions' had begun in earnest. Leigh Hunt, De Quincey, and Macaulay died; Dr Livingstone reached Lake Nyasa; Mr Gladstone was Chancellor of the Exchequer. The same thrifty, ambitious, materialistic businessmen who made a best-seller out of Samuel Smiles' newly published *Self Help* also welcomed Landseer's lions to Trafalgar Square. Patriotism and trade were indissolubly linked, and the foundation of the Volunteers that winter was prompted as much by concern for investments as a direct war scare. In the purely literary field two poems crystallized the official and 'irresponsible' elements of intelligent society: on the one hand Tennyson, with the first *Idylls of the King*, on the other Edward FitzGerald's translation of the seductively *fainéant* Omar Khayyám.

There is, indeed, more than a hint of the Persian poet's philosophy about Cunningham Grahame himself. He made a sufficient income without over-exertion; and for the rest there were his family, his many friends, the pleasures of Edinburgh society. Yet, as his subsequent behaviour showed, his was a far from tranquil nature; like many Scots he possessed a deep streak of pessimism, and his black moods were akin to fashionable modern *Angst*. It must have been some such mood which drove him to apply for a post which uprooted his family from Edinburgh. In May 1860, when Kenneth was little more than a year old, his father was appointed Sheriff-Substitute of Argyllshire, an unprecedented alien in Campbell country. The move took place at once.

The Sheriff-Substitute's seat of office was at Inveraray, not far from the castle of the Dukes of Argyll. But Cunningham Grahame decided to build his own house there: and for three years the family lived in temporary quarters down Loch Fyne, first at Ardrishaig, later in Lochgilphead. The Campbell workmen were clearly in no hurry to oblige a foreigner.

Kenneth's earliest memory, he declared in after years, was of 'shiny black buttons, buttons that dug into dusty, blue cloth', probably the upholstery of the railway carriage in which he travelled from Edinburgh. He also recalled the little paddle-steamer that delivered them to the quayside; and I suspect that a striking image from *The Wind in the Willows* may have been prompted by the first night he spent in this new and unfamiliar home, 'a child that has fallen happily asleep in its nurse's arms, and wakes to find itself alone and laid in a strange place, and searches corners and cupboards, and runs from room to room, despair growing silently in its heart'. But he soon settled down happily to this new life; indeed, the wild skies

INVERARAY CASTLE.
When the Grahames moved to Inveraray they were automatically invited to dine at the castle with the Duke and Duchess of Argyll. Mrs Grahame charmed the Duchess, who invited her to bring the children visiting.

and hills that ringed Loch Fyne, and more still the ever-present sea, left a powerful impression on his memory—'wind-shaken water, whip and creak and rattle of shrouds, flap of idle sails in halcyon spells, cry of gulls at pasture on the pale acres that know no plough ... a certain haunting smell of tar and weed'. Those were the happy years, years spent 'among the gleaming lochs and sinuous firths of the Western Highlands, where, twice a week maybe, the strange visitant crept by headland and bay, a piece of the busy, mysterious outer world'.

Here the young boy found what he was always in after-life to cherish: tranquillity. Here—already a little aloof from his brother and sister—he would wander along the beach, where the 'big black-sided fishing-boats' lay, or loaf on the pier, 'with its tranquil "lucid interval" between steamers, the ever recurrent throb of paddle-wheel, the rush and foam of beaten water among the piles, splash of ropes and rumble of gangways'. The local policeman was courting his nursemaid; so from time to time, as a treat, he would be rowed out into the bay, golden seaweed shimmering fathoms below, and look at the white yachts lying at anchor. It is not surprising that he hated the occasional trips away from this magic place to Edinburgh or elsewhere, and conceived a lively scorn for trains. Neither friendly porters nor the coat of arms emblazoned on the carriage door could endear this 'ungainly rattle-trap' to him; his only consolation was 'when suddenly it

Loch Fyne.
Under the wild skies and among the hills that ringed the loch the young Kenneth Grahame first acquired that habit of solitude which he was to preserve throughout his life.

rattled past some dingy town, [and] over the reeking house-tops there appeared a tangled tracery of masts, while a delicate waft of tar and harbour-mud breathed of the authentic, unsuspected Paradise at hand'.

Between Ardrishaig and neighbouring Lochgilphead, where they found better accommodation after a year or so, the Grahames spent the years 1860-62. Willie and Kenneth made friends with local fishermen, who carved model boats for them; there were cairn terriers at home, and gingerbread to be bought on the pier, and the fascinating spectacle of Highland girls baiting hooks with lug-worms. Kenneth's father would sometimes walk the harbour with him, quoting scraps of poetry, as he gazed at the masts and brown sails; it was here that Kenneth first heard, soon after its publication, a poem that was to haunt him all his life, Longfellow's 'Sea Memories'.

> I remember the black wharves and the slips
> And the sea-tides tossing free;
> And the Spanish sailors with bearded lips
> And the beauty and mystery of the ships
> And the magic of the sea.

In that remote spot the events of the outer world must have seemed immeasurably distant, almost irrelevant: Garibaldi's final triumph, the American Civil War, even the terrible Lancashire cotton famine. Perhaps only the death of the Prince Consort had any reality for the isolated family. Here, without doubt, Grahame first acquired that habit of solitude which he was to preserve throughout his life. We may suspect too that the Hesperides of which he so often and wistfully wrote derived at least in part from the dour yet romantic background of Loch Fyne, fjord-deep between tall dark hills, unchanging, hardly touched by the disease (as he saw it) of modern industrialism, instilling its own slow sea-rhythm into his childish consciousness.

The new home at Inveraray was ready in May 1863: a big house of Scottish granite, backed with pinewoods, and looking out over the loch. The Grahames were automatically invited, after a suitable interval, to dine at the Castle, and Bessie Grahame described the occasion in a letter to her mother: the Malcolms and MacNeils who were their fellow-guests, the silent young man whom she took (on account of his silence) to be a curate. We get the impression of a quick humorous eye, a highly vivacious personality. At any rate, Mrs Grahame charmed the Duchess. Not only was she invited to bring her children visiting the very next afternoon, but was offered the services of a Ducal gardener 'to help with the flower-beds at the new house'.

The Grahames' last child, Roland, was born on 16 March 1864, nearly five years after Kenneth. A day or two later his mother collapsed under a virulent attack of scarlet fever. Complications set in—scarlet fever was at that period still a highly dangerous disease—and on 4 April Bessie Grahame died. Her last, characteristic, words were: 'It's all been so lovely.' The same day Kenneth caught the infection, and for several weeks his life, too, was despaired of. Cunningham Grahame wrote to his own mother in Edinburgh, and the old lady came West to nurse her grandson.

Slowly, very slowly, the young Kenneth passed his crisis and began to mend. But the disease had weakened him permanently, leaving behind a characteristic legacy of recurrent bronchial complaints. In all other respects he was healthy enough; in fact he was to prove something of an athlete. But throughout his life his chest remained alarmingly vulnerable to any change of weather, and at least once, in the year of his marriage, he was again very near the point of death. It is, perhaps, not surprising that after such a childhood experience he developed so tenacious and full-blooded a love of the visible natural world. He was never consumptive as Richard Jefferies was, but he acquired something of the consumptive's intense interest in what can be seen, felt, tasted, absorbed: sunlight, good food and wine, Mediterranean landscapes, the small intricate life of field and hedgerow.

Cunningham Grahame was shattered by his wife's death. Like many essentially weak men, he was ill-equipped to absorb emotional shocks, and had clearly used his devotion to Bessie as a safeguard against aimless self-indulgence: her going seemed to destroy any vestige of ambition or responsibility he possessed. Plainly his attitude to her did not extend to his children; as soon as was decently possible he made arrangements for them all to go south to live with their maternal grandmother at Cookham Dene in Berkshire. A letter of Helen Grahame's suggests that he made little financial provision for them. He probably had always resented his children for diverting even part of Bessie's affections from himself; in a man of his type, intelligent, weak-willed, emotionally immature, the phenomenon is well known. Roland at least he may well have seen, in his misery, as the direct cause of her death; they were all an intolerable reminder of what he had lost, to be pushed out of sight and forgotten. When they were gone he himself remained at Inveraray, indifferent to the shocked whispers of his neighbours, alone in the great granite house with his cellar of claret and his black self-pity.

Not once in all his published work does Kenneth Grahame mention either his mother or his father; yet their absence can be felt in nearly everything he wrote. At the beginning of *The Golden Age* comes the one direct hint, a notable and characteristic understatement: 'Looking back to those days of old, ere the gate shut to behind me, I can see now that to children with a proper equipment of parents these things would have worn a different aspect.' From the loss of his mother he never, in fact, altogether recovered: his attitude to his wife was at least in part that of a son. His father he seems to have excluded from his emotions altogether; twenty years later the diary entries made on the day of Cunningham Grahame's death display a cold, clinical indifference. But for the moment the child's natural resilience was uppermost. On the way south, in Stirling, he was preoccupied to the exclusion of all else by a large rubber ball in a toyshop, and before he reached Cookham Dene was speculating wildly on the superlative, ideal qualities of this new grandmother. The reality, as he hinted many years later, he found 'a slight disappointment. Of course by this time we are well aware of the superlative and abiding charm of our grandmothers; or else we have learnt by sad experience not to expect very much from any of our relations.'

Granny Ingles, of The Mount, Cookham Dene, was certainly a formidable character, 'a strong-minded woman and had her own way as far as she could', her grandson Reginald recalled in after years. And Helen, with that brisk meiosis so characteristic of the ex-matron, wrote in 1936: 'I don't suppose she could be described as a child-lover.' This was, perhaps, not entirely just, and indeed Helen herself modifies her verdict: 'It was hard no doubt at the age of sixty, having brought up her own family of five sons and a daughter to have us landed upon her, enough to try anyone's temper ... our grandmother's income was a small one and if our uncle had not helped us I don't know what would have become of us.' Mrs Ingles had certainly been highly attached, in an authoritative sort of way, to her own children. Most of her sons had careers in the Armed Services, and her granddaughter Bessie Luard (who thought her 'a very wonderful woman') recalled having heard 'my Father often say in joke that she sat on the steps of the Admiralty and the War Office till they did what she required for her sons.' All sources of evidence agree that she was, in her own way, very sociable and an excellent talker, who used to tell her adopted brood 'stories about Wallace and Bruce—as Scottish history'. She was a Presbyterian, but for some inscrutable reason of her own always went to the Church of England Low Church. Helen admitted that Mrs Ingles 'was not strict except about our table manners,' but Helen herself by this time was already being enrolled as an adjutant to Authority, and probably found the disciplining of her unruly younger brothers a congenial task. Nevertheless, her summing up—'if she treated us with "kindness according to the needs of the flesh" as Kenneth says we could not expect more'—seems to reach the heart of the matter.

However strictly the family obligation might be honoured, the four Grahame children must have strained the charity of a not particularly well-off woman in her sixties. She did her duty by them, in the outward sense; but she could not summon up the emotional warmth on which children so desperately depend. She was clearly a strong-willed and autocratic woman, used to getting her own way, and impervious to argument. The financial burden which her grandchildren represented cannot have sweetened her temper towards them; and her Presbyterian conscience may well have been satisfied by the more material aspects of parental care But there is no reason to suppose that the young Grahames suffered the kind of childhood that Kipling or even 'Saki' did. There was no cruelty in the positive sense, merely emotional deprivation of a rather subtle kind, and in the background a nagging sense of money-trouble.

Granny Ingles of The Mount, Cookham Dene.
Mrs Ingles became the formidable guardian of the Grahame children after the death of their mother in 1864.

There is, too, much to suggest that in ways those short years at The Mount were among the happiest of Kenneth's life. Certainly they made the most profound impression on him. In 1907, a year after he had returned to Cookham Dene as a married man, with a son of about the same age as he himself had been in 1865, Constance Smedley records him as saying: 'I feel I should never be surprised to

THE MOUNT, COOKHAM DENE.
The short years that Kenneth spent here as a boy were among the happiest of his life. When he returned in 1907, his memories were so clear that he 'should never be surprised to meet myself as I was when a little chap of five, suddenly coming round a corner...'.

meet myself as I was when a little chap of five, suddenly coming round a corner ... The queer thing is, I can remember everything I felt then, the part of my brain I used from four till about seven can never have altered. Coming back here wakens every recollection. After that time I don't remember anything particularly.'

What was it about The Mount which affected him so powerfully? Following the best romantic tradition, it was probably the place itself and the countryside round it. All through his adult life this exiled Scot never strayed far from the soft hills and rich soil of Berkshire, so different from the sea-lochs and granite he had known as a child in the Western Highlands. It was as if he deliberately sought out the warm, friendly, tolerant south as an antidote to that repressive puritanism he always associated with his own background.

To such a child his first glimpse of The Mount must have been unforgettable. For all Mrs Ingles' penuriousness, it was by any standards a beautiful and spacious property. The house was originally a hunting-box, and a great tree in the grounds, 300 years old, marks the former edge of Windsor Forest. The gardens and orchard cover several acres; the eye travels over wide lawns and trim yew hedges to a glimpse of Cliveden on a distant hillside. Round the house stand magnificent copper beeches, and the garden descends in terraced levels, decorated with flagged lily-ponds, low Italian walls, and ponderous stone flower-pots. The orchard is wild enough to contain any number of buffalo or pirates, while the house itself might have been specially made for children. The leaded windows, the old Dutch tiles, the heavy beams made out of ships' timbers, the twisting staircase leading up to a dusty, vaulted attic under the eaves—all must have been a paradise through which the young Grahames roamed in a private dream, only occasionally bothered by the claims of their latest governess or tutor.

'Hunt Them as Bisons Scattered Over the Vast Prairie'
E. H. Shepard's drawing for 'Dies Irae' in *Dream Days*.

As Kenneth lost sympathy with this new adult world, so he retreated more and more into his own 'countries of the mind'. The conditions were perfect for the incubation of just such a dream-world as was to haunt Grahame for many years to come. The imaginary City which recurs again and again in his work (most notably, perhaps, in 'The Roman Road') was first built in that roomy attic at The Mount, known to the children (whose private domain it became) as 'the Gallery'. Chalmers writes: 'The City was ... kept strictly in the Gallery. Except on Sunday. On Sunday it became mentionable beyond the Gallery door, but only upon the way to church, but only if out of earshot of elder persons. Then, on the dusty churchward mile, the previous week passed under close review; then all mortals encountered, Sunday to Saturday, in a world of workaday, were weighed in the balance. Those found worthy were forthwith proposed and elected freemen of the City. Those found wanting—was there not a savage pleasure in excluding them, in having the golden barriers clash to...?' The natural inclination which children have to form a world of their own was here intensified by the feeling the Grahame children must have had of *not belonging:* they were thrown, in several senses, on their own resources.

This general atmosphere tallies so exactly with that of *The Golden Age* and *Dream Days* that it is essential to clarify how far the two books can be admitted as biographical evidence. We cannot, obviously, treat them as pure autobiography, though there is no doubt that they are largely based on the Grahames' life at Cookham Dene.

The best point from which to start, is the anonymous narrator; though even here we must make allowances for Grahame's desire to idealize his childhood self. In 1931 he wrote to a curious enquirer: 'The "boy" somehow never had a name, so I suppose at this late period he must just go on being anonymous.' But at the time of composition he had been less reticent, as Helen Dunham recalled after his death in a letter to his wife: 'We first met in 1896, after *The Golden Age* had come out ... I remember speaking to Mr Grahame of "The Roman Road"—and he said: "Ah I'm glad you like that because it was more or less myself", and when I said something of having been afraid that he might grow up, he said "No—I don't think I shall—I've just been writing about a circus and I found I didn't feel a bit grown up".' We can assume, then, that in a broad sense the 'I' of *The Golden Age* and its sequel at least represents Grahame's early attitude to life as he himself later recalled it.

This boy has a strongly marked and individual character. He simultaneously resents and envies the arbitrary power exercised by his elders. He has the emotional precocity often to be found in orphans or foster-children. His tendency to solitariness is pronounced, and causes him some twinges of conscience; these children live by a positively hierarchical common code, and the individualist is not encouraged: 'I waited until they were both thoroughly absorbed, and then I slipped through the hedge out of the trodden highway, into the vacant meadow spaces. It was not that I was unsociable ... but the passion and the call of the divine morning were high in my blood.' This is the authentic Wordsworthian note; Kenneth was to wander 'lonely as a cloud' for the rest of his life. From the beginning his love of Nature—that ambivalent abstraction—was considerably higher than his love of humanity.

The *alter ego* of *The Golden Age* also goes out of his way—beyond the normal derision natural to a young boy—to mock and sneer at girls in general and the whole network of personal social relationships they involve one in. Girls are the inferior sex in every way. 'I can't make out what they find to talk about', Edward complains, and the Narrator replies: 'What they'll be when they're men'. His own infatuation, in 'Mutabile Semper', provokes him to a devastating piece of satire, all the more effective for its feather-light obliquity. The girl in question is made to reveal in turn her squeamishness, her passion for worming out secrets and then giving them away, her shameless capacity for emotional blackmail. She is house-proud, materialistic, and possessions-conscious; bossy and egotistic; sharp-tongued, authoritarian, flirtatious. She has all the ghastly feminine failings known to mankind, and unrolls them in the space of ten pages. The largest concession this premature misogynist will make is that 'when you have girls about the place, they have got to be considered to a certain extent'.

Other characteristics can be gathered from chance allusions. He is indifferent to the morality of property rights, but suffers guilty qualms at the sight of a village whipping-post; he likes to strum at random on a piano because scales are associated with adult discipline; he supposes that sundials wind up, and tends to take the worn clichés and metaphors of his elders at their literal face value. He dislikes the

'You Haven't Been to Rome, Have You?'
The imaginary City which recurs again and again in Grahame's work is the backdrop for the meeting of the boy and the artist who had been to Rome. Grahame admitted that the boy was 'more or less myself.' The illustration for 'The Roman Road' is by Maxfield Parrish.

moral precepts with which they hedge anything to do with money. He is liable to periodic fits of violent depression and pessimism. He hates all 'courtesies, welcomes, explanations and other court-chamberlain kind of business'—a trait which he later passed on to Badger. He is naturally generous, and (though loath to admit it) genuinely attached to his brothers and sisters. He is conscious of an occasional temptation to act as a buffer between them and the grown-ups, to play the 'Blameless Prig'. He is an expert on the fauna of the American continent, and a willing but incompetent hand with a paint-box. His natural temperament is conservative; he has an absolute passion for stability, discipline, the sense of a fixed order in life; and his worst fits of brooding and misery are provoked by such occasions as the departure of a governess, or Edward's metamorphosis into an alien schoolboy—when he is left to contemplate the 'raw new conditions of our changed life'. The acuteness of his misery can be gauged from the fact that it is for him something physical—it leaves a dull bruise, it is like a beating, it gives one 'a dull, bad sort of pain low down inside', a pain which can even resemble 'a corporeal wound'.

Some of these qualities may derive from adult hindsight but in general they square very well with what we know about the conditions of the Grahames' existence at Cookham Dene. They suggest how violent in fact was the emotional wrench that uprooted these children from their family atmosphere and transplanted them to the thin soil of relatives' charity. Nevertheless, the 'Olympians' that Kenneth actually knew were far from being monsters; at the worst they were unimaginative and irritable. There is every reason to suppose that he later fictionalized them almost completely in order to extend his satirical attack to a specific class of contemporary English society.

Who, in fact, among his relations was he in constant contact with during this period? His grandmother, indeed, was omnipresent; but the only other relative that we know to have actually *lived* at The Mount (and even then for two years only) was her son David, Bessie Grahame's twin brother. The Rev. David Ingles was in his early thirties, a graduate of Edinburgh Academy and Trinity College, Cambridge, where in 1860 he had acquired a rowing Blue. His previous curacy had been at Stoke-on-Trent; he was appointed to Cookham Dene in 1864—an appointment which suggests that Mrs Ingles could charm the ecclesiastical authorities no less than the War Office. He lived with her and the Grahame children till his marriage in 1866. Helen Grahame recalled that he 'made a great deal of us, taking us on the river and to see his friends at Bisham and elsewhere'. Perhaps it was from Uncle David that Kenneth first acquired his passion for 'messing about in boats'.

No other relative appears to have been in contact with the Grahame children with sufficient regularity to justify Kenneth's resentment and hatred of relatives as a class. But this resentment rises to almost pathological levels—openly in *Pagan Papers*, with greater discretion in *The Golden Age*.

The most concise statement Grahame makes anywhere about his personal objections to relatives as such as in a piece called 'Justifiable Homicide', written in 1891, where he puts forward humorous arguments (reminiscent of De Quincey's 'Murder as One of the Fine Arts) for their extinction. They are abominably stingy; they 'have crammed their victim full of precepts, rules of conduct, moral maxims, and most miscellaneous counsel; all which he intuitively suspected at the time, and has ascertained by subsequent experience, to be utterly worthless'. This summing-up, while it largely confirms the evidence of the other books, adds one very interesting fact: Grahame resented meanness over money in adults. Perhaps he

COOKHAM VILLAGE, c1883.
In May 1906, after thirty years of London life, Kenneth Grahame returned to the country at last. With the whole of the Home Counties to choose from, Grahame went back to the very centre of his childhood: Cookham Dene. As he wrote of Mole in *The Wind in the Willows*, 'the wafts from his old home pleased, whispered, conjured, and finally claimed him imperiously.'

looked on half-crowns as a tangible substitute for that affection which the Olympians could not give, a substitute which they were in duty bound to provide. Yet, ironically, it was one of the few unlikeable traits which in after years he himself acquired: something more than good Scots thrift. We always tend to condemn our own weaknesses most violently in others.

In December 1865 one of the chimneys at The Mount fell in a heavy gale, and old Mrs Ingles became nervous about the others. It was at this point that Uncle John Grahame, Cunningham Grahame's brother, persuaded her to move to a different and considerably smaller house. John Grahame was a Parliamentary Agent, a partner in the firm of Grahame, Currie and Spens; and it is clear from a letter of Helen Grahame's that he had made himself at least partially responsible for the *ménage* at The Mount. It seems probable that he had been exerting pressure on Mrs Ingles for some time, and found that the chimneys did the trick.

At all events, in the spring of 1866 Mrs Ingles and her brood of grandchildren left The Mount and its spacious acres for Fernhill Cottage, Cranbourne. Once again, after putting down tentative roots in Berkshire soil, Kenneth and the rest were (as it seemed to them) arbitrarily transplanted once more, as if they were part of the luggage, without feelings or free will. To a child with Kenneth's passion for the fixed order of things such migrations—and the half-knowledge that they were forced by financial pressure—must have been profoundly disturbing.

Nevertheless there were compensations. The cottage was leased from Mr Algernon Gilliatt, who was a cousin of Uncle David's newly-married wife Anna, and became a close friend of the family while they remained there. It was at Cranbourne, too, that David Ingles introduced the Grahames to a man who was to influence the course of Kenneth's life irrevocably: William Lidderdale, the future Governor of the Bank of England. Helen writes: 'Mr Lidderdale's only connection with Cranbourne was that his wife's mother Mrs Busk lived at Ascot Place, Winkfield, about two miles away. The Lidderdales used to come to stay with her in the summer and we went over to see our old nurse Ferguson and the Lidderdale children. But Mrs Busk was an old friend of Grannie's and we were always at Ascot Place.'

By this time Kenneth's literary tastes had begun to show themselves, chiefly in his disconcerting habit of chanting such infectious stuff as *The Lays of Ancient Rome* on walks through the pinewoods. Conyngham Ellis, the Vicar of Cranbourne, may have fostered this tendency, though Helen asserts, oddly, that Kenneth never had lessons in Cranbourne. She herself seems to have viewed her brother from this moment on with some suspicion. 'It was at Cranbourne', she writes, 'that Kenneth began to spout poetry, first Shakespeare, then Macaulay's *Lays,* then Tennyson', as if such behaviour was somehow reprehensible. In later years she was to observe to enquiring friends: 'Oh we don't go in for Kenneth, you know.' Yet Helen herself wrote some charming occasional verses—in private. The family tradition of the Grahames did not encourage literature: they believed in pterodactyls, not dragons.

Kenneth seems to have struck most response at this period from his cousin Reginald Ingles, who was several years his junior. Major Ingles recalled of his visits to Fernhill Cottage that Kenneth 'was the nice one, who was always kind, and who we were always delighted to see—and to go out with, who never ticked us off, and was always ready to help one in little things. ... Willie and Helen we did not like very much ...'. Already, it seems, Kenneth was becoming isolated from those he most needed emotionally.

Then came a fresh surprise, which momentarily raised Kenneth's hopes only to disappoint them once more. In that same summer of 1866 an unexpected letter reached Cranbourne from Inveraray: James Cunningham Grahame had suddenly decided to summon his family home. We cannot be certain of his motives. He may have felt a genuine fit of remorse and affection; he may have supposed that the presence of children would help him to fight his crippling alcoholism. At the lowest level, it may have been a move to make some show of social respectability, and so safeguard his official position.

At all events, the children left Fernhill Cottage and travelled north once more, as Kenneth recalls in 'The Romance of the Rail', 'through the furnace-lit

Midlands, and on till the grey glimmer of dawn showed stone walls in place of hedges, and masses looming up on either side; till the bright sun shone upon brown leaping streams and purple heather, and the clear, sharp northern air streamed in through the windows.' They went with excitement and high hopes; but it was useless. Their father's resolution soon spent itself when they were present in the flesh, and by now, too, the time had almost been reached when through his heavy drinking he would no longer be fit for the duties of a Sheriff.

For nearly a year they stayed at Inveraray, witnesses to their father's slow moral and physical disintegration; then Cunningham Grahame resolved the dilemma himself. He resigned his post in the spring of 1867, and went abroad. For twenty years he scraped a wretched living in France, probably by teaching English, and died alone in a cheap Le Havre apartment house. As far as we know none of his children saw or communicated with him throughout the whole of those twenty years. But Kenneth, at least, could not rid himself of the vain dream with which he had travelled north. Not for the first time in the young boy's life there had been an ugly split between hope and fulfilment, dream and reality. He was eight years old. Who can blame him if he clung with desperate and increasing intensity to the dream?

Quarry Wood, Cookham Dene.
Approached from Marlow, Quarry Wood forms a dark band above the flat meadows of the Thames valley. The wood formed the basis of Grahame's description of 'The Wild Wood'.

'Crossing the Hall, They Passed Down one of the Principal Tunnels.'
Colour plate by Arthur Rackham. Kenneth Grahame's description of Badger's house was possibly based on Welbeck Abbey. The eccentric activities of the fifth Duke of Portland, who disappeared for weeks at a time and who built himself underground rooms and passages at Welbeck, came to light during a court case in 1907.

Cliveden Reach.
From Cookham Lock the River Thames flows past the steep,
wooded slopes that form part of the Cliveden estate.

Sculling Boat Amongst the Willows.

The Thames at Cookham.
During his early childhood at Cookham, Grahame first acquired
his passion for the River Thames which lasted until his death at the
riverside village of Pangbourne, further upstream.

Cookham Backwater.
Below the weir at Cookham, away from the frothy mainstream, the shallow
backwater flows under the shady willows and alder.

II

THE SPELL OF OXFORD

1868–75

Nothing made a deeper impression on Grahame's mind than the beginning of his school-days: they mark the close of an era. Henceforward dream and reality are separated for ever, and the precarious private world the children had created exists only in memory. Once again it is an adult decree which shatters their defences. In 1868 (probably at Uncle John Grahame's urging) 'the word had gone out, the school had been selected; the necessary sheets were hemming even now, and Edward [*i.e.* Kenneth and Willie] was the designated and appointed victim'. At that grisly farewell scene on the station platform the narrator recalls: 'Fortunately I was not old enough to realize ... that here on this little platform the old order lay at its last gasp, and that Edward might come back to us, but it would not be the Edward of yore, nor could things ever be the same thing.' (It is interesting that Grahame describes *from the spectator's viewpoint* a departure in which he himself was involved: as if in fact his true self was being left behind.) And indeed he is only too well justified in his forebodings; when Edward does come home after one term he is translated into an alien being 'ragged of attire and lawless of tongue, a scorner of tradition and an adept in strange new physical tortures, one who would in the same half-hour dismember a doll and shatter a hallowed belief'.

Here, in fact, is the first whiff of the Olympians' own world: arbitrary, pragmatic, unimaginative, custom-bound, and strongly hostile to the pleasures of fantasy. Because it is laid down by immutable decree, this ordeal of school is unavoidable: henceforth one must live in the enemy's camp, wear his colours and mouth his public shibboleths. What is more insidious is the possibility that one may come to believe in them—'can it be that I also have become an Olympian?' Though the inner self clings to its old truth still, and the double personality preserves its countries of the mind, a permanent conflict has been set up. The pleasures of maturity, as Grahame made very clear in his two childhood books, have their own peculiar seductiveness for the youthful imagination.

It was 'on or about Michaelmas Day, 1868,' Grahame wrote in 1932, a few months before his death, when 'a bright and eager (sullen, reluctant, very ordinary-looking) youth of nine summers sprang lightly (descended reluctantly, was haled ignominiously) onto the arrival platform of the Great Western Railway

Station at Oxford.' During the weeks of anticipation dread had been mixed with hopeful excitement. 'According to some it meant larks, revels, emancipation, and a foretaste of the bliss of manhood. According to others—the majority, alas!—it was a private and peculiar Hades, that could give the original institution points and a beating.' Certainly at first the majority seemed to have been the more accurate prophets. St Edward's School had only been recently founded, and somewhat anarchic conditions still prevailed there. The Headmaster, Mr Fryer, 'would hide pence and halfpence and turn us all out in the dark to look for them. ... Pits were dug and filled with mud and water, and over them, and into them, the unsuspecting ones were lured.' The upper boys were liable to go on strike; one, who was believed to wear a corset as a protection against caning, 'being told to report himself to the Head seized the easel and announced aloud that he would knock the Head down with it'. Notwithstanding this, St Edward's was a highly religious foundation; about one boy in seven took orders, and twenty masters were ordained during residence.

It was not, perhaps, an entirely sympathetic atmosphere; and Grahame has left us a picture of 'a small school-boy, new kicked out of his nest into the draughty, uncomfortable outer world, his unfledged skin still craving the feathers whereinto he was wont to nestle. The barrack-like school, the arid, cheerless class-rooms, drove him to Nature for redress; and, under an alien sky, he would go forth and wander along the iron road by impassive fields, so like yet so unlike those hitherto a part of him.' The discipline in this respect was easy-going. Within certain limits boys were allowed to wander where they liked, and Grahame took full advantage of this: there was, as he noted, no games tyranny.

At first he was very much a hermit-crab *sans* shell, clearly unused to the conventions prevailing in such an establishment. But within a day or two of his first arrival Kenneth had a taste of discipline fiercer and more arbitrary than his domestic Olympians could ever have conceived. In a prize-giving speech at St Edward's School he related:

> The junior form, or class, was in session, so to speak, and I was modestly occupying that position, at the very bottom, which seemed to me natural enough, when the then Headmaster entered—a man who had somehow formed an erroneous idea of my possibilities. Catching sight of me, he asked, sternly, 'What's that thing doing down there?' The master in charge could only reply that whether it was crass ignorance or invincible stupidity, he wotted not, but there it was. The Headmaster, who was, I was persuaded, a most illogical man, and could not really have studied that immortal work, the *Republic* of Plato, in which the principles of ideal justice are patiently sought out, merely remarked that if the thing—meaning me—was not up there or near it, pointing to the head of the form, before the close of work, it was to be severely caned; and left the room.

It is pleasant to record that the rest of the form achieved undreamed of heights of stupidity in order to avert the worst; but Kenneth, who was unused to being 'savaged by big, beefy, hefty, hairy men called masters', promptly burst into tears

KENNETH GRAHAME
as a new boy at St Edwards School, Oxford. Grahame described himself as a 'small school-boy, new kicked out of his nest into the draughty, uncomfortable outer world. ...'

of horror and bewilderment. 'What maggot had tickled the brain of the Headmaster on that occasion,' he wrote, 'I never found out. Schoolmasters never explain, never retract, never apologize.' He was, as he himself admits, a little chap, and unused to physical punishment. He had been doing his best, 'and at home I had not been considered an absolute fool'. Now he had run full tilt into the public school tradition of arbitrary assault. It was a salutary shock, and he quickly adapted himself to this new, unbelievable world, horseplay and all. But he never jettisoned his own basic beliefs; he merely learnt that in public they must either be concealed or presented indirectly.

It is a tribute to his toughness, resilience and inner resources that he not only survived his seven years at St Edward's, but did extremely well there in every way. After his rough initiation, he settled down to prove himself as conventional a public schoolboy as the best of them. He gained his 1st XV Colours for Rugger ('a useful forward; always upon the ball, lacks weight and strength'); was Secretary of the 2nd XI at cricket; shot at Wimbledon; and spent his last four terms, from Michaelmas 1874 onwards, as Senior Prefect, or Head of School. He won prizes for Divinity and Latin Prose in 1874, and the Sixth Form Class prize in 1875. It was a solid and respectable progression. Yet I suspect strongly that much of this performance was executed at least partially tongue in cheek. Grahame's first known appearance in print, at the age of fourteen, was with an essay entitled 'The

Good and Bad Effects of Rivalry', which was printed in the school *Chronicle*, 'to encourage care in ... composition', Even a St Edward's master, writing in 1913, admits that this 'shows no promise of the exquisite prose that was to be in later years the delight of thousands.' What he fails to add is that it displays a breathtaking and calculated sanctimoniousness.

'...It certainly is a very difficult thing in practice to feel kindly towards a rival, and to anyone but to one who always bears in mind one of the chief duties of a Christian, to love one another, and keeps a good control over himself, it is a very difficult thing...' writes the future author of *Pagan Papers*, who knew, no less than Stalky, what would please the muscular Christians set in authority over him. Nowhere else does he display anything but amused contempt for the official creed as practised in the 'days when one was young and Godless, and went to church'. Of his elders he observed: 'No irresistible Energy haled them to church o' Sundays; yet they went there regularly of their own accord, though they betrayed no greater delight in the experience than ourselves.' He constantly attacks the empty social formula which the Victorian Sabbath had become, the aesthetic tastelessness of the services: but his most biting satire is reserved for Puritanism—hell-fire preachers, missionaries, Original Sin, the discipline of 'barbed-wires and Sunday schools'.

Even so it was impossible for Grahame to preserve a completely orthodox front; the anti-authoritarian streak in him was too strong. He found a convenient and legitimate outlet in the Debating Society, where his most outrageous opinions could pass as cheerful coat-trailing. He 'considered a lawyer was only doing his duty when he defended a client whom he knew to be guilty'. He supported cremation, a more provocative thing to do then than now: but 'the hideous utilitarian phantom was banished by a large majority'. He bombarded the House with statistics on Free Trade, and 'thought the custom of duelling had gone far to sustain the honour of the country'. Only once, in 1875, did he show his hand on a religious topic, but then he by no means minced his words. In a debate on the relative merits of Queen Elizabeth and Queen Mary, we read:

> K. Grahame, who was on the opposition side of the house, said there was nothing to choose between the characters of the two Queens. One was a bigoted Catholic, the other a spiteful Protestant. He read to the house a passage from a work entitled 'The Student's Hume', but did not justify the opposition view of the question by drawing any deductions from his quotation.

Even in 1875 Hume, who explained moral principles in terms of habit and social custom, and supposed that religion arose 'from the incessant hopes and fears which actuate the human mind', would have been fairly strong meat for an orthodox Anglican schoolmaster. Perhaps wisely, the young empiricist only released this broadside in his last term.

At the same time, that is when he was in the Sixth, he was devoting a good deal of his time and energy to the *Chronicle*, which had been started by a contemporary of his, Trant ('Tichy') Chambers. Chambers edited it, and Grahame supplied many original contributions, all unfortunately anonymous. We can hazard a guess, but no more than a guess, at the identity of some of them. 'The Dress and Manner of the Man', for instance, agrees very well with Grahame's early dandyism. 'Tomorrow,' he told a friend on the eve of Gaudy Day, 'tomorrow I shall be superb.' It is a touch worthy of the young Beerbohm. 'On the Road', too, strikes a note we shall find recurring again and again later: 'Let us then have done for a while at least with the hurry-scurry of artificial locomotion, with railway, coach, or bicycle, to wit, and use our natural powers of movement.'

It is interesting and characteristic that Grahame's memories of his school-days are far more concerned with visual impressions of places and objects than anecdotes about his contemporaries. 'Misty recollections of friends—clear and distinct of desk, stair, cistern, room' he noted. He shows a lively curiosity about the old school building in New-Inn-Hall Street, which was abandoned for a better site, known as Summertown, in 1873:

> On the left, or west side, first you have the buildings composing the Hall itself, the 'Tavern' of Verdant Green's days, where the buttery was open all day; then the grounds and solid Georgian vicarage of St Something-le-Baily ... —a pleasant jumble. On the right or east side were two little two-storied white gabled houses, of the sort common enough in Oxford then, and of which a few specimens still remain, running up to the old, fifteenth-century, back gate of Frewen Hall. Then came St Edward's, a stone-built mansion of two stories, reaching to the end and then 'returned', as architects say.

Here, in this pleasant Queen Anne house, Kenneth Grahame spent five of his seven years at school. Everything, 'in those troglodyte days', as he puts it, was very primitive. There was no Sixth Form, merely Big Boys. The house was obviously overcrowded: the boys slept five or six to a bedroom, and conditions upstairs were 'rabbit-warrenish'. The matron, Mrs Reece, seems to have been a kindly soul, and in sympathy with the boys rather than the masters. She used to come and help the smaller fry wash in the morning, and would occasionally smuggle a particularly dispirited urchin into the kitchen where (like Martha in *The Golden Age*) she proceeded to regale him with bread and treacle. If a master was heard approaching, a heap of dirty towels served as camouflage.

There were at that time few organized games, which may explain why the boys were allowed to spend so much of their free time exploring the neighbourhood. In 'Oxford through a Boy's Eyes' Grahame includes an anecdote which shows how quickly he conformed with the new régime:

> Some sort of stable, or garden, gateway gave issue on the street northwards; but this was never used, and I only happen to remember it because on my first Guy Fawkes Day we boys attempted a private bonfire, thinking, in our artless way, that in Oxford bonfires were the rule rather than the exception. The authorities, however, thought otherwise, and firemen and police battered at the stable gate aforesaid till explanations ensued and till, I suppose, somebody was squared as usual.

After the move to Summertown, a more organized curriculum was introduced, in which games played a larger part. Grahame, as we have seen, showed himself an excellent all-round sportsman; but he probably looked back with nostalgia to the more leisured days at New-Inn-Hall Street, a supposition confirmed by the fact that he nowhere gives a description of life at Summertown. The well-ordered White House cricket ground, for instance, could never replace in his estimation those hilarious games played on Port Meadow. The sole advantage Port Meadow possessed as a cricket pitch was an absence of boundaries:

> If an ambitious and powerful slogger wanted to hit a ball as far as Wolvercote, he could do so if he liked; there was nothing to stop him, and the runs would be faithfully run out. The chief drawback was that the city burgesses used the meadow for pasturage of their cows—graminivorous animals of casual habits. When fielding was 'deep', and frenzied cries of 'Throw her up!' reached one from the wicket, it was usually more discreet to feign a twisted ankle or a sudden faintness, and allow some keener enthusiast to recover the ball from where it lay.

It is a scene which would have delighted A. G. Macdonell.

But nothing, not even Port Meadow cricket, could compare with the delights of 'exploring, exploring, always exploring, in a world I had not known the life of before'. Inveraray and The Mount had contributed their share to Grahame's undiscovered City; now it was Oxford's turn, and Rome would come later. On a page of notes for the memoirs he never began Grahame scribbled, apropos his schooldays: 'What one took away: the Spell of Oxford;' and another fragment he left pays the city tribute:

> In that gracious grey old city of our abiding, well-watered, of pleasant approach by bridge that bestrode the brimfull river or causeway through standing water lily-starred, grey straying side-streets looped or nestled all along the four noble thoroughfares rich in tower and steeple—the home of restless jackdaws forth-issuing day-long; the organ-mouth of bell-music vocal through daylight most passionately appealing at the quiet close of evening. ...

Oxford in Grahame's schooldays was indeed a fascinating lure for an imaginative boy. To begin with, all the streets (except the newly macadamized High) were still paved with mediaeval cobbles: even the Broad and St Giles. This was not only picturesque; it discouraged traffic. The few ancient hansoms and flies were mainly in demand for the beginning and end of term, to make the long trip between the colleges and a decently secluded railway station. There were no bicycles, and—if one can imagine Oxford without them today—no cars. Morris-Cowley still lay in the womb of time. As R. W. Macan pointed out: 'Unless you were wealthy and kept a horse, you trusted mainly to your own legs for locomotion. Pedestrianism was still the joy of the reading man in the Oxford of the "seventies". But then, he still had the unravished country of the Scholar Gipsy to wander over, with or without a companion. ... Oxford was still a duodecimo city in those days. The country began just beyond the bridges.'

In this mediaeval paradise Grahame wandered, hour after hour, rapturous and obsessed. With no one to ask questions, as at home, or make 'tedious talk of delphiniums and greenfly and such', he strolled in and out of the Fellows' Gardens;

HIGH STREET, OXFORD, c1885.
The 'good grey gothic' of Oxford contributed its share to Grahame's undiscovered City. Grahame wandered, rapturous and obsessed, 'along the ... noble thoroughfares rich in tower and steeple—the home of restless jackdaws forth-issuing day long'.

he sampled the Arabian Nights' catholicity which, then as now, characterized the Market. 'It seemed,' he recalled, 'to have everything the heart of man could desire, from livestock at one end to radiant flowers in pots at the other.' He window-gazed in the High, lingering at the smart tailors' displays. Before he was ten he knew by heart 'all the stately buildings that clustered round the Radcliffe Library', even finding time for wonder at the 'exceeding nigritude and decay' of the Sheldonian Caesars, and the general blackness of the University buildings; this, he thought, 'might have been put on with a brush, in a laudable attempt to produce the "sub-fusc" line required in the attire of its pupils'.

Brasenose Lane held flesh-creeping delights; in this gloomy *couloir* Grahame and his friends were shown the precise window at which a horned and hoofed Devil appeared, one Sunday night, to the members of the Hell Fire Club. Here a stray traveller witnessed the fearful scene: Old Nick caused the blackest sinner to collapse in convulsions on the floor, and extracted his soul slowly through the bars (says Grahame, with all the relish of anticlimax) 'as a seaside tripper might extract a winkle from its shell with a pin'. It was a tale precisely calculated to tickle the

MERTON STREET, OXFORD, c1880.
The mediaeval cobbled surface of the streets of Oxford discouraged traffic. The few hansoms and flies were mainly in demand for making the long trip between the colleges and the railway station. There were no cars and no bicycles.

boy's anti-Puritan instincts; yet he remained enough of a Scots Calvinist to get a genuine *frisson* out of it.

During his second year at school, in 1869, Grahame visited St Giles's Fair. It was the first fair of importance he had ever seen, and stirred in him a passion for the world of circus and fair-ground which persisted all his life. Freaks were then the mainstay of the show: Grahame recalled 'giants, dwarfs, fat ladies, tattooed ladies, mermaids, six-legged calves and distorted nature of every variety.' Not possessing enough pockey-money to investigate the side-shows for himself, he wandered down the rows of painted booths, drinking in their wildly imaginative advertisements, which depicted 'the object within under conditions and in surroundings hardly quite realizable, one was tempted to think, within the limitations of a caravan. Three mermaids combed their hair on rocks, or swam lazily about in warm tropic seas; there boa constrictors wound themselves round the bodies of paralysed Indian maidens, in the depths of Amazonian jungles.'

Perhaps he had the best of the bargain. For him the mermaids remained mermaids, the jungles were truly parrot-haunted, and the lagoons through which he swam in imagination were golden and tropical. It is faith, not money, which

St Giles's Fair in 1865.
Kenneth Grahame first visited the fair during his second year at school in 1869. Not possessing enough pocket-money to investigate the side-shows, he retained the romantic image portrayed by the wildly imaginative painted booths uninfluenced by the clumsy fakes ... and sickly animals cooped in packing cases'.

can move mountains: the bystanders who paid their sixpences and went inside soon re-emerged disillusioned. What *they* saw were 'clumsy fakes, dried fish, abortions in bottles, mangy and sickly animals cooped in packing-cases'. The whole story crystallizes, in precisely applicable terms, just that conflict of dream and reality which continued to haunt Grahame's imagination.

There were, too, other more strictly indigenous spectacles than fairs. In 1870, for instance, Oxford celebrated a particularly sumptuous Commemoration of Founders and Benefactors. The new Chancellor, Lord Salisbury, was there, with diminutive but impeccably blue-blooded pages to hold up his train; there was a Gala Ode composed by the Professor of Poetry and set by the Professor of Music; there was a recitation of the Newdigate Prize Poem, and honorary degrees for such notables as the PRA and Mr Matthew Arnold. Oxford can muster some impressive pageantry and processions for such occasions, of a kind to impress a boy already (without knowing it) in love with Pre-Raphaelism.

Nevertheless, the spirit of Arnold, Ruskin, and Morris was powerful enough at Oxford in the seventies to captivate an impressionable schoolboy, already soaked in Virgil and Horace. And there were too, perhaps a more potent influence than any other, what T. S. Eliot calls 'a strong brown god'—the River. As Grahame wrote:

> The two influences which most soaked into me there, and have remained with me ever since, were the good grey Gothic on the one hand and, on the other, the cool secluded reaches of the Thames—the 'stripling Thames', remote and dragon-fly haunted, before it attains to the noise, ribbons and flannels of Folly Bridge. The education, in my time, was of the fine old crusted order, with all the classics in the top bin—I did Greek verse in those days, so help me! But these elements, the classics, the Gothic, the primeval Thames, fostered in me, perhaps, the pagan germ that would have mightily shocked the author of *The Sabbath.*

To his last days Grahame preserved a deep, not entirely articulate passion for 'this sleek, sinuous, full-bodied animal, chasing and chuckling, gripping things with a gurgle and leaving them with a laugh ... glints and gleams and sparkles, rustle and swirl, chatter and bubble'. The river is in one sense a symbol of life, in another an emblem of constancy: it is faithful and steady-going, it never 'packed up, flitted or went into winter quarters'. It is also the last natural refuge from speed and mechanization; a system of toll-gates and locks ensures leisurely progress, free from dust and clatter, to the quiet upper reaches by Lechlade or Abingdon. The roads have been ruined; the River remains what it was. All running water affected Grahame almost hypnotically: he could stand and stare at it for hours.

It seems possible too, from his own account, that Grahame, while still a schoolboy, contrived to indulge his lifelong passion for 'messing about in boats'. The exploration of the Thames to which he alludes is unlikely to have been conducted entirely from the landward side. There is a fragment of MS in which he pictures himself gliding lazily through Oxfordshire harvest hayfields in a canoe—a craft which he would have disdained later, when he had become a sculling enthusiast. In this canoe we can picture the slight, dark-haired schoolboy paddling (as he described) past labourers busy about the harvest, and occasionally exchanging a cheerful word with them. One, 'who stood kneedeep in fragrant hay tossed up to him by moist helpers below, catching sight of my canoe ... was fain to cheerily observe, "Ah, if I had lots o' money that's the way I should travel"'. The young Grahame retorted, enviously, that there were worse ways of going about than on a haycart, and that he (the labourer) didn't know how lucky he was to have spent so much time in such a pleasant occupation. 'Rejoinder he doubtless could have supplied—but the remorseless stream bore me out of hearing. That is one of the special charms of the stream: the river of life has remorseless eddies and backwaters which forbid your escape from such disputes.'

So the canoe would drift on, between meadows thick with loose-strife, beyond Pinkhill and Eynsham Lock and Wytham Great Wood, past Hagley Pool and the Trout Inn by Godstow Bridge, till Port Meadow and Osney Lock brought 'noise, ribbons and flannels' once more, and waters desecrated with 'lobster-claws, gold-necked bottles, and fragments of veal pie'. Here we can leave him, leaning over New Bridge, where Cromwell's levies once tramped, and meditating on the

THE TROUT INN BY GODSTOW.
Grahame pictured himself gliding lazily through Oxfordshire harvest fields in a canoe. His return to Oxford ran past the inn and through Godstow Lock to Port Meadow.

OLD GODSTOW BRIDGE.
The bridge crosses the Thames at the point at which it divides into two streams by The Trout Inn.

Oxfordshire landscape: 'Typical of the country, which has changed not at all—and why should it—hay, and the rural Pan for ever'.

During the Christmas holidays both Kenneth and Willie were often guests at Uncle John Grahame's London house in Sussex Gardens. They were taken to Drury Lane for the pantomime, together with Uncle John's children, Edward, Walter, Bessie, and Agnes. Mr Bilton, Uncle John's head clerk, was given afternoons off to escort them to the Zoo, the Tower of London, and other such urban delights. Kenneth caused amusement, and a certain degree of raised eyebrows, by his somewhat precocious wit, probably sharpened in the Debating Society: 'Some dull family friends,' Chalmers writes, 'kindly folk who, of their garden's plenty, gave surplus vegetables to their neighbours, were on the agenda. "They have their points," declared someone at the dinner-table. "Have they?" said Kenneth doubtfully. "Well, dear," he was told, "they gave us this excellent asparagus." "*Pointes d'asperges,*" Kenneth is said to have retorted as he helped himself.' Perhaps for this, perhaps for less definable reasons, he found himself from the beginning out of sympathy with Uncle John, a downright practical man who believed in hard work, physical exercise, and no nonsense. Agnes, however, liked him considerably: 'a tall good-looking boy of kind and charming disposition' is her description of him at this period.

The Grahame boys seem not to have come near Sussex Gardens during the summer holidays. In August, when not at Cranbourne, they were often to be found in Portsmouth, where Uncle Jack Ingles was a Commander aboard HMS *Hercules.* Reginald Ingles, Uncle Jack's son, recalls a visit he made to the wardroom with Kenneth, when Uncle Jack gave them a sumptuous breakfast of omelettes (which Kenneth had never tasted before) and devilled kidneys; and afterwards turned them over to the gunnery-lieutenant, who failed to appreciate their calling his armament 'cannons'. From the scanty evidence, one gets the impression that Granny Ingles found it somewhat overwhelming to have all four Grahame children in residence for the whole span of a holiday. She probably farmed them out, *privatim et seriatim*, to the many relatives available—a process which may have supplied material, eventually, for *The Golden Age*.

At the beginning of 1875, Kenneth's last year at St Edward's, Willie died. He had been forced to leave St Edward's in 1871 because of chronic recurrent bronchial trouble; and during the Christmas holidays of 1874, which he and Kenneth were spending with Uncle Jack, he went down with severe inflammation of the lungs and on New Year's Eve he died without rallying. He was sixteen years old. The funeral was held early in January, and Willie was buried beside his grandfather in Highgate Cemetery, where many Grahames lie. 'Close by,' Grahame noted laconically, when he visited the site on 22 April 1887, 'is the grave of Rossetti's father, mother, and wife.' Another bond had been broken; and yet more disillusion was to come. The Golden Age was fast dissolving in the stress of adult realities, and its memory became increasingly precious as time drew relentlessly on.

III

A LONDON PRELUDE

1876–8

It seems clear that, all through his school-days, Grahame assumed himself to be destined for Oxford. His natural aptitude for the humanities would, indeed, have gained him an easy entrance, and he would in all likelihood have done well enough there to emulate Lewis Carroll and become a don. Such an existence he would have found congenial above all others: in later years he envied his friend Sir Arthur Quiller-Couch, who so comfortably blended his academic and literary lives. The social aspects of Oxford also appealed to him; he once wrote to Sir Sydney Cockerell that 'as a manner of life I like Feasts and going on to rooms, and could contentedly spend most of my existence that way.'

We should not forget, either, that to an intelligent upper-class English boy of the period an Oxford education was taken for granted: it was a part of the natural order of things, and Grahame, with his passion for traditional English observances, must have leaned heavily on such an assumption—so heavily that (like most adolescents) he failed to reckon the financial cost which four years at Oxford would involve. Uncle John, however, was not an upper-class Englishman but a middle-class Scot, and therefore less indifferent to such mundane details. He informed his nephew bluntly that Oxford was out of the question. Kenneth pleaded with him desperately, promising to live, while up, with the strictest economy, to take a brilliant degree, to become a distinguished member of a High Table, or one of the learned professions. But Uncle John, that dour and practical business-man, was adamant. Granny Ingles induced her son David to put in a word with Mr Lidderdale, and Kenneth was in due course nominated to a clerkship in the Bank of England. There was a waiting-list, however: no vacancy would occur till 1879. Uncle John proposed that Kenneth should spend the two intervening years in his, Uncle John's, office at Westminster, and Kenneth had no option but to agree.

This was the most crushing blow that Grahame suffered, perhaps, in his whole life; nothing else had such radical and far-reaching consequences. It not only meant that he was condemned to enter the Bank; it effectively deprived him of escape from it at a later date. To do any of the things which Grahame envisaged as his life's work—to pursue an academic career above all—an Oxford or Cambridge degree was absolutely essential. 'I think at one time', wrote his cousin, Annie

WILLIAM LIDDERDALE.
As governor of the Bank of England, Lidderdale gave Grahame the opportunity to enter the Bank and thereby irrevocably influenced the course of his life.

Grahame, 'he hoped to get a post as Inspector of Schools, but whenever he applied for anything he was turned down through no fault of his own because he had never been to College and taken his degree. I've always thought it splendid of him to stick to his work at the Bank as he did.' Chalmers claims that he was 'always too big for a less than philosophical view of life'; but the testimony of relatives, no less than his own early work, makes it plain that, for the first few years at any rate, he resented bitterly the uncongenial task thus forced upon him.

The nature of this resentment requires careful examination. Grahame's bitterness is not general but specific. He is not, like Housman, cursing 'whatever brute or blackguard made the world', he is damning his relatives. And he is not (when we go into the matter more closely) damning them, out of spite, for their unfortunate poverty; on the contrary, the burden of his complaint is precisely that they had the money, but refused to use it for his benefit. 'During his minority he has lain entirely at their mercy: has been their butt, their martyr, their drudge, their *corpus vile.* Possessing all the sinews of war this stiff-necked tribe has consistently refused to part: even for the provision of those luxuries so much more necessary than necessities.' The phrasing of this passage suggests that Grahame was thinking of his late adolescence rather than his childhood, that the martyrdom and drudgery were the duties imposed on him as a clerk; and that the valuable luxury for which his elders would not provide was a university education. Now we have seen already that Granny Ingles, on Helen's testimony, was really poor. The inference is clear enough: Uncle John put his high-falutin nephew into a practical job to bring him to his senses, and teach him his role in society as a *de facto* orphan. It was not that he could not afford to send Kenneth to Oxford; he disapproved of such a step on principle.

If this conjecture be true, it explains why Kenneth indulged in such ferocious compensation-fantasies about his relatives, why he went out of his way to satirize the Olympians as materialistic, arbitrary, and mean.

'Schoolboy hopes these,' he wrote in 'A Funeral', 'comically misshapen, tawdry and crude in colour—let the pit receive them, and a good riddance! ... It is time to have done with fancies and get back to a world of facts. If only one could! Well, one can but try. It will be easier, now that they are really buried all. Hail and farewell to the short-lived dead!' It is not surprising that relatives speak of strained relations between uncle and nephew; nor that old Dr Kingdon, the Surgeon to the Bank of England (and not a man to suffer whimsy gladly), should have observed that Kenneth's uncle did not seem to understand the boy. Indeed, the *mores* of his class and age entirely sanctioned Uncle John's attitude. As Mr John Marlowe has pointed out, 'much of the energy and driving force of the Victorian middle class was derived from the feeling of servility which was associated with financial dependence. This attitude of mind meant that the whole subject of money and property became hedged about with a peculiar sanctity ... a man losing his money was the equivalent of a woman losing her virtue.'

Both socially and financially Grahame was completely helpless. The need to adhere to the traditional dogmas of family loyalty, discipline and conformity was at least as strong as the anarchic individualism which complemented it, and the tension set up by these two forces in conflict was an essential element in his creative process. When the tension slackens, and more particularly when the dilemma is finally resolved, the impulse to write dwindles and dies.

But in 1876 the emotional tug-of-war had only begun, and its effects were as yet incalculable. What it seems to have done right from the beginning was to establish a violent dualism in Grahame's mind, a dualism that invaded every aspect of his personality and work, and manifested itself in several distinct forms. One of the most interesting is the habit he developed of setting the two halves of his ego arguing; sometimes obliquely, disguised as separate characters, sometimes in open schizophrenia. Grahame was not (as has sometimes been supposed) a wistful anarchist who lacked the courage of his convictions; the division, the battle, was in himself. Only half his nature fought against the things he satirized; a fact recognized by a reviewer of *Pagan Papers*, who observed in *The Critic* that while posing as an unregenerate child of Nature, he had every appearance of respectability.

The climate of the age encouraged this split approach to life, and Victorian literature is full of it: the result was what Holbrook Jackson described as 'a glorification of the fine arts and mere artistic virtuosity on the one hand, and a militant commercial movement on the other'. In *Virginibus Puerisque* Stevenson summed it up in a strikingly relevant phrase: 'Shrilly sound Pan's pipes; and behold the banker instantly concealed in the bank parlour'. Arnold had crystallized the attitude of the opposition, locating the evil in industrialism, purely material ideals, the repression of instinct, the spiritual sterility that was a direct product of a puritan cash-morality. He saw, too, the force of repressive public opinion and the dualism it was liable to produce. The age that produced Grahame's *The Golden Age* also threw up Stevenson's *Dr Jekyll and Mr Hyde*.

The result of this atmosphere was to produce a pregnant contrast between the business-man and the country vagabond, entirely to the latter's advantage; and a whole crop of stories appeared in which stockbrokers and similar urban figures broke loose, lost their memories, went West or South, kicked over the traces, and in various ways displayed a pretty blend of fugal neurosis and resurgent natural instincts. This literary symptom of the current social malaise is well represented in Grahame's work. Rat, in 'Wayfarers All', is so painfully affected by the Call of the South that his eyes change colour, and he displays other interesting hysterical symptoms. A stockbroker ('a good portly man, i' faith: and had a villa and a steam launch at Surbiton') disappears from home and business to be found weeks later in ragged country clothes, by a Hampshire river-bank, tickling trout with village urchins; 'and when they would have won him to himself with horrid whispers of American Rails, he answered but with babble of green fields'. Nevertheless, inevitably, Throgmorton Street gets him back in the end. He has had his fling; but the social fabric must be preserved.

THE WATER RAT AND THE SEA RAT.
E. H. Shepard's line drawing for *The Wind in the Willows*.

Not nearly enough has been made of Grahame's successful career at the Bank of England. To the individual, the anarchic artist in him, it must have been the equivalent of selling out to the enemy for a handful of silver. The Bank was the very nerve-centre through which operated the speculators and big business firms to whom industrialism was the breath of life. It was the Bank that in 1842 decided to lend up to £250,000 on railway development—a sum which by 1851 had swollen to £3,070,000 in debentures spread among eleven railway companies. As Sir John Clapham observes, 'over 9000 miles of line were authorized and nearly 1900 miles opened in Britain between 31 December 1843 and 1 January 1848.' It was the Bank

Willows on the Thames.

Port Meadow, Oxford, from Godstow Lock.
The vast meadow, overrun with cattle, was used by St Edwards School as a cricket pitch whose sole advantage was the absence of boundaries.

Merton College, Oxford.
The gothic architecture of Oxford was drawn into Grahame's picture of his imaginary City.

High Above the Quadrangles
the tower of St Mary the Virgin rises to look down into Brasenose College.

River Meadows north of Oxford.
To his last days Grahame preserved a deep passion for 'this sleek, sinuous, full-bodied animal'.

The Thames near Eynsham.
Kenneth Grahame, as a schoolboy, explored the 'stripling Thames'.

he served for so long which directly supported what Grahame described as 'the iron tetter that scurfs the face of our island [and] has killed out the pleasant life of the road.'

Yet there was no breaking away from the prescribed order of things. Grahame was enough of a child of his time to accept unquestioningly the bonds against which his spirits chafed. Besides, he had banking in his Scots blood; there was always present in his character an element which, far from opposing middle-class mercantilism, was largely identified with its interests, and which became increasingly predominant as time went on.

It may be doubted whether Uncle John could have chosen a profession for Kenneth which more aptly symbolized everything against which the boy's instincts rebelled. Yet we should not condemn his action out of hand. By his own lights he acted for the best. Oxford, it should be remembered, did not enter into the Grahames' scheme of things. The academic life meant nothing in their tradition. Like most middle-class Calvinist families, they either served God or Mammon, and occasionally defied Holy Writ by doing both: especially when practising at the Bar. To John Grahame his nephew's request must have seemed not only fanciful but reprehensible, mere dilettantism. Besides, it was high time the boy was earning his keep. So he probably argued, bewildered and annoyed at the trick Nature had played by placing this literary cuckoo in a solid, respectable Scots nest.

What passed between the two of them at that crucial interview will never be known. But at all events things were arranged in such a way that Kenneth was not obliged to live with Uncle John till he found his own feet in London. Another of his father's brothers, Uncle Robert, offered him accommodation in his own house, Draycott Lodge, and Kenneth gratefully accepted. No doubt John Grahame, too, was relieved at not having so reserved and enigmatic a boy under his roof as a permanent guest. He probably saw quite enough of him during working hours at Westminster.

Robert Grahame was a merchant who had spent much of his life abroad in Manila. Robert and his wife Georgina had one daughter, Annie, with whom Kenneth struck up an immediate friendship; and this continued for many years, long after Kenneth had moved elsewhere. He remained at Draycott Lodge till his entry into the Bank; it was conveniently handy for Westminster, an old-fashioned house between the King's Road and Fulham. In 1876 Fulham was still a small village in the midst of market gardens; since then the market gardens have vanished, and Draycott Lodge with them.

If Kenneth had to live in London, Chelsea and Westminster were far more pleasant than most districts; but what stuck in his throat was having to live in London at all. It was a penance he endured as well as he could, and indeed made the best of: but a penance it remained. Eighteen years later, in *The Yellow Book*, side by side with Grahame's own 'Roman Road', John Davidson wrote a ballad of a thirty bob-a-week clerk which exactly caught the mood shared by Grahame and thousands more urban workers, now as then:

For like a mole I journey in the dark,
 A-travelling along the underground
From my Pillar'd Halls and broad suburban Park
 To come the daily dull official round;
And home again at night with my pipe all alight
 A-scheming how to count ten bob a pound.

We shall meet that mole again; but it is not till 1908 that he finally bursts into the light and enjoys the sunny, uninterrupted pleasures of total irresponsibility.

The prevalent attitude of writers to London ever since the Industrial Revolution had been one of moral and physical disgust, symbolized by Cobbett's clinically exact image of the 'Great Wen'. The agricultural slump was largely caused by the draining of countrymen into the towns for higher wages, and accelerated by the import of cheap American grain. Add to this the impact of the railways, the spread of the suburbs, and the passing of the Union Chargeability Act in 1865 (which 'finally detached the labourer from his place of settlement ... and created mobility of labour'): the result was the end of village life (as Hardy, Rider Haggard, and Richard Jefferies all perceived) and, in Dr Trevelyan's words, 'the general divorce of Englishmen from life in contact with nature, which in all previous ages had helped to form the mind and the imagination of the island race'.

To intelligent and sensitive writers who knew the full meaning of this upheaval, who could gauge just what intangible element was being lost for ever from English life, and at what cost, London stood as the visible symbol of the Enemy, the Destroyer. Its swarming slums, its granite pavements, its foul fogs and polluted air, its counting-houses and banks, its prostitutes and gin-palaces, its ceaseless noise, all summed up the new way of life which was spreading like a cancer to engulf the old in the sacred name of Progress.

In this Goyaesque sub-world grim new forces were stirring, that fed on poverty and despair. In 1867 the first volume of *Das Kapital* appeared; in 1871 an engineering strike paralysed north-east England; in 1875 the right to picket and strike was firmly established by law, in an Act that was also concerned with 'Improving Artisans' Dwellings'. Everywhere there was change, unrest, disruption of tradition. Grahame could hardly have enjoyed the atmosphere of this London, so far removed from Dunbar's 'Queen of Cities all'. But he had no choice in the matter: and London became his home (though he escaped from it whenever possible) for the next thirty years. It was only two years before his retirement that he escaped permanently to Berkshire and the quiet backwaters of the Thames.

Nevertheless, if he was unhappy in London, he took some trouble to conceal the fact. He dined with Uncle John at Sussex Gardens on every second Sunday, both before and after he went into the Bank; and to him he presented a front of Stoic cheerfulness and determination over the *fait accompli* of his career which won the older man's admiration. 'Pluck and steadiness' were the words Uncle John chose to describe Kenneth's attitude; and his cousin Agnes recalled of these conditions that 'it was a pleasure to see him come into the room, he looked so happy and pleasant. He was neither too talkative nor too reserved.'

Already the public mask was slipping into place, the gap between appearance and reality widening. 'I have never heard him talk about himself', Agnes added, and we can see this reticence as characteristic of something more than modesty. The nearest Kenneth came to telling the truth about himself was, paradoxically, in his published work. Through this stylized *persona* he could speak more honestly than when he wrote as himself, even as a diarist or in his love-letters.

Certainly there was no apparent rupture during this difficult period between Kenneth and any of his relatives. Christmas 1876 found him, together with Roland, staying at Halstead Vicarage in Essex, where Uncle David and his family had migrated two years previously. Granny Ingles was a frequent visitor there also. The following September was spent in Scotland, where Uncle John had rented a holiday house near Pitlochry. Besides Agnes and Walter, his own children, and Kenneth, Helen, and Roland, he had also invited his niece Annie—Uncle Robert's daughter—who wrote of this visit: 'We certainly didn't bother ourselves about politics or anything abstruse (presumably a reference to Uncle John's profession)—but I had been reared on old Scotch ballads and stories and folklore which appealed to Kenneth also, and later on at any rate formed a bond of union between us.' The holiday was apparently a success; at any rate it was repeated, probably in 1881, and on this occasion, Annie remembered, 'Kenneth brought with him a copy of *Uncle Remus* which had just come out, I think;—at any rate none of us had ever heard of it;—and he was continually reading and quoting from it.'

While he was attached to the firm of Grahame, Currie, and Spens—the attachment, to judge by Cousin Agnes' recollections, was a decidedly vague one—Kenneth occupied some of his time in learning shorthand, but authors in Uncle John's opinion, were *flâneurs*, not really gentlemen, and liable to immorality. The boy was obviously leading too sedentary a life; it was making him liverish and unsettled. The best thing he could do would be to join the Volunteers—plenty of good hard drill.

Kenneth, as usual, took up the suggestion without fuss, and worked at it with dogged conscientiousness. Besides, at least half his own nature was highly suspicious of journalism and professional authors; to the end of his life he held that writing was a gentleman's spare-time occupation, not to be contaminated with money or deadlines or hack-work. This did not prevent him habitually bargaining for unusually good terms, even with the publishers of his first book: he was, after all, a Scots banker as well as an English essayist.

The Volunteers as a body had been founded, as we have seen, in 1859, and had since grown and proliferated considerably. Kenneth and Roland naturally joined the London Scottish. In the photograph of Kenneth in uniform, he has grown a small military moustache to go with the part, and sits facing the camera with military self-assurance—hands on spread knees, the swagger-stick between, bonnet cockily askew. But the eyes are remote and defensive, the face set in blank expressionlessness; one senses the mask again. Kenneth threw himself into drill, and boxing, and fencing, with abandon: such activities kept him healthy and occupied.

KENNETH GRAHAME
of the London Scottish Volunteers.

(In that sense Uncle John had been quite right.) Later he became a sergeant; and there is a delightful story of his leading a most unorthodox sort of charge in Hyde Park.

It came about in this way. Kenneth and Roland were regular guests at the Lidderdales', and had made great friends with their two baby daughters who were now in the care of the Grahames' old Scots nurse, Ferguson. One day when they were drilling in the Park, Ferguson wheeled the Lidderdale girls over to watch, in their large, shiny double perambulator. This was more than Sergeant Grahame could resist; when he recognised his admirers, he

> ordered a complimentary charge to be made on the perambulator. His platoon, flourishing its muskets, therefore advanced with leaps, bounds and loud cheers. The two objectives in the perambulator were enchanted. Not so their guardian, who thought that her Master Kenneth had 'gone gyte'.

Kenneth seldom 'went gyte', and when he did let himself go in this way it was more often than not with children, who could be relied on not to mistake his mood.

London offered other compensatory pleasures to the imaginative. Grahame had discovered Soho, as we might expect, immediately on arrival. He developed a passion for wandering through the Italian quarter, fascinated by exotic little restaurants, the unfamiliar but beautifully cadenced language, the warmth and friendliness of the atmosphere. It offered him something more than cheap but delicious wine and food; it kindled that passion for the south which sustained him steadily throughout his long years in the City, and led him on those first breath-taking pilgrimages he made to Florence and Rome during his summer vacations. He formed the habit of dining in Soho once a week if he could afford it; and at one of these dinners he made the acquaintance of a most remarkable man, a huge, grey-bearded heavily-muscled lion of about fifty, who attracted Grahame's attention by his Johnsonian dogma and Rabelaisian wit. Their eyes met over a joke; the stranger invited Grahame to join his party; and they finished the evening (after putting away a good deal of cheap red wine) by solemnly exchanging cards. The stranger's name was Furnivall, and the meeting took place towards the end of Grahame's first year in London.

Frederick James Furnivall has been aptly described as a 'living and talking library, more comforting, indeed more delightful and cheering, than a visit even to the British Museum.' His interests were certainly wide. He read mathematics at Cambridge, was later called to the Bar, but abandoned both when he became involved in the Christian Socialist Movement led by F. D. Maurice. He also developed an early interest in music and philology, and in 1849 began a long friendship with Ruskin, which lasted till the latter's death. He 'lectured on English poetry from Chaucer to Tennyson', and in the sixties began exploring early and middle English literature, particularly the Arthurian romances. His editing labours soon crystallized in the founding of the Early English Text Society, with Tennyson and Ruskin among the first subscribers. Some three years before his meeting with Grahame he had also launched the New Shakespere Society, which became especially associated with dating Shakespeare by metrical tests. This practice called out a great deal of petulant ridicule from pre-dominantly aesthetic critics.

The oddly assorted pair took to each other instinctively. Furnivall was everything that the Olympians were not: a wild man of letters, a prodigious scholar, a natural odd man out, a Bohemian, a drinker, a savant who held court on the first floor of the New Oxford Street ABC, who took slum children to Kew Gardens, marched round London in red shirt-sleeves, and was likened by one country wag to the Prophet Jeremiah. Once he started talking 'the difficulty was to stop his flow of speech, as many a chairman found to his dismay. He was irrepressible. Relevance never troubled him.' Strangest of all, and a supreme attraction as far as Grahame was concerned, he was a champion sculler, and devoted to the life of the river; yet, paradoxically, he had never learnt to swim.

As early as 1845 he had devised and helped to build two sculling boats of a new

FREDERICK JAMES FURNIVALL
introduced Kenneth Grahame to sculling. This wild man of letters with his white beard was an inspiration for Grahame's 'Pan' in *The Wind in the Willows*.

and radical design. Sir Sidney Lee records that 'a wager boat on Furnivall's lines was soon built for the champion sculler, Newell'. From 1861 onwards Furnivall ran a highly successful working man's rowing club on the Thames. He conducted a ferocious campaign against the Amateur Rowing Association for excluding artisans from the 'amateur' class in sculling; his vitality won him as many friends as his tactlessness made him enemies. Warm-hearted, fiery-tempered, humane, irreligious, a scholarly radical and radical scholar, he was exactly the fermenting influence which Grahame needed.

TOAD SCULLING.
E. H. Shepard's drawing.

Grahame joined the New Shakespere Society on Friday 9 June 1877, and the records of the Society show that his cousin Annie, who shared his literary interests with such sympathy, became a member at the same time. For three years he attended the Friday meetings at University College in Gower Street; and then in 1880 Furnivall invited him to become Honorary Secretary of the Society. He accepted, and continued to discharge this office till the Society's final dissolution in 1891. During all this time he never once delivered a paper or voiced a personal opinion on any subject, which must constitute something of a record. He may well have been walking warily, like Agag, to keep out of the way of the polemical brickbats buzzing round his President's head; for about the time Grahame became Secretary the quarrel with the aesthetes was assuming vast proportions. Swinburne, who at first supported Furnivall, had suddenly made a *volte-face* and published a satirical skit on the Society; Furnivall replied with a fine piece of invective, and was soon referring to Swinburne, in print, as 'Pigsbrook'. By 1881 complaints were reaching Browning, the senior vice-president of the Society, of Furnivall's 'coarse and impertinent language'. Furnivall went on exactly as before, and many of the Society's more distinguished vice-presidents (though not Browning himself) resigned. From this scandal the Society never fully recovered, though it struggled on for another decade.

Grahame's specifically literary debt to Furnivall is obvious and considerable. It embraces his close acquaintance with (at one end of the scale) Malory, Hakluyt, the Arthurian romances, and above all Shakespeare; and (at the other) his passion for Browning, Shelley, Ruskin, and Morris. Furnivall founded both the Browning and

Shelley Societies, and would probably, given the chance, have extended his organizing activities to his other favourites. So, too, it was through Furnivall's agency that Grahame gained his *entrée* to the outer circle of that literary society which revolved round Tennyson and Browning, and first met the bright young men and women who were later to be his fellow-contributors to the *National Observer* and *The Yellow Book*. And at some point during their early acquaintance Grahame showed Furnivall, very tentatively, his own unpublished jottings, and asked his advice on what to do with them.

In a 'small ledger book, no doubt originally bound for the baser uses of the Bank and its balances'—and therefore not begun before 1879—he had taken to scribbling down odd quotations that caught his fancy, short anecdotes, scraps of highly personal prose, and a series of poems composed by himself. This ledger disappeared at some time after Mrs Grahame's death in 1946. Chalmers, however, quotes from it liberally, and Mr Roger Lancelyn Green (who also examined it, albeit hurriedly and under difficult conditions) has made notes of the poems. He describes them (with reservations) as '*very* artificial in type, rather the pretty-pretty Dobson kind of thing', an opinion on the whole confirmed both by the extracts Chalmers prints, and by such complete poems as survive in various periodicals. In the circumstances it is not surprising that Furnivall, while recommending Grahame to send his work to editors, strongly advised him to give up poetry and stick to prose. Posterity has confirmed his purely literary verdict. The ledger book included a quote from an Ode by Horace which deals with the beginning of the boating season which was dear to Grahame's heart. Grahame loosely paraphrased it in a rhymed triplet (his only known translation) as follows:

> Gone are the snows and April come is she;
> The West Wind blows and, down loud beaches, we
> Once more our prows propel to their blue sea.

So—This—Is—A—River.
E. H. Shepard's drawing.

'Boats,' he wrote, many years later, to a little girl who had sent him a letter about *The Wind in the Willows*, 'boats are the only things worth living for—any sort.'

Grahame's own contributions to the ledger show considerable range of mood. At one extreme is his pessimistic poem 'As You Like It', which was published in the *National Observer* in 1891. The first stanza runs:

> Life's a jungle, life's a dance,
> See the mummers everywhere
> Hopping, tossing bells in air—
> How the hobby-horses prance!
>   I advance
> Somewhat sick the round to share.

This image of 'life' as a shadow-show played out by mummers recurs elsewhere: 'our daily round,' Grahame wrote in 'Concerning Ghosts', 'is passed among such gibbering simulacra that to foregather with a ghost would be a mild but very real and pleasant relief.' Appearance and reality, in fact, are becoming inverted, or, from another viewpoint, acquiring Platonic values. The 'real' is a permanent disappointment when measured against the 'ideal'; dreams are the only true ideals; Fairyland has probably invented us rather than *vice versa*.

There is (as nearly always) a flicker of cheerful irreverence running through even the most pessimistic of Grahame's utterances, and the tone of this poem is subtly modified by recognition that it probably derived in part from a song of W. S. Gilbert's in *The Gondoliers:*

> Try we life-long, we can never
>   Straighten out life's tangled skein,
> Why should we, in vain endeavour,
>   Guess and guess and guess again?
> Life's a pudding full of plums,
> Care's a canker that benumbs.
>   Wherefore waste our elocution
>   On impossible solution?
>   Life's a pleasant institution,
> Let us take it as it comes!

Occasionally, too, Grahame tries his hand at the consciously humorous anecdote, somewhere between *Punch* and the *Dolly Dialogues*. It does not show him at his best: it is written (as Alan Pryce-Jones observed of *Pagan Papers*) 'in that irritatingly facetious style which is the chief objection to trying to be funny in English':

> T'other day I was about to cross the Channel—the usual crowd at the quay. A lady approached me in evident distress—a pretty woman too. 'Sir,' she said, 'my husband disappeared from my side ten minutes ago and I can perceive no trace of him—and now my black poodle has slipped his collar and escaped!' 'Madam,' said I, severely, 'you are most unreasonable. I can supply the place of your husband to a limited extent but I'll be hanged if I'll play at being a black poodle for anyone.'

Apart from this, there are several biographically suggestive love poems and two fragments of prose, one of which is a revealing passage on Friendship. The dead, says Grahame, are dearer than the living, 'for though, through circumstance and the sorry, sordid rubs of life, the former may start away, or pale and change till they are perhaps even actively hostile, derogatory, scornful, and love sickens and grows cold, still the dear dead always approve; their sympathies are sure'. And not only the dead, we can deduce. Children grow up, change, forget their old nature, die (in a sense) from what they were. But once they are caught and set down in words, they are fixed for ever, like the figures on Keats's Grecian Urn, in a pose which preserves that ideal moment.

Yet Grahame cannot bear the thought that these idealized companions have failed as adults; and so he transfers the failing to himself: 'The friends of our youth ... live somewhere yet in the flesh, might be seen and talked with, if we would. But we will not have it, at least yet. Because of the very height of the ideals we shared together, we cannot face them yet, while not one solid step has been made.' To confront remembered dream-children with their real, changed, adult counterparts is a perilous proceeding; and we shall see Grahame more and more uneasy, as time passes, when in the company of his brother and sister. His family were never quite able, or eager, to live up to the private ideal he set them.

How many of these fugitive pieces had been written when Grahame showed Furnivall the ledger we cannot be certain: probably not many, since London editors first began to accept his known work in 1888, and some poems from this source were published as late as 1891—2. It is interesting (and squares with all we know of them) that Grahame had found no one in his own family to whom he was willing to show his prentice work, or who could be expected to take any interest in it: nor, apparently, was there any like-minded spirit at the Bank or among his colleagues in the Volunteers. If he let Cousin Annie share his secret, he certainly did not admit the fact to Furnivall: but since they had been drawn together by their literary interests, it seems likely enough that the ledger had passed through her hands before the Doctor pronounced on its contents. At any rate, from this time forward, Grahame began to submit essays, articles, even stories for publication: and it is possible that some of these early pieces actually appeared in obscure periodicals and have not been traced. Trant Chambers, for instance, referred to 'a pretty little storyette of yours about an aristocratic little girl who made friends with a poor little lad, who subsequently died.' For several years—perhaps not entirely surprisingly if this is a fair sample—'five out of six of my little meteorites,' as Grahame put it, 'came back to me.' Meanwhile the material world had closed in on the would-be author, and diverted much of his time and energy into more practical channels. The Olympians, for the time being at least, had the upper hand.

IV

THREADNEEDLE STREET

1879–87

Kenneth Grahame entered the Bank of England as a gentleman-clerk on 1 January 1879, and Threadneedle Street welcomed him with the thickest, yellowest fog that had been seen that winter. Since he had acquired the habit of walking to work (partly for economy's sake and partly for the exercise) he had found it advisable to move his lodgings somewhat nearer the City. From Draycott Lodge, with its clear air and market gardens, he transferred himself to a 25s-a-week flat in Bloomsbury Street, which he later shared with Roland when the latter also entered the Bank. On that first morning, conscientious as ever, the new clerk allowed himself ninety minutes to walk a mile and a half through the fog. He arrived in Threadneedle Street on the stroke of ten, and found himself alone in his department, with no superior to report to. 'An hour later', writes Chalmers—a banker himself—'he was to learn from a youthful colleague in a frock-coat and flourishing whiskers, the first principle of Finance. Which is that a London Particular excuses all things dilatory in a banker and especially is it indulgence, extenuation and ample justification for an extra hour in bed and a leisurely breakfast.' It was a lesson which Kenneth was quick to learn.

He had acquitted himself with distinction in the entrance examination, and his English Essay paper actually gained full marks—a unique achievement, without precedent in the Bank's history, and never afterwards to be repeated. The subject was 'India', and we may hazard a guess that its political sentiments were as acceptable to that most conservative of institutions as its literary style: Grahame's views on coloured people were not so much hostile as comfortably superior. Miss R. M. Bradley, daughter of the then Dean of Westminster, recounted how 'he once startled a lunch-table at which the habits of a European potentate then visiting London were under discussion, by announcing "Well, he's a Black", as if that settled the matter. On being asked to explain so inaccurate a statement, he replied blandly: "I divide the whole population of Europe into English people and blacks."' She added in explanation that, despite his wide travels in Southern Europe, this was no pose; he perversely expected a different code of manners from his own countrymen.

There has been a general tendency (largely fostered by Grahame's own early

THE BANK OF ENGLAND.
When Kenneth Grahame entered the Bank of England as a gentleman-clerk on 1 January 1879, Threadneedle Street welcomed him with the thickest, yellowest fog of that winter.

essays) to regard his sojourn at the Bank as an unrelieved grind, the mere means by which he earned a living; and thus to disregard this aspect of his life entirely when considering his literary work. The unspoken inference is, of course, that the two had no connection. A more misleading assumption could hardly be made. When a man spends nearly thirty years in a given profession it leaves its mark on him; and when he is appointed to one of its three highest offices while still under forty we cannot suppose that he treated it as nothing but a bread-and-butter chore. On the one hand, there was banking in Grahame's blood; and on the other, there was much about the Old Lady of Threadneedle Street that was calculated to appeal to the romantic side of his nature. To the spirit of finance, and the disfiguring urbanization it bred, he remained profoundly hostile; but the Bank itself, the visible manifestation of a great and ancient tradition, with its ritual, its liveries, its vaulted strong-rooms packed with gold would at first have fascinated him but finally—and probably long before the end—bored him by her very immutability and solid assurance. Yet in those earlier, creative years, though he may (as he himself represents) have been a galley-slave, part of his nature at least rejoiced in its chains; and they did not, when all is said, chafe very heavily. Bankers' short hours are proverbial, and even the Old Lady's most junior employees enjoyed a surprising amount of leisure.

The general atmosphere of day-to-day life in the Bank at this period—certainly in the lower echelons—was not by any means so prim, stuffy, or Gladstonian as we might suppose. Eccentricity was common, and rowdyism not unknown: the clerks behaved surprisingly like medical students of the Bob Sawyer vintage, and many of their superiors could have sat for Leech or Boz. The Old Lady, in fact, was so ultra-conservative in her traditions that by 1880 a distinct whiff of the Regency still lingered about her. Allan Fea, who became a clerk two years after Grahame, and first worked in the Private Drawing Office, paints an extraordinary picture of the Bank as it then was—an aspect of Threadneedle Street which the official histories tend to overlook. In *Recollections of Sixty Years* he writes:

> In 1881 the Bank was very different from the orderly place it is now, and the above-mentioned department [*i.e.* the Drawing Office] was one of the rowdiest of the lot. The pandemonium was a little startling to a novice—jokes shouted from one end of the office to the other; the singing of a line from some popular song winding up with 'Amen' in a solemn cadence of about a hundred voices. If you were not good at dodging you were liable at any time to have your hat knocked off your head by a flying Pass-book. ...

Such horseplay was mild in comparison with some of the extra-curricular activities in which the clerks indulged. Drunkenness was extraordinarily prevalent; it was 'by no means uncommon in the eighties to see fellows in the washing-places trying to sober themselves with douses of cold water, or lying prone upon a table for a while, ere they dare return to their desks'. It was not so long since fighting dogs had been chained by those desks, waiting for after-hours bouts down in the lavatories. Some clerks ran small farms outside London, and turned up stinking of the midden; others used to buy their meat in bulk at Billingsgate, and leave it lying about the office: 'It was a very ordinary thing' recalled Fea, 'for the householders in an office to carve up half a sheep downstairs in the washing department'.

Though many of the clerks had private means, and entered the Bank for purely vocational reasons, there seems to have been a scattering of extraordinary rough diamonds about when Grahame entered on his apprenticeship. (There was an old tradition that till the seventies the Bank had advertised vacancies by a notice on the railings outside; that anyone could apply; and that once a butcher had left his meat with the porter, gone in, and found himself a clerk five minutes later.) Table-manners were appalling, and one man had such objectionable habits of hawking and spitting that the head of his department ordered—not a reprimand, but a free daily issue of sawdust to be scattered round his desk.

I suspect that a good deal of Grahame's distaste for his job during the early years may have been due—curiously enough—not to the air of starched Victorian rectitude which one normally associates with banking in the eighties, so much as this atmosphere of crass and Philistine licence. Paganism was one thing, this kind of behaviour (as Grahame made clear in 'The Rural Pan') quite another; Pan and Mercury have little in common, and Grahame's Calvinism was strong enough still to gag at these swillings and oafish crudities of behaviour. On the other hand, he must have realised the more harmless eccentricities in which the Bank abounded; the ancient and decrepit stockholders who appeared on dividend day; one old lady, Amelia Macabe, who dressed like a girl, with a hat like 'a strawberry basket trimmed with white muslin', and distributed booklets of her own poems among the clerks; the raffles before pay-day, at which one enterprising young fellow auctioned his uncle's cremated bones; the strange nick-names—'Job Lot', 'The Dead Horse', 'The Dook', 'The Stiff'un', 'The Ghost', 'The Maiden Aunt', or 'The 'Orrid Old 'Og'—which the clerks bestowed on each other and their chiefs.

There were, too, plenty of loopholes for escape during working hours. Business was often very slack, and always slack enough to allow time for shopping after lunch—a leisured lunch taken at one of those famous old chop-houses, long since destroyed: the Bay Tree, with its open grill and comfortable pew-seats, where you could get the best steaks in the City; Baker's, whose old-world waiter seemed to belong more to coaching times than Victorian London; Birch's, with its punch and cheese-cakes; Thomas's, where huge chump chops were served off pewter. Full and cheerful, the clerk with his wits about him could always manufacture some errand or other which would leave him free for an hour or two. While officially collecting money from some counting house or other he might explore the by-ways and back-streets of old Holborn which have since been demolished to make way for the Strand and Holborn. He might take a 'penny steamer' up to Westminster or down from the Old Swan Pier to Wapping and Shadwell. How even the minimal amount of work required actually got done it is difficult to imagine.

Over the week-ends Grahame's beloved Thames was within fairly easy reach. It seems clear, from chance allusions scattered through *Pagan Papers*, that Grahame escaped to the peace of the river and the Berkshire countryside whenever he could. Oxford, on the other hand, he never revisited for ten years after he left school. Perhaps he could not bear to go near a place that had held out such hopes to him, and won his affection so entirely, only to fade like a mirage when he stretched out his hand to touch it; the wound of disappointment, however well concealed, remained raw and aching.

But as time passed Oxford, too, became incorporated in his private myth. 'During (say) the last five years of those ten' [*i.e.* from about 1880 to 85], he wrote in a letter to Helen Dunham, 'I constantly at night ran down to a fairy Oxford—the real thing, yet transformed, and better, because the Gothic was

PANGBOURNE.
Grahame made regular week-end trips to his beloved Berkshire Thames sometimes exploring the river by boat instead of from the river-bank.

COOKHAM LOCK ON A BANK HOLIDAY c1885.
Even in Grahame's day he had cause to complain that the Thames could sometimes be too busy and noisy.

better—a maze of lovely cloisters and chapels and courts. I used to spend a long day there and come back next morning. At the end of those ten years I happened to revisit the real Oxford several weeks in succession—I spent several weekends there—and at once the fairy Oxford vanished, and is only just beginning to return now [1896], when I have not seen the real thing for two years. I like the fairy one better!'

This is a curiously prophetic passage; it confirms what one suspects of Grahame's art—that it throve best on deprivation, nostalgia, the ideal never quite attained. He knew the danger himself. 'Think of living in Italy,' he remarked during his first visit to Florence, 'when you might have it to go to.'

Meanwhile London offered not only pleasures but a panorama of life which, for the observant eye, contained its own drama and aesthetic appeal. Standing in Trafalgar Square he watched the flash and tumble of pigeons, sunlight flaking from their opalescent wings, or a crocodile of schoolgirls tripping by, with restless eyes, glancing ankles, a susurrus of chatter—'and oh, that wave of red hair that flaps on one cool white neck!' Close by the steps of the National Gallery, then as today, a pavement 'screever' was busy with his gaudy chalks. Above, a sky of crystalline blue, and the year's first real sun alchemizing the sooty London wilderness: the young clerk stared entranced, and later caught the scene perfectly in a short essay called, appropriately enough, 'Pastels':

> The buses whirl up and recede in vivid spots of red and blue and green; tawdry house-fronts are transmuted into mellowest shades of blue-grey and tawny; or, freshly-painted, throw up broad masses of dazzling white. A butcher's cart, a child's Tam-o'-Shanter, a mounted orderly jogging from Pall Mall—all join in the conspiracy of colour; and woman everywhere, realizing what she was created for, flecks the canvas with pigments unknown to the dead and buried year. The artist, meanwhile ... rubs in the white round the widow's cap, brings out the high lights on the greensod, and adds corners of the proper droop to the mouth of the orphan in his old masterpiece—'Her Father's Grave'.

The pavement artist's activities seem to have fascinated Grahame beyond measure, and he describes the pictures in detail: a cut half-salmon ('with special attention to the flesh-tints at the divided part'), the Charge of Balaclava, the portrait of Lord Wolseley that could be transformed at need, by the addition of a beard, into the Duke of Saxe-Coburg. 'It has always been my longing,' Kenneth wrote to his friend Graham Robertson, 'to have been able to draw and paint'—but the kind of painting he had in mind was something very like the screever's work, itself first cousin to that of the school-room.

At all events Grahame seems to have stayed there, absorbed in the scene, while 'the afternoon haze mellowed everything with an illusion of its own', putting him in mind of old-world châteaux and pre-Revolutionary France; till darkness fell, the red tail lamps of hansoms dotted the gloom, and the pavement artist departed in search of the nearest four-ale bar. If he moved at all it was into the National Gallery itself, a favourite haunt of his. Like the Baltic stockbroker he describes in 'The

Iniquity of Oblivion', he 'only went in to be amused, and was prepared to take his entertainment from all schools alike, without any of the narrow preferences of the cultured'. ['Did the British artists in Suffolk Street', he remarks laconically in his diary entry for 22 April 1887.] 'From the very first, however, the Early Tuscans gripped him with a strange fascination, so that he rarely penetrated any further.' Elsewhere he recalled that

> before the National Gallery was extended and rearranged, there was a little 'St Catherine' by Pinturicchio that possessed my undivided affections. In those days she hung near the floor, so that those who would worship must grovel; and little I grudged it. Whenever I found myself near Trafalgar Square with five minutes to spare I used to turn in and sit on the floor before the object of my love, till gently but firmly replaced on my legs by the attendant.

Grahame never, as he says, strayed down the tortuous by-ways of Art; but he acquired a wide working knowledge of many artists' works, from Carpaccio or Botticelli to Watteau, Fragonard, and Lancret. He had a then unfashionable obsession with Blake, disliked the Manchester School heartily, and (presumably under Ruskin's influence) considered the Northern and Flemish schools influenced by the 'toil and stress of weather'. He praised the realism and modernity displayed by such artists as Turner or Frith—when their work is compared with the equivalent writing of the time we can see his point—and believed, characteristically, that one of the main purposes in art was to save the past from entire oblivion:

> When, wandering through some gallery [he observed in a speech at the opening of an exhibition of the work of Eric Kennington] we come suddenly on the depicting of some once well-known and loved piece of nature or achitecture, now swept away by so-called improvements or developments, we must have felt some glow of gratitude to the painter, over and above any joy in his work, for having fixed and recorded, for practically all time, a beauty now in itself vanished for ever.

Yet not all his reactions followed this simple and practical pattern. The Italian Primitives seem to have moved him so strongly that he refers to the sensation as a 'possession'. Grahame was shy of self-analysis: 'the man', as he says on this occasion of his thinly disguised *alter ego*, 'was not apt in the expression of subtle emotion'. The peculiarly spiritual quality which early Italian painting displays makes it likely that there was, in the widest sense, a religious element involved. Calvinism and social anglicanism between them had damned Grahame's natural spring of faith at the source; what he suffered from, paradoxically, was severe religious repression, which sometimes found very odd outlets. For so resolutely commonsensical a pagan he appears surprisingly familiar with obsessive, hysterical, and generally abnormal emotional states: there is even a hint, in 'The Piper at the Gates of Dawn', that he underwent at least one intense visionary experience of a semi-mystical nature.

But such moments of awareness or self-exploration were comparatively rare, and there were less demanding amusements available than the National Gallery. Grahame's tastes were well-marked and London, despite everything, had its attractions: the circus, the freak-show, the illusionist, anything instinct with fantasy, oddness, the romantic or the macabre. He was fascinated by the Crystal Palace, and visited it frequently; and he almost certainly went to the old Polytechnic, where there were Haunted Castles, strange scientific experiments, a genuine 'Pepper's Ghost', and blood-curdling performances of such immortal works as 'The Mysteries of Udolpho' and 'Baron Münchhausen', complete with electrical effects. A Miss Alice Bath, as Allan Fea tells us, often figured in these scenes, and appeared as 'Undine, the Spirit of the Fountain': an ingenious arrangement of a large glass shade with a hose playing on the top. There was also the life-sized acrobat, 'Leotard', 'who performed stiff-jointed exercises and evolutions as he swung across the Central Hall'—and gave his name to a smaller, more domestic version who appears in *Dream Days*. Grahame found mechanical toys of any kind irresistible:

> He was an acrobat, this Leotard, who lived in a glass-fronted box. His loose-jointed limbs were cardboard, cardboard his slender trunk; and his hands eternally grasped the bar of a trapeze. You turned the box round swiftly five or six times; the wonderful unsolved machinery worked, and Leotard swung and leapt, backwards, forwards, now astride the bar, now flying free; iron-jointed, supple-sinewed, unceasingly novel in his invention of new, unguessable attitudes. ...

It was early in 1882 that young Reginald Ingles, at the age of sixteen, began to visit Kenneth and Roland in their Bloomsbury Street lodgings. (Uncle Jack, now a captain, was on a long course at Greenwich, and he and his family were living in Blackheath.) Kenneth went out of his way to make the younger boy at home; late in life Major Ingles recalled that his cousin 'always treated me just as an equal, though I know now that I was rather young and foolish.' This instinctive, unforced sense of equality was one of Kenneth's most deeply ingrained assumptions: we meet it again and again in his work. As far as Reginald Ingles was concerned, it meant pleasant visits to *Faust* at the Lyceum, or dinner at Kenneth's favourite Italian restaurant in Soho, where they 'had about ten courses for 1s. 6d. and drank Chianti out of a basket bottle'; or long hours of talk in the evening, when the air would grow heavy with the smoke of Honey Dew and the smell of fresh-ground coffee-beans. Kenneth was fussy over his coffee, always insisting on making it with an earthenware strainer; occasionally his tidy nature must have protested at his visitor's clumsiness, but good manners, somehow, always prevailed. Major Ingles relates:

> I remember Kenneth lending me a long churchwarden clay pipe with red sealing-wax on the stem. It was one of his treasures ... But I unfortunately broke the bowl off by tapping it on the fire-grate to knock the ash out. Kenneth, though he looked just slightly annoyed, was awfully nice about it and said that it did not matter a bit.

According to Major Ingles, Grahame was certainly writing in 1882, but whether or not with any success is uncertain from the way he phrases it: 'I think at that time he used to write a little to magazines and some literary pages'. He had begun that habit of walking-tour holidays which he only abandoned when he later went abroad regularly; and despite his drill and fencing, he had, during this period, two severe illnesses, 'what they called in those days inflammation of the bowels—one time I believe he was very bad and nearly died'. Despite his fine physique, it is clear that Grahame was never a completely well man all his life.

Partly because of his health, partly through that instinct for solitude which was so strong in him, he soon after this left Bloomsbury for a top-floor flat at 65 Chelsea Gardens, off the Chelsea Bridge Road. Probably there was already some slight clash of temperament between Roland and himself; if so, he would have wanted at all costs to avoid an open quarrel. But more urgent, certainly, was the need to find what he had never truly possessed, a place of his own.

His longing for domestic ties crystallized themselves in a persistently recurring dream which he later noted down in some detail. To judge by his letter to Helen Dunham—who confessed to a similar experience—he seems to have investigated the possible causes of his dream with great care. 'I'm not surprised at all,' he wrote, 'that you too have a room. Scientific people deny the repetition, and say that the one dream has along with it, and as part of it, a confused sense of many previous ones—that it is a mirage, in fact. But *we* know better.' Here is the dream as he remembered it:

> First, there would be a sense of snugness, of cushioned comfort, of home-coming. Next, a gradual awakening to consciousness in a certain little room, very dear and familiar, sequestered in some corner of the more populous and roaring part of London: solitary, the world walled out, but full of a brooding sense of peace and of possession. At times I would make my way there, unerringly, through the wet and windy streets, climb the well-known staircase, open the ever-welcomed door. More often I was there already, ensconced in the most comfortable chair in the world, the lamp lit, the fire glowing ruddily. But always the same feeling of a home-coming, of the world shut out, of the ideal encasement. On the shelves were a few books—a very few—but just the editions I had sighed for, the editions which refuse to turn up, or which poverty glowers at on alien shelves. On the walls were a print or two, a woodcut, an etching—not many. Old loves, all of them, apparitions that had flashed across the field of view in sales-rooms and vanished again in a blaze of three figures; but never possessed—until now. All was modest—O, so very modest! But all was my very own, and, what was more, everything in that room was exactly right.

It is characteristic of Grahame that his wish-fulfilment dream should invent a past as well as a future: that the ideal room should not only be perfect but *familiar* (even down to little details like the oak balustrade on the stair) though in fact he had never known anything resembling it. To make the illusion yet stronger, he played an elaborate charade with himself, based on the assumption that the room *did* exist, that he *had* been there, and only unaccountable absentmindedness prevented his remembering the circumstances. He would consult his accounts for details of rent payment; but found, conveniently, that he did not keep accounts. (This was a plain evasion: he kept meticulous accounts, as we would expect. But the next sentence gives away the truth: 'statistics would have been a mean prosaic way of plucking out the heart of this mystery'—especially when there was nothing to pluck out.) There followed investigations in the back streets of Bloomsbury and Chelsea, but, naturally, without result. If only there were some clue, 'some touch, scent, sound, gifted with the magic power of recall': but no clue presented itself. And again the strange split in Grahame's mind, so consciously conceived, is presented in an arresting image:

> It waits, that sequestered chamber, it waits for the serene moment when the brain is in just the apt condition, and ready to switch on the other memory even as one switches on the electric light with a turn of the wrist. Fantasy? well—perhaps. But the worst of it is, one can never feel quite sure. Only a dream, of course. And yet—the enchanting possibility!

Once again, and not for the last time, we have seen the genesis of a theme that was only to be developed fully in *The Wind in the Willows.*

Meanwhile the flat in Chelsea Gardens served as some kind of substitute, and at least had the virtue of inaccessibility. 'It was like climbing the stairs of a lighthouse,' one visitor recalled. 'There was no lift and the dirty stone staircase swept up in endless spirals.' As some compensation Kenneth had a superb view out over the Thames and Battersea Park; and he was already, within his limited means, beginning to stamp his personality on his rooms—a few prints, and one or two pieces of good furniture acquired from friendly relatives, or bought cheap in the Portobello Road. Chief among these purchases was a Chippendale bureau which, so tradition had it, once belonged to the Duke of Wellington; and this bureau sheds an interesting side-light on his methods of composition. After his death a secret drawer was discovered in it, which contained a small hoard of odds and ends: 'a set of Maundy Money, a handful of small sea-shells, minute models of *filets-bleux* (Breton fishing-nets), the Rules of Roulette (in miniature), a colourful prayer-card of Tobias and the Angel, &c.' Now this is almost certainly the bureau which figures in *The Golden Age*, and which also contains a secret drawer with treasure-trove; but since Grahame bought it while he was living in Chelsea Gardens, it follows that he used the experience to enrich the memory of his childhood, that it was transferred from another setting. Similarly with the sumptuously illustrated volume in 'Its Walls Were as of Jasper': it was composed (Grahame himself wrote) 'of several books, or rather memories of them—a little town or two—and some early Italian pictures'.

There is one curious passage in 'The Secret Drawer' which confirms this duality. The fictional narrator, a nine-year-old boy, suddenly breaks off in the middle of persuading the boudoir bureau to give up its secret and reflects: 'Was it any good persisting longer? Was anything any good whatever? In my mind I began to review past disappointments, and life seemed one long record of failure and of non-arrival.' Such sentiments are startingly out of key in the story, even when one has accepted Grahame's technique of moving to and fro contrapuntally between his adult and childish outlook; but in their proper context—a depressed young clerk furnishing his flat—they are only too appropriate. This is one of the clearest instances of Grahame's failing to disguise his source-material; in general he very carefully obliterated all tell-tale clues.

An interesting example of the process at both stages has survived. During his early years at the Bank Grahame took considerable interest in the legends of eccentricity which the older hands recounted. He went to the trouble of grubbing about in the official records in order to supplement oral tradition, and was sometimes richly rewarded. Of one former Bank employee he wrote:

> In his office there was the customary 'attendance-book', wherein the clerks were expected to sign each day. Here his name one morning ceases abruptly from appearing: he signs, indeed, no more. Instead of signature you find, a little later, writ in careful commercial hand, this entry: 'Mr——did not attend at his office today, having been hanged at eight o'clock in the morning for horse-stealing'.

Now we should not have known for certain that this episode referred to the Bank (though we might have guessed it) had we not possessed both original draft and published version of another anecdote relating to 'the same establishment'. These are so revealing when compared that they are worth quoting at length. The first is from the 'ledger diary', and shows the original germ of the idea:

> A certain old clerk in one of the pay departments of the Bank of England used to spend his yearly holiday in relieving some turnpike-man of his post and performing all the duties pertaining thereto till recalled to Threadneedle Street. This was vulgarly supposed to be an instance of slavery to one's accustomed work—of 'pay and receive'—and spoken of pityingly. But that man doubtless knew what he wanted, knew one way of seeing Life. And what better way? And if all he was good for was to pay and take payments at least he recognized the fact, accepted it, boldly built thereon and went for it in its best shape.

This fragment was afterwards worked into an essay called 'The Eternal Whither', published in the *National Observer* on 9 July 1892. By then the text had been modified in several ways. The exact location had been carefully concealed, the style had become far more prolix and ornate, and—perhaps most significant of all—the final stoic resignation had been completely reversed:

> There was once an old cashier in some ancient City establishment whose practice was to spend his yearly holiday in relieving some turnpike-man at his post, and performing all the duties appertaining thereto. This was vulgarly taken to be an instance of mere mill-horse enslavement to his groove—the reception of payments; and it was spoken of both in mockery of all mill-horses and for the due astonishment of others. And yet that clerk had discovered for himself an unique method of seeing Life at its best, the flowing, hurrying, travelling, marketing Life of the Highway; the life of bagman and cart, of tinker and pig-dealer, and all cheery creatures that drink and chaffer together in the sun. He belonged, above all, to the scanty class of clear-seeing people who know both what they are good for and what they really want.

The first version is perhaps more honest than the second, which seems to be propagating a carefully cultivated personal myth; yet who can tell, when dealing with Grahame, exactly where the borderline between myth and actuality can be drawn? He came to see himself as Ulysses in Threadneedle Street, the romantic wanderer pinned down to an urban routine by duty and necessity, the defeated rebel; but later in life, at least, he quite consciously urged the use of 'the countries of the mind', of day-dreams and fantasy, as a psychological therapeutic for those exhausted by the workaday world which they must accept whether they will or not.

His life between 1882 and 1887 fell into a well-ordered routine. There was the ferry-steamer to and from work, boarded at Chelsea Embankment or London Bridge; evenings visiting relatives, or dining in Soho, or drilling with the London Scottish; the business of the New Shakespere Society, and Furnivall's always stimulating company. In 1884 he added a new interest to the others: perhaps at Furnivall's suggestion he undertook voluntary work at the newly founded Toynbee Hall, in Stepney.

He is not listed among the distinguished lecturers who addressed the East End poor on English literature or current affairs; his was a more practical bent. He took the chair at sing-songs, and even sang himself; he fenced, boxed, and played billiards with the young toughs of Whitechapel and the Commercial Road. His one encounter with a literature class was mildly disastrous: he undertook to address a particularly rowdy group of girls. Perhaps his flustered good looks were irresistible; at any rate, almost before he could open his mouth, his audience mobbed him cheerfully, smothered him in kisses, 'at the same time chanting, to the tune of *Men of Harlech,* "What is one among so many?"' Grahame's only comment on this episode was that it considerably increased his affection for the London Scottish.

Sidney Ward, a colleague of his in the Bank, also did similar work at Toynbee Hall, and reveals in his reminiscences that Kenneth took some interest in Canon Barnett's early exhibitions of modern art, which were held in what has now become famous as the Whitechapel Gallery. But even so, Ward remarked—and we recognize the trait at once—'he liked a solitary life as a bachelor, with his books and writing, so that, friends as we were, I never saw a great deal of him outside our office life. He was probably the better pleased to see me because I didn't dig him out too often.'

His reticence was absolute unless he chose to reveal something of his inner thoughts. It is worth recording that as late as 1898 a director of the Bank purchased *The Golden Age* under the impression that it had something to do with bimetallism.

In August 1884 Grahame spent the first of several summer holidays at the Lizard, in Cornwall. He and Helen went together, and stayed with a friend of Helen's named Mary Richardson. Helen must have fallen as deeply in love with the place as Kenneth did: when she retired from nursing she took a house at the Lizard and remained there till her death in 1940. Kenneth at once developed a passion for deep-sea fishing: he learnt to whiff for pollock and mackerel, and the difficult art of dealing with conger. (He maintained that 'the fun with a twenty-five pound

MULLION COVE, THE LIZARD, CORNWALL c1880.
On one visit to The Lizard, Kenneth Grahame took great delight in being mistaken for a genuine Cornish fisherman by the Principal of Hertford College, Oxford.

conger only really began after you got it into the boat.') He became adept at baiting and hauling a mile-long sea-line, and at times he went out with the pilchard fleet, dressed like a local fisherman in rough warm blue jersey and peaked cap. On one of these occasions the Principal of Hertford College, Oxford, who visited the Lizard regularly and took a great interest in the fishermen, mistook Kenneth for the genuine article. Kenneth, poker-faced, touched his cap and answered Dr Boyd's somewhat patronizing questions in a fine Cornish burr; but the real locals, unable to keep this joke to themselves, told the truth to the Doctor, who came back to apologize in an agony of embarrassment. Kenneth had never been so flattered in his life. Fishermen were real people, untouched by the canker of urbanization; it was a rare compliment to be taken for one of them.

Miss Richardson gives an interesting description of him at this period, when he was about twenty-five:

> He was a tall ... fine looking young man, a splendid head, broad and well-proportioned—carried himself well—a good healthy complexion, large widely opened rather light grey eyes, always with a kindly expression in them. Not exactly handsome but distinctly striking-looking—sensitive hands and mouth, rather short clever nose. ... Distinctly reserved, until he trusted you—he seemed to me at times as if in his younger days he had been teased, and his boyish aspirations trodden on. ...

So the Lizard, too, was gathered in to Grahame's private world of release and romance, its memories cherished like those trinkets in the secret drawer which were, in a sense, the symbol of this larger myth which sustained him. Night fishing by lantern-light, trolling off Kynance Cove, the great and mysterious sea-beast which broke his line one stormy evening, the cargo of African fleeces washed ashore for salvage—Kenneth went out to the wreck with the coxswain of the lifeboat, his seventy-four-year-old fishing companion Tom Roberts—the soft-spoken Cornishmen in whose homes he came to be welcome: all were woven into a pattern of remembered happiness, remote as a star, which warmed him through a London winter.

He remembered the swifts flying above the estuaries, the gorse and the gales and the pounding breakers—and especially he remembered the food: Cornish cream, 'thunder and lightning', pilchard pie, leek pasties. He haunted the Cornish bric-à-brac shops, too, and his Chelsea rooms were soon littered with inkstands and candlesticks carved in serpentine. About this time his habit of collecting knick-knacks becomes generally noticeable. One of his manias was for those hollow glass rolling-pins with painted designs, known as 'Sailors' Farewells'; at a sale in 1920 he put up nearly forty for auction. The normal psychological explanation for this magpie practice is an urge to compensate for emotional deprivation, which fits well enough in Grahame's case, and is supported by his obsessional preoccupation with food.

It was in 1866 that Grahame first visited Italy: a momentous event in any sensitive northerner's life, doubly so for one who had his peculiar passion both for the South and for classical antiquity. He went with Helen to stay in the Villino Landau, near Florence, a 'little old farm-house' as Annie Grahame described it, which had been discovered by her mother and taken by Robert Grahame on an extended lease. It was a long, low, two-storied building, from which a paved courtyard sloped gently down to an old stone archway. Georgina Grahame was a passionately devoted gardener, and the whole place was a mass of madonna lilies, tea-roses, narcissi, jonquils, and sweet lemon plants.

On the second Sunday in May Kenneth and Annie Grahame made an expedition to the Festival of the Madonna del Sarso in the hill country behind Fiesole. Annie describes this expedition to the Madonna in amusing detail, and concludes: 'We got back about 7 pm, none the worse for the long day, which Kenneth had beguiled with delightful fairy tales'. His own? Perhaps; we cannot tell. At all events the genial air of Tuscany was working its magic on him, and it may be that his cousin's company, sympathetic as always, stirred him to inventiveness, as they walked those steep hill paths to the Madonna and her ancient Festival.

Characteristically, Kenneth had spent weeks before this visit acquainting himself with Florentine history and art; as a result he knew exactly what he was looking for and where to find it, an achievement which highly impressed Mrs Grahame, who wrote of the visit in glowing terms as 'in more senses than one, a "Golden Age" visit', and added wistfully that 'such red-letter times do not come every day.' Yet Kenneth was able to lift his nose from his Ruskin and Burckhardt long enough to observe and note down that 'the smells of Italy are more characteristic than those of the South of France', a statement which time has done nothing to refute. It was during this visit, too, that he bought the little blue-and-white majolica plaque—one of Cantazala's reproductions of a Madonna and Child by della Robbia—which he some years later put up, like a modern Greater London Council memorial tablet, outside his house in Kensington Crescent: an echo of those disturbingly intense moments he had spent in the National Gallery contemplating the Italian Primitives.

THE PIAZZA AND THE PORTA DEL POPOLO, ROME, c1900.
The glorious dream-Rome of *The Golden Age* could be approached by no reality.
'Even the beauty of Rome was not just that particular beauty that we had caught a glimpse of through the magic casement of our idealism'.

Either that year or the next, Grahame also had his first sight of Rome: and though this was a Rome which has long since vanished, a Rome of the *contadini* that still preserved an authentic whiff of the atmosphere which Shelley knew, I suspect that, as well as delight, Grahame experienced a secret twinge of disappointment. The glorious dream-Rome of *The Golden Age* could be approached by no three-dimensional reality, however august, sunlit, and picturesquely ruinous; Grahame admitted as much, years afterwards, in a lecture delivered before the Keats-Shelley Literary Association—in Rome:

Which of us, even today, when about to visit some new far-distant city or country, does not form, sometimes deliberately but usually almost unconsciously, a picture of it, more or less vivid, beforehand? ... I suppose that all of us here can remember our

> coming to Rome for the first time in our lives, and the preconception of the place that we brought along with us. Do we not all remember, when we reached Rome at last, the same two things—the absence of that strangeness which I have called the fantastic element and which somehow we cannot keep out of our imaginings, and secondly, the slight touch of disappointment that even the beauty of Rome was not just that particular beauty that we had caught a glimpse of through the magic casement of our idealism?

The warning was clearly given; and yet in after years it was ignored, and the vision lost. Grahame should have remembered that it was Stevenson who said that it is better to travel hopefully than to arrive.

On the eve of his departure for Florence, Grahame let himself become involved, in a minor capacity it is true, in a roaring theatrical scandal—a production of Shelley's *The Cenci*. Perhaps he had some idea of putting himself in a properly receptive mood for Italian culture; more probably he was incapable (like most people) of saying 'No' to Furnivall, who, as we might expect, was behind the occasion. Since the Lord Chamberlain refused to license *The Cenci*, the usual solemn mummery of a 'club production' was gone through. The play was produced by the Shelley Society on 7 May, at the Grand Theatre, Islington; it was Browning's birthday, and with him in the audience were Lowell, Meredith, Shaw, Andrew Lang, and Sir Percy and Lady Shelley. Hermann Vezin played the Count, and Miss Alma Murray, Beatrice; Kenneth took the part of Giacomo, one of the Count's sons. Dr Furnivall, somewhat mischievously, considering the incestuous subject-matter of the play, sent his housemaid to see it, and as Annie Grahame relates, 'being anxious to learn what impression it had made on her asked her what she though of it. She said: "Mr Grahame did look so handsome walking up and down the stage in his best clothes".' The result of the play was (as Furnivall had obviously hoped) a fine advertisement of the society; but Annie Grahame wrote that there was also 'a howl of disgust from various critics, and a spirited controversy on the propriety of the play and Vezin's interpretation of his part, in the *Pall Mall Gazette*'. During the subsequent uproar in the correspondence columns, Grahame was in all likelihood only too thankful to slip away to Italy. It was, as far as we know, the only time in his life that he ever appeared on a public stage: it was certainly the last.

The following year, 1887, marked the end of a major, if silent, influence in his life. On Sunday 27 February, he took a walk after lunch through Fulham and over Putney Bridge to Barnes Common, ending up at Hammersmith Bridge and returning along the towpath as far as Putney. He stayed out to tea with a friend, and on his return home found a telegram saying that his father had had a serious apoplectic stroke. It was from Mr Currie, a partner of Uncle John's, who had been in the Le Havre office when Cunningham Grahame first fell ill; he sent the wire, he told Kenneth afterwards, 'from a feeling of considerateness'—which at least suggests that Kenneth and his father had not previously been in any kind of communication. Shortly afterwards, however, a second telegram arrived, with the information that Mr Grahame had died during the afternoon. Kenneth wired back to Currie to say he was coming, wrote to Helen, and the following night crossed from Southampton to Le Havre, where his father had died, and where all but the first two years abroad had been spent. He noted down in his diary the following account of that Tuesday's events:

> Mr Currie met me, and we drove straight to my father's room, where I was able to see his face before the coffin was finally closed. He seems to have died quite instantaneously, no signs of life having ever shown themselves after those who heard the noise of his fall had reached his room and raised him ... At three o'clock we drove to 32, Rue Bougainvillea where for want of room inside, the coffin was placed in the little turfed garden or yard outside the house, and Mr Whelpton (the resident Methodist minister) read passages and prayers, chiefly those included in the Church of England Burial Service. ... We then drove to the little cemetery of Sainte Adresse on the heights over-looking the sea, near the lighthouses. With us were some clerks from Mr C(urrie)'s office who had known my father ... and the old landlady Madame Bazille, with her son and daughter-in-law. At the grave Mr Whelpton completed the service—I bade adieu to the other mourners at the gate of the cemetery. After speaking to Madame Bazille I put a £5 note into her hand. This had been approved of by Mr Currie, who spoke warmly of her affectionate care for eighteen years.

Next, Grahame went down to Mr Currie's office, where his father's papers and books had been brought. The books, he notes, were mostly school-books—dictionaries, grammars, and so on—and he brought away a few only. He seems to have been disappointed in his search for private and legal documents, though with Mme Bazille's son he made a thorough search of his father's room. 'I made over the clothes to the Bazilles, and also the money in his purse—only 15 frs—Mme Bazille showed me a small photo of himself which he had given her, and which she wished me to take if I had not got one. I begged her to keep it.' There followed some routine business at the Mairie and British Consulate, after which Grahame, like any sightseer, went off for a tour of the docks with a man named Holmes, from Mr Currie's office. He returned to London the following day.

Nowhere in these bleak, practical diary entries is there the least hint of regret, hatred, or strong emotion of any kind: merely a cold and businesslike indifference. The ritual had to be gone through, and Grahame went through it quickly, efficiently, and economically, even to the picking of the cheapest available cemetery. On the surface it does not seem that his father's death affected him one way or the other. Yet is it entirely coincidental that the following year he began to be published, and that from then on essays and stories poured from him in an ever-increasing spate? While he lived, Cunningham Grahame still exercised a psychologically inhibiting influence on his son, even from across the Channel; the prose style of Grahame as diarist is tight, spare, restrained—almost, one had said, repressed. But after his father's death there is an immediate sense of release, the blowing away of a black cloud.

To judge by the scrappy entries in his April diary, Grahame's mood was one of relaxed cheerfulness. He still either walked to work or went by boat; and on

Monday 18 April, a day of bright sun and white frost on the ground, he 'got up at 6, and went a delightful walk by the river before breakfast'. Life was suddenly—he probably could not have explained how or why—opening out into a pattern of brighter colours, wider interests.

To all events, one day, his mind running on the Berkshire Downs in December, where 'the furrows still gleam unbroken, touched each, on the side the share has polished, with warm light from the low, red, winter's sun', he sat down and wrote a country essay, entitled 'By a Northern Furrow', which he sent to the editor of the *St James's Gazette*: and this time there was no rejection slip.

V

PAGANS AND PHILISTINES

1888–93

In June 1887 Queen Victoria celebrated her Golden Jubilee, and the London Scottish were on duty, as Kenneth wrote, 'during the whole short summer night prior to the Great Day.' They were later inspected by Lord Roberts, and Kenneth described the occasion, in which both he and Roland participated, as 'full of music, marching, and much true and affectionate loyalty and patriotism.' Yet this picture of stable harmony was far from the whole truth. Enormous forces were beginning to disrupt the Victorian class-structure, and as a Londoner Grahame could witness at first hand some of their uglier manifestations. In the Jubilee year itself jingoistic complacency was shattered by Bloody Sunday and the Trafalgar Square riots; and though few people, perhaps, saw a connection between the founding of the ILP and that of the Arts and Crafts Movements, whose originators thought it 'more honest to learn to weave or make furniture than gamble on the stock exchange', they were undoubtedly part of the same great protesting ferment.

Since Grahame's arrival in London, this atmosphere of opposition had become more violent and more articulate. At one end of the scale came the hierarchic social round, with its stilted compliments, its snobbish etiquette, its conversational clichés and elaborate sexual gambits; at the other were the Salvation Army, the Irish Land Act, the first Rowton Houses, and the Fabian Society. In the middle Sir Gorgius Midas sat, coining money from sweated labour, lampooned in the pages of *Punch*, and pertinaciously buying his way into the higher echelons. Between these three class-divisions were basic fear, hatred, and distrust; but in a real emergency the rich and the privileged would always unite against the radical element. The days were passing when a tenant, suspected of trades-unionism, could be quietly ousted from his tenancy; in 1880 in *Hodge and His Masters* Richard Jefferies noted that 'respect for authority is extinct. ... There used to be a certain tacit agreement among all men that those who possessed capital, rank, or reputation should be treated with courtesy. ... But now, metaphorically speaking, the labourer removes his hat for no man. ... The cottager can scarcely nod his employer a common greeting in the morning.'

Things were indeed different now; when the first Fabian pamphlet appeared in 1884, a year after Marx's death, it contained these words: 'We live in a competitive society with Capital in the hands of individuals ... the time approaches when Capital can be made public property ... the power is in your hands, and chances of using that power are continually in your reach'. As time went on this movement became more angry and violent. Anarchists proclaimed their intention of 'sending the privileged classes to heaven by chemical parcel post', strikes and riots increased, political murders were not unheard-of, and an attempt was even made, in 1882, to assassinate the Queen.

Meanwhile, for the mercantile middle-class, material progress remained the watchword. By 1884 the railway companies were practically exhausted after four decades of cut-throat competition, leaving a legacy of deserted roads, ruined countryside, and disrupted local traditions. The industrial towns were spreading their tentacles further and further into hitherto rural areas, and the flow of labour away from the land continued unchecked. The counties in 1885 defied squire and farmer and voted Liberal; the following year came the Pall Mall Riots, with a furious mob looting the shops in Piccadilly.

It seems clear in retrospect (though it was not probably realized at the time by either side in the struggle) that the privileged classes of the eighties and nineties were frightened as well as angered by such demonstrations; and that it was fear, the subconscious nightmare of the upsurgent mob, which hardened their resistance. Radical change of any kind—especially change which involved their rural economy—they regarded with the deepest suspicion. It was not only the county families (broadly speaking) who adopted this attitude of militant chauvinism; the intellectuals and writers largely followed them. As Osbert Burdett percipiently observed in *The Beardsley Period*, they 'could not conceive society in other than aristocratic terms, and their preference for aristocracy persisted side by side with hatred of the plutocracy that apes it. Thus they became destroyers of the remnant of what they loved, without identifying themselves with the disruptive forces that were preparing the ground for a different society.'

Nostalgia, fear, anger, wish-fulfilment, escapism in the broadest sense: these were their driving motives. It was as if by taking thought they could alter the unwelcome pattern of their age, as if words were magic weapons which could break up the nightmare and bring back daylight once more. It was these brutal facts which underlay the whole drift towards fantasy, 'art for art's sake', the Celtic Twilight, the hair-splitting over Appearance and Reality, the *Looking Glass* doubt as to who was in whose dream, the widening gap between the artist and a society which he hated and feared, yet could not wholly escape.

In one way or another nearly all the writers of the later Victorian period attacked the new radical trends; and even those who, like William Morris, actively supported radicalism still disassociated themselves from the industrial urbanization which produced it. This put them in an impossible position. Their 'ideal' society was aristocratic, rural, and pre-industrial. The actual society to which they belonged was a solidly materialistic and intolerant bourgeoisie. They were simultaneously committed to a doctrine of material progress, and debarred from any kind of progressive thinking, by temperament no less than social pressure:

mechanical development was accompanied by hardening of the religious and political arteries. They knew their civilization had taken the wrong turning, not in their brains but in their blood: every physiological instinct they possessed rebelled against the retreat from natural rhythms to the seasonless maelstrom of the metropolis.

Yet their protests did them no good, and not a little harm. When Morris spent his time weaving on a handloom, or turning out superb editions from the Kelmscott Press, or living in a pseudo-mediaeval revival of his own making, he was certainly at peace with himself, but he was out of step with his society. That is the tragedy of the post-industrial age: a man who satisfied his natural creative or pastoral instincts, who set out to be craftsman and maker, would by that act cut himself off from his fellows. He could fulfil himself, or he could conform with his society; but he could not do both, though both were essential to his well-being. The point had been reached at which they were mutually contradictory.

The attempt to romanticize industrial phenomena by absorbing them into a traditional myth—whether Lionel Johnson's 'iron lilies in the Strand' (*i.e.* lamp-posts) or the pyloned landscapes of the thirties—is simply a form of self-protection. Kipling was a pioneer of this kind of social therapy which was based on a carefully developed conviction that the repulsive reality is in fact infinitely desirable. The easiest answer, however, was to contract out of society altogether and later the vast majority of writers considered art, literature and religion as 'a refuge, a sort of cloistral refuge, from a certain vulgarity in the actual world'. An art that cuts off its own roots soon withers away into sterile repetitiveness: nothing is more subtly destructive than a closed circle of artists feeding on each other. An excessive preoccupation with stylistic ornament; a tendency to derive themes from the work of previous writers; an evaporation of moral seriousness into mere hedonistic froth; a species of emotional corruption induced by the necessary search for new sensation: these are some of the more obvious dangers inherent in the formula of 'Art for art's sake'.

Those writers who could not reconcile themselves with this *déraciné* aestheticism, and yet remained temperamentally opposed to the radical view, tended to throw their energies either into satire or the kind of swash-buckling romantic imperialism made popular by Disraeli.

The imperialism represented the positive implications of this rather negative carping, and apart from Kipling its main exponent was that remarkable character W. E. Henley: poet, journalist, encyclopaedist, art-critic, playwright, essayist, lexicographer, anthologist and—last but not least—editor. It was in this editorial capacity that he first met Grahame, whose 'little meteorites' had at last come to rest in the office of Frederick Greenwood, editor of the *St James's Gazette.* James Payn at the *Cornhill* had fobbed his would-be contributor off, a month or two earlier, with a polite bromide: 'Your little paper', he wrote, 'is too short and slight for the *Cornhill*, but the humour it exhibits has struck me as being exceptional and leads me to hope that I may again hear from you.' The *Cornhill* never had another piece by Grahame till the posthumously published 'A Dark Star' in 1933; what is interesting about Payn's letter is its reference to *humour*, which seems hitherto to have excited no comment.

The two early essays which Greenwood published, 'By a Northern Furrow' and 'A Bohemian in Exile', though not without a quiet wit, could hardly be described as humorous, even by the standards of 1890. A great deal of Grahame's journalism at this period was anonymous but one essay has been identified as Grahame's. It shows that Grahame *was* a humourist and confirms his interest in contemporary and political affairs.

Sidney Ward, in his unpublished recollections of Grahame, gives this account of the episode: 'It was at the time of the great Parnell divorce, and the papers were full of sensational accounts of how the great man escaped from Mrs O'Shea's house, through a window, when the Captain arrived unexpectedly. A day or two afterwards there appeared in the *St James's Gazette* an alleged "Conversation between a Balcony and a Waterspout". It was clever and witty and scurrilous and altogether delightful. I turned to K. G. and said: "I say, Grahame, did you see that gorgeous conversation between a balcony and a water-spout in the *St James's* last night?" "Yes," said K. G., "I wrote it!"' The issue in which it appeared was that of 19 November 1890:

A PARABLE

(OVERHEARD AND COMMUNICATED BY OUR OWN CAT)

"Well, old fellow," said the Waterspout to the Verandah, "and how do you feel, now it's all over?"

"Very poorly indeed, thanks," said the Verandah mournfully. "Just look at my nice paint! I'm scratched and kicked all over."

"Paint, indeed!" said the Waterspout, with scorn; "what does paint matter? Now look at me. I'm all twisted and bent like a bayonet. If it hadn't been for our old friend the Fire-escape there, who took some of the work, I should have been old iron long ago."

"Well, it's splendid exercise," put in the Fire-escape meditatively; "*I* don't mind if he thinks it does him good. But, really, I didn't think he had it in him. He's a marvellous man!"

"Oh, *you* don't mind, of course!" remarked the Waterspout; "escaping is your business. But it's not mine, and I don't want to take it up. And now my old friend the sparrow, who's built in me these five years, has had to go. Says she didn't mind the racket so much; but there will be a young family to bring up next spring, and she must think of them."

"Quite right too," said the Verandah. "Good old sparrow! But between ourselves, now, it was very funny sometimes, wasn't it? First of all *He* would slip in, in a modest and unassuming manner, as if he had called to tune the piano; then he—I mean Shea—would come and kick at the door; then she would open it for Sh—I mean him; and *He* would come sliding down our friend here, like a lamplighter. Then *He* would pick himself up and ring the visitors' bell; and Shea would open the door for *He*—I mean him; and all would be surprise, delight, and harmony. And the next night he'd give the Fire-escape a turn."

> "He gave *me* a turn once or twice," said the Waterspout reflectively. "I've had a burglar down me, and a schoolboy or two, but never the idol of a nation's hopes and aspirations. The boat that carried Caesar and his fortunes will have to take a back seat now."
>
> "By the by, old chap," said the Verandah, "what will the other old Waterspout say? The Grand one, you know—the head of your family." [This refers to Gladstone, who as a Liberal supported Parnell—but depended largely on the Non-conformist vote. The line of Liberal papers such as the *Manchester Guardian* and *Freeman's Journal* was that Parnell's private life had nothing to do with his politics.]
>
> "Why," put in the Fire-escape, "he'll say that the subject is one of vast human interest, and he would like nothing better than to hear it fully and freely discussed. He fears, however, that at his time of life he must leave to younger and more vigorous—"
> The measured tread of the policeman approached down the quiet lane, and silence reigned once more in the peaceful little suburb.

This piece, ephemeral enough in itself, sheds a most interesting light on its author in the context of his subsequent development. It shows his first crude use of fable as a vehicle for satire, complete with the characteristic *non-human* viewpoint which always, in one form or another, gave edge and perspective to his criticisms. It also explodes that faint haze of otherworldliness, in the purely sentimental sense, which his more disastrous admirers are liable to attribute to him. Grahame, we should never forget, was one of the first English writers to pepper his essays with quotations from Rabelais: this aspect of his nature was firmly suppressed by his wife and biographer after he died, and Sidney Ward's unfortunate disclosure remained in the obscurity of a private letter-file. There was a general air of French farce about the Parnell proceedings which must have caught Grahame's fancy; Parnell's horses were called Dictator, President, and Home Rule, while Mrs O'Shea's maid declared under cross-examination that her mistress 'said there was a secret society about, and it was necessary to have the door locked'. Politically, too, he found irresistible the opportunity to poke fun at Gladstone and Parnell simultaneously.

This brings us back to Henley. He was installed as editor of the *Scots Observer* in 1888 and he moved the editorial offices in 1890 to London and rechristened the paper the *National Observer.*

The *National Observer* was from the first stamped with Henley's pugnacious and idiosyncratic prejudices on every page, whether political, artistic, or moral. He was violently anti-Socialist, so he lost Shaw as a contributor. He could reconcile—or even equate—Toryism with Radicalism, as 'a broad doctrine of individual freedom within the fabric of a firm but self-reformative social structure', but he had no tolerance for the *practical* Radical. Henley's somewhat ambiguous position gave his satirical guns a wide field of traverse. At one and the same time he was prepared to attack Gladstone (that 'Pantaloon'), Sir Wilfred Lawson the teetotal MP, General Booth of the Salvation Army, W. T. Stead ('Bed-Stead'), the famous journalist, and Richard Le Gallienne. His real enemy was Puritanism, which he instinctively associated in an unholy trio with Labour and Humbug.

The *National Observer*, though its circulation was never high, had a dazzling gallery of contributors, ranging from Stevenson and Kipling to Yeats, and managed to blend literary virtuosity with slashing political indictments, such as Kipling's poem *Cleared*, on the Parnell Commission. It lasted for four years; and it finally failed because the intellectuals who should have supported its literary star were all progressives, politically speaking, while the Tories at whom it was aimed stuck to *The Times*, *Punch* and the *Illustrated London News*. Beerbohm, as so often, had the last word on it: 'The paper', he wrote, 'was rowdy, venomous, and insincere. There was libel in every line of it. It roared with the lambs and bleated with the lions. It was a disgrace to journalism and a glory to literature.'

Henley's views all struck a responsive chord in Grahame. He had clearly been going through that tiresome initial process of finding a congenial editor. Nothing, in all probability, attracted him more than Henley's slashing attacks on Puritanism. In Grahame's own words—'and it's so true—and the whole truth—that the *N.Obs.* left a hole, never yet filled up. They were good times, those; and I don't see the same output now.' Elsewhere he admitted that Henley 'was the first Editor who gave me a full and a free and a frank show, who took all I had and asked me for more: I should be a pig if I ever forgot him'.

Grahame's first known contribution to the *Scots Observer* was 'Of Smoking', which appeared on 18 October 1890. 'The Rural Pan' was not published by Henley till 25 April 1891; and by then five other contributions had preceded it, all submitted in that neat holograph which had so impressed a sub-editor on the *St James's Gazette,* and given doubts to an old Scots ledger-clerk at the Bank of England ('It's no' the hand of a principal, young Grahame'.) Henley and Grahame had met, and taken a personal liking to each other; indeed, after a little, Henley first made Grahame a regular contributor, and then tried to argue him into giving up his career at the Bank and becoming a professional writer. But Grahame, who had strong views on the writer's amateur status, who 'held himself to be a spring and not a pump', for once held out against all Henley's persuasions and curses, and yet contrived—rare diplomacy—to remain his friend.

Henley, as Stevenson observed, was a man of tremendous energy and presence; and Grahame wrote, remembering him: 'My personal recollection of W. E. Henley is vivid enough still—perhaps because he was so very vivid himself. Sick or sorry—and he was often both—he was always vivid. The memory of this, and of his constant quality of stimulation and encouragement, brings him best to my mind.' The lame, irascible, diehard poet, with his bawdy enthusiasms, his vitriolic satire, and his nostalgia for the heroic simplicities of Homer's age, when 'men were not afraid of nor ashamed of death, and you could be heroic without a dread of clever editors', made a deep impression on Grahame: there was something in Henley of Furnivall's tremendous yet always compulsive unorthodoxy. Grahame became a regular guest both at the Friday dinners held in Verrey's Restaurant for contributors, and at those more select gatherings on Sunday evenings in Henley's house.

These Sunday 'At Homes' have been described by Yeats, who also attended

KENNETH GRAHAME.
A gentleman of the *Scots Observer*.

them, and who 'disagreed with Henley about everything, but admired him beyond words'. 'We gathered ...,' he wrote in *Autobiographies*, 'in two rooms, with folding doors between, and hung, I think, with photographs from Dutch masters, and in one room there was always, I think, a table with cold meat ... he made us feel always our importance, and no man among us could do good work, or show the promise of it, and lack his praise.' According to C. L. Hinds, who was a guest in September 1891, it was easy to distinguish the literary amateurs from the professional writers. 'They looked more comfortable; they ate their food in a more leisurely way; they were readier to praise than to blame, because literature was to them a delightful relaxation, not an arduous business.'

W. E. HENLEY.
Henley, editor of the *Scots Observer*, was the first to publish Grahame's work. This 'irascible diehard' is caricatured (right) by 'Spy' (Leslie Ward) for *Vanity Fair* in 1892.

Among these 'leisure-hour gentlemen of the pen', Hinds noticed, was

> a tall, well-knit, blonde man, who moved slowly and with dignity, and who preserved, amid the violent discussions and altercations that enlivened the meetings of the group, a calm, comprehending demeanour accompanied by a ready smile that women would call 'sweet'. And yet this blonde, temperate, kindly-looking man had also a startled air, as a fawn might show who suddenly found himself on Boston Common, quite prepared to go through with the adventure, as a well-bred fawn should do under any circumstances, but unable to escape wholly from the memory of the glades and woods whence he had come. He seemed to be a man who had not yet become quite accustomed to the discovery that he was no longer a child, but grown-up and prosperous.* Success did not atone for the loss of the child outlook. Every one of us has his adjective. His adjective was—startled.

*This report contains two inaccuracies. Firstly, Grahame's hair was dark until it turned prematurely grey; secondly he was not prosperous at the time of the meeting although by 1921 when Hinds was writing, Grahame had become so.

It is one of the clearest and most characteristic descriptions of Grahame which have come down to us: modified, perhaps, by Graham Robertson's slightly more robust appraisal:

> He was living in London where he looked all *wrong*—that is to say, as wrong as so magnificent a man could look anywhere. As he strode along the pavements one felt to him as towards a huge St Bernard or Newfoundland dog, a longing to take him away into the open country where he could be let off the lead and allowed to range at will. He appeared happy enough and made the best of everything, as do the dogs, but he was too big for London and it hardly seemed kind of Fate to keep him there.

Fawn or St Bernard—it is significant, yet not surprising, that each attempt to convey his personality has recourse to an animal image.

Between 1890 and 1896, the years which marked Grahame's most intensely creative period, everything he wrote that did not go into *The Yellow Book* first appeared in Henley's *National Observer,* or, after that failed, in its successor, the *New Review.* (This division of loyalties, between Decadence and Counter-Decadence, is a fairly accurate analogue of Grahame's literary temperament.) There can be no doubt that Henley's editorial influence on his young Scots essayist was profound, and by no means always beneficial. Like certain American editors today, he had a habit of 'subbing' and touching up his contributors' material till it carried the Henley stamp.

It is quite plain that Grahame's material underwent this processing: his contributions to the *St James's Gazette* are easily distinguishable from those in which Henley had a hand. As soon as Grahame begins to publish in the *Scots Observer* his archaisms and quaintness take a sudden leap skywards. It is not difficult to guess why. To do him justice, he protested against this tinkering with his text. In the corrected proofs of 'A Funeral' we can see the battle going on, with Grahame excising or modifying the more blatantly archaic conceits which Henley had presumably inserted before sending the MS to the printer. But Grahame was still only on the threshold of the literary world, and cannot be blamed for not pressing his point more strongly.

There is, indeed, a good deal of evidence that he fell under Henley's hypnotic spell after a while. The older man certainly fired him with a portentous enthusiasm for Stevenson, his former star contributor. Much of *Pagan Papers*, both as regards style and theme, reads like a variant gloss on *Virginibus Puerisque,* where we also find essays on Pan, walking-tours, smoking, and the pleasures of idleness.

Today, when we go through these stock themes—food and drink, tobacco, sleep, travel, walking, nature-mysticism, and the rest of them—it becomes clear that they are all regarded as *drugs*, either stimulant or soporific, escape-routes from an intolerable everyday reality. Grahame knows this perfectly well. There is, as he says, 'a certain supernal, a deific state of mind' which can only be produced 'after severe and prolonged exertion in the open air', followed by an evening at some village inn described in 'The Romance of the Road':

There, in its homely, comfortable strangeness, after unnumbered chops with country ale, the hard facts of life begin to swim in a golden mist. You are isled from accustomed cares and worries—you are set in a peculiar nook of rest. Then old failures seem partial successes, then old loves come back in their fairest form, but this time with never a shadow of regret, then old jokes renew their youth and flavour. You ask nothing of the gods above, nothing of men below—not even their company. Tomorrow you shall begin life again: shall write your book, make your fortune, do anything; meanwhile you sit, and the jolly world swings round, and you seem to hear it circle to the music of the spheres.

It is the same with tobacco, which is 'the true Herb of Grace, and a joy and healing balm, and respite and nepenthe': an opinion echoed by Calverley, Arthur Machen, and, most strikingly, Lionel Johnson, in *The Yellow Book:*

The blue smoke curls and glides away, with blue pagodas, and snowy almond bloom, and cherry flowers, circling and gleaming in it, like a narcotic vision. O magic of tobacco! Dreams are there, and superb images, and a somnolent paradise. ... Perhaps the cigarette is southern and Latin, southern and Oriental, after all; and I am a dreamer, out of place in this northern grey antiquity.

Again there is the contrast between the grey puritan North and the colourful, abandoned Mediterranean; between the exotic dream and the intolerable reality.

When one reads widely in the literature of the period there emerges a nightmare picture—and perhaps a not entirely false one—of writers and artists doping themselves silly on liquor and tobacco, walking themselves into a muscle-bound stupor every week-end, turning Nature into a kind of personalized God: and why? To produce bigger and better compensation-fantasies for the disgusting deadness of urban life; to blunt their senses enough to make existence bearable; to stimulate their imaginations into producing an inner lotus-land to which they could retreat at necessity.

The protests made by a minority are fatally easy to misinterpret; and what began as an ideal is always liable to corruption in practice. When Grahame wrote his essay on 'Loafing', his perfectly valid proposition was that the exclusive emphasis on material progress, the acceleration of the tempo of living beyond man's natural capacity, were starving and stunting the human soul.

The essays which Grahame wrote in this period are a clear enough guide to his own preoccupations and interests, and present a surprisingly coherent picture. On the whole he avoided the extremes represented by rural fantasy on the one hand and Henley's muscular sword-waving on the other. His comments are shrewd and realistic, with occasional whiffs of fantasy or angry satire as the mood took him. Like the Homeric heroes he and Henley vicariously admired, he is disturbed profoundly by the thought of death; 'from no love of them, but rather with a shuddering fear, he must be busy with all the emblems of mortality'.

The lure of the open road, the call of the simple life, away from hammering modern ugliness and competition and smoke and complexity: that is what draws Grahame again and again, perhaps nowhere more effectively than in 'A Bohemian in Exile', the story of Fothergill, the modern scholar-gipsy, who had had the courage to break loose and contract out of society. Fothergill at one point is lured back to property and respectability, but soon begins to mope in his cage, and vanishes once more.

The most interesting thing about Grahame's approach in this essay is its practicality. The whole thing is treated as a possible plan of action, not as fantasy; when Fothergill meets the narrator on the Berkshire Downs, and tells him of his experiences, he seems to be opening a gate into a tangible and realizable paradise:

> The old road-life still lingered on in places, it seemed, once one got well away from the railway; there were two Englands existing together, the one fringing the great iron highways wherever they might go—the England under the eyes of most of us. The other, unguessed at by many, in whatever places were still vacant of shriek and rattle, drowsed on as of old: the England of heath and common and windy sheep down, of by-lanes and village-greens—the England of Parson Adams and Lavengro.

It is the last glimpse of the past, the death-throes of real country life; and Grahame was young enough to have caught its authentic flavour before it was lost for ever.

Grahame's life moved on tranquilly enough during these years. In 1888 he was transferred to the Chief Cashier's office: the Chief Cashier was Frank May, who five years later resigned under something of a cloud, having been in the habit, *inter alia,* of advancing high overdrafts on his own authority without consulting the Governor. Here Grahame made friends with Gordon Nairne, who was in later years to be Chief Cashier himself when Grahame was Secretary. Nairne, in his reminiscences about Grahame, hints that he allowed more interpenetration between imagination and business than has generally been supposed. On one occasion Grahame 'had to write a very brief memorandum concerning the affairs of a pensioner of the Bank who had been under me. He asked whether I thought the facts were clearly stated and I remember being much struck by the touch of romance with which he invested the official life of a very ordinary man.' And, conversely, there was romance to be culled from the Bank in his writings: the magic evocativeness of words like 'bullion' or 'ingots', the perennial thrill of a place 'where gold was thought so little of that it was dealt about in shovels'.

Grahame did not remain in the Chief Cashier's office long; the following year he was transferred to the Secretary's office, and here he remained. At first he was occupied with the cataloguing of books in the Directors' Library; and, in Nairne's words, 'as these were mainly on dry-as-dust subjects, I doubt if the task proved very interesting to him.' However, it was here that he first met Sidney Ward. Perhaps because of Ward's delicacy and respect for Grahame's solitude, the two of them were soon intimate enough to go for long week-ends together on the Berkshire Downs. Ward recalls an occasion on which Grahame had borrowed a fourteenth-century cottage in the main street of Streatley, and they walked twenty miles along the Ridgeway before returning to 'chops, great chunks of cheese, new bread, great swills of beer, pipes, bed, and heavenly sleep'.

This week-end, and others like it, supplied the material for several essays. We can sketch in something of what Grahame did and felt on these occasions from his own record: the comfortable breakfast in shirt-sleeves, the stroll through the village street, punctuated by exchange of courtesies with various dogs; the irritation of a bicycle-bell, shattering the rural calm with its metal reminder of cities, speed, and progress. This is his cue to climb a gate and make his way towards solitude and the breezy downs, following the age-old Ridgeway:

> At once it strikes you out and away from the habitable world in a splendid, purposeful manner, running along the highest ridge of the Downs, a broad green ribbon of turf, with but a shade of difference from the neighbouring grass, yet distinct for all that. No villages nor homesteads tempt it aside or modify its course for a yard ... Where a railway crosses it, it disappears indeed-hiding, Alpheus-like, from the ignominy of rubble and brick-work; but a little way on it takes up the running again with the same quiet persistence.

Then comes the characteristic touch of animism, the anthropomorphic image: 'Out on that almost trackless expanse of billowy Downs such a track is in some sort humanly companionable: it really seems to lead you by the hand.'

After a while exercise accomplishes its task, and the moment for contemplation has come. This mild yet intense communion with nature is characteristic not only of Grahame but many of his contemporaries; none perhaps more than Richard Jefferies, whose spiritual autobiography, *The Story of my Heart,* was first published in 1883 and appeared in a second edition about the time Grahame's two 'Ridgeway' essays were written.

About 1890 Grahame visited Venice for the first time. Here he met mastiffs that—incredible to relate—flourished on a diet of *oar-blades*: they lived in a garden separated from the canal by an ilex-hedge, and passing boatmen, knowing their habits, would push old oars through the hedge for them: 'whereupon the great dogs, seizing the blades, would crunch them up as though they did but eat biscuit'. And one September day, barefoot and paddling (supreme pleasure!) in the crinkled, sandy shallows of the Lido, his mind full of Ulysses, Grahame encountered an expatriate Englishman who gave him the material for 'Long Odds'—one of his oddest and most revealing stories:

> He was barelegged also, this elderly man of sixty or thereabouts; and he had just found a *cavallo del mare,* and exhibited it with all the delight of a boy; and as we wandered together, cool-footed, eastwards, I learnt by degrees how such a man as this, with the mark of Cheapside still evident on him, came to be pacing the sands of the Lido that evening with me. ...

Just how much of the subsequent narrative was prompted by the actual, historical meeting, and how much added by Grahame's personal obsessions and fears, we cannot exactly determine. The old man is presented as a former Secretary of a City company dating from Henry VII; and one of his particular duties was 'ticking off, with a blue pencil, the members of his governing body, as they made their appearance at their weekly meeting'.

STREATLEY, BERKSHIRE c1885.
Kenneth Grahame borrowed a fourteenth-century cottage in the main street of this Thames-side village and used it as a base for long walks on the Downs.

THE BERKSHIRE DOWNS AT STREATLEY, c1880.
The view from the Thames towpath at Goring Lock shows the slopes of the Downs rising immediately behind the village of Streatley.

This function gave the old man a very sizable neurosis. First he lost all sense of time, which seemed to speed up into a nightmare gallop: some members dropped out of the Board, new ones appeared, 'the whole business was a great humming zoetrope', life was slipping through his hands like water spilt in the desert. Then he had a full-scale visual illusion: he saw Death personified while on an Underground train, and Death was ticking the Secretaries themselves off with a blue pencil; and he knew that when his own name was reached he would die. He jumped out at St James's Park with one name between him and destruction, and made his way to the Park itself; and there on the bridge over the water he halted, mopped his brow, and gradually recovered his peace of mind:

> Beneath his feet a whole family of ducks circled aimlessly, with content written on every feature; or else, reversing themselves in a position denoting supreme contempt for all humanity above the surface, explored a new cool underworld a few inches below. It was then (he said) that a true sense of his situation began to steal over him; and it was then that he awoke to the fact of another life open to him should he choose of grasp it. ... The very next Board day he sent in his resignation, and with comfortable pension. ... crossed the Channel and worked South till he came to Venice, where the last trace of blue-pencil nightmare finally faded away.

How far does this passage reflect Grahame's own predicament? To begin with, it is uncannily prophetic. It was written in 1895, when Grahame was not yet Secretary of the Bank—that came several years later—and thirteen years before he resigned and began travelling round the Mediterranean. What it may well indicate is the last kick of his imprisoned *alter ego* against the claims of respectability. Grahame was not yet Secretary: but he must have known he soon would be. The future stretched ahead, mapped out, predictable. time raced dizzily, the blue pencil wagged like a metronome. Thoroughly scared, Grahame took a holiday in Venice: but, unlike the old man on the Lido, he came back. We cannot be certain how far 'Long Odds' is an accurate description of Grahame's state of mind: but much of it rings unpleasantly true. Once again he had driven his instincts down, deep below the surface: and this time they remained there, alive, but invisible. The period of open conflict was over.

VI

THE RURAL PAN

1893–4

On 19 January 1893 Kenneth Grahame wrote to John Lane & Elkin Mathews, offering them a selection of his essays for publication in book form. It was a nervous, awkward, tentative letter: another Rubicon to be crossed, and always the chance of rebuff and failure:

> Dear Sirs I wonder whether you would care to publish a quite small selection of articles that I have had in the *National Observer* and *St James's Gazette* during the past few years?
>
> They are, I think, just sufficiently individual and original to stand it.
>
> Mr Henley suggested to me once, that a 'blend' of these short articles with verse would perhaps make a 'feature' that might take. But that is a detail I have no particular feeling about, one way or the other.
>
> The two journals mentioned would, I think, give friendly reviews.
>
> I can, of course, leave the things with you anyway, to look over.
>
> Your attractive 'format'—which you maintain so well—has mainly prompted my suggestion.

John Lane must have been amused by the naïve blend of flattery, self-advertisement, and shyness—not to mention the heavily underlined hint of friends at court. (It is hard to remember that the author of this letter was soon to be Secretary of the Bank of England.) But Lane perceived the quality of the essays themselves, and agreed to publish them in his autumn list.

The first edition of *Pagan Papers* (as the collection was entitled) contained, in addition to the early essays, six stories which were afterwards to be incorporated in *The Golden Age*: these, in fact, were what many of the critics at once fastened on. But Lane could not have foreseen this when he accepted Grahame's MS, for the simple reason that at the time only one of them, 'The Olympians', had been written. (It had appeared anonymously in the *National Observer* on 19 September 1891, and was an instantaneous success with the literary world.) The remaining five* were composed in a kind of creative frenzy between February and September

*'A Whitewashed Uncle', 'The Finding of a Princess', 'Young Adam Cupid', 'The Burglars' and 'Snowbound'.

1893, and incorporated in *Pagan Papers* in time for its publication at the end of October. This was Grahame's first real appearance under his own name before a critical public: all his work hitherto (with the exception of one or two poems) have been unsigned.

Henley, the born editor, saw that in 'The Olympians' lay the kernel of something entirely new, the blueprint on which a whole magic structure could be erected; and he used all his powers of persuasion to guide Grahame along the path he should take. The emotional crisis, which Grahame's fable of Death on the Underground indicates, would appear to have caused a change in his approach to writing.

Hitherto the statement direct had sheltered behind simple anonymity: Henley changed all that. He made Grahame cast his children's world in the form of fiction—characters, dialogue and all: this at once provided a *persona* of a far more subtle kind. Grahame could, without anxiety, now come out into the open, safe in the knowledge that his 'real self' was not addressing an audience direct. Precisely because of this, his imagination—and the only too well buried instincts on which it fed—could work far more freely. In *The Golden Age* the process was only half-complete; later, in *The Wind in the Willows*, it reached its full, logical conclusion.

Why Grahame expressed such gratitude to Henley in after years was because he knew—perhaps not consciously—that the lame editor had turned the one psychological key, at the one possible time, which released his full inner creativity. Henley knew Grahame's limitations no less than his talents: he guessed at once that here was a supreme miniaturist, who would destroy his own unique vision if he attempted to inflate himself into a fashionable 'major' writer, or continued to elaborate his ideas too consciously. Like every born editor, Henley's first concern was to realize his contributors' potential *on their own terms,* not his. When he cut Yeats's verses about it was, paradoxically, in the belief that he was making them more Yeatsian. He may have been wrong; but his intention was wholly innocent. Sometimes the process failed; sometimes—and *The Golden Age* is a shining example—he succeeded to perfection. Grahame at one stroke came back to something very near the vernacular; and Henley left his copy untouched.

Between acceptance and publication of *Pagan Papers* Grahame had a full and busy year. In Threadneedle Street there was a sizable flutter over the Chief Cashier's resignation, and another, of astronomical dimensions, over the decision to employ woman for clerical and sorting work: this caused violent conservative disapproval, and a spate of tiresome jokes. (It also was probably responsible in part for Grahame's one 'adult' short story, *The Headswoman,* which he was completing about this time, and which has sometimes been taken as an allegorical skit on the feminist movement.) He was acting as a secretarial go-between for Sidney Lee and Furnivall over the latter's newly projected critical edition of Shakespeare—Lee was writing introductions for about five plays. He returned towards the beginning of autumn from an Alpine holiday by the Rhône, cheerful and tanned, and ready for whatever the critics might say. He wrote to Lane in September that 'Henley asks me to let him see a set of sheets of the book before it appears. He is anxious to see how it turns out.' His royalty agreement was an unusually good one for John Lane in those days: on a limited edition of 450 copies he got 10 per cent. for the first 200, and 20 per cent. thereafter. 'I don't call this a grasping proposal,' he claimed '—especially from a Scotchman.'

Pagan Papers was a pleasantly printed and produced little volume, which flaunted an arresting frontispiece by Aubrey Beardsley. Beardsley's elegant and Satanic Pan made a piquant contrast with the rural essay to which it mainly referred: the incongruity is significant. To judge by a passage in *The Golden Age*, Grahame was as excited by his advance copies as any schoolboy. Edward, when about to depart to school for the first time, acquired a trunk and play-box with his name painted on them in large letters:

> After their arrival the owner used to disappear mysteriously, and be found eventually wandering round his luggage, murmuring to himself, 'Edward—', in a rapt remote sort of way. It was a weakness, of course, and pointed to a soft spot in his character; but those who can remember the sensation of first seeing their names in print will not think hardly of him.

And soon the reviews began to come in. *Pagan Papers* got a very mixed reception indeed. The oddest assumption, shared by Grant Richards in *Great Thoughts* and the anonymous critic of the *Literary Echo,* is that the essays are not, in fact, pagan—'for,' says Richards (can he be joking?) 'it was in the pages of Mr Henley's ever-English organ that [their] contents made their first appeal.' Those who enjoyed the book praised its vitality, gusto, and colour; but others were not slow to attack its derivativeness, preciosity, and affectations, while the *Scotsman* declared, with Calvanistic rectitude, that the essays 'do not manifestly appear to be the work of a Christian'. 'Certain jewels,' observed the *Pall Mall Gazette,* 'are endurable only under certain lights; but Mr Grahame loves to display all his jewellery by every light that fills his sky or his chamber.'

What strikes one most about these notices is their essential triviality. The only periodical that came remotely near the heart of the matter was the short-lived *Critic,* in a review written six years after publication—surely a record delay?—which at least touches on one main theme implicit in the book's title:

> Mr Grahame shows that the old gods, for so long slaves of the ink-pot, have yet some work left in them, and, if harnessed all together and touched up with the whip of invention, may be made to drag a conceit through the ruts and bog-holes of a dozen paragraphs. Being capable of so much, he is surely capable of better. Let him turn the gods out to grass, and go, himself, in the shafts.

The aesthetic movement had converted the natural impulses of anti-industrialists into a convention of 'literary paganism', which was no less remote from reality than the profiteering Philistines it opposed. Grahame only succeeded inasmuch as he preserved his paganism from urban faking and coterie art. He was quite explicit as to the main impulse behind this concept of life: it was an antidote to 'the shadow of Scotch-Calvinist-devil-worship' on which he had been brought up.

What Grahame failed to see was that neo-Paganism implied something more than a relaxation of puritan taboos and the sensuous appreciation of nature's bounty. It had almost nothing in common with the pre-Christian ethic on which it was supposedly modelled. It was not, as Huxley suggested, Catholicism with the Christianity taken out, but a conscious *anti*-Christianity that made the antics of Aleister Crowley and the rest of the Black Magic brigade logically only too admissible. License was precisely what the rebels wanted, and they found it easy enough to manufacture an extenuating myth in support of their activities.

Today their daring naughtiness, so hedged about with an ingrained aptitude for respectable public behaviour, strike us as comic and a little sad—sad, because they reveal so clearly the desperate underlying need for a charitable and nourishing faith.

In 1891 W. F. Barry published an extremely sensible article on neo-paganism in the *Quarterly Review*. This traced its literary genesis (from the moral viewpoint) in Hume, Rousseau, Voltaire, Goethe, and Lessing; and, though overtly hostile to the core of natural passion which informed it, hit with deadly accuracy on the weaknesses inherent in its excesses. Of the retreat to mediaevalism Barry wrote: 'Despite its gorgeous tones we are conscious of an unreality. The masked figures, who are so well made up, cannot take off their visors without the enchantment vanishing .... They could not raise the dead, but they found huge delight in imitating their grave-clothes.'

Great Pan was dead; and not the combined ministrations of rebels, aesthetes, pastoralists, and Satanists could ever wish him into life again, though they tried every trick they knew for more than thirty years. 'Pan', in fact, was a convenient short-hand term for their own anarchic emotional urges: he had become a literary symbol, without any highest common factor except a vague full-blooded animalism. The frequency of references to him in the literature, the recurrent representations of him in the art of the period offer an interesting side-light on that pantheistic nature-worship of which, over the years, he had become the convenient and accepted deity. The tradition ran unbroken from Coleridge and Wordsworth through Keats, Shelley, Arnold, the Brownings, Swinburne, and Stevenson. The Goatfoot peeped out in Brooke and 'Saki' and E. M. Forster's early short stories. He inspired countless poems, including a volume by Miss Eleanor Farjeon. Maurice Hewlett and Richard Le Gallienne flirted with him. John Buchan had a personal experience of Panic terror while climbing in the Bavarian Alps: 'Sebastian the guide had seen the goat-foot god, or something of the kind—he was forest born, and Bavarian peasants are very near primeval things—and he had made me feel his terror.'

The drawings and paintings told a similar story. Osbert Burdett said of Beardsley's 'The Mysterious Rose-Garden' that 'it is conventional art listening to the whisper of creative imagination in the familiar and formal garden of Victorian times: it is the return of Pan, the repudiation of authority'. This was the period that could find no room for the grotesque, that held Dickens in some suspicion and distrusted *Punch* till it had been thoroughly institutionalized. Sometimes, as in Beardsley, Pan's healthy phallicism was subtly converted into urban pornography.

Sometimes—and C.H. Shannon's woodcuts in *The Dial* are the most striking examples—he was portrayed as a dark, cruel, towering, monolithic figure: 'Pan Mountain' shows him crouched, merging with the rocky hillside, his pipes turning to pendent rock pinnacles, his half-crossed legs to wild foothills. The Earth-symbolism is obvious.

In *The Wind in the Willows* Grahame brings us to a third aspect of Pan which the neo-pagans emphasized: his rôle as protector and healer of herds and country folk. (I will discuss the Pan of *The Wind in the Willows* later.) Pan is associated by Grahame with the spring, but not in any crudely regenerative sense; and in 'The Lost Centaur' he is treated as a demigod

> in whom the submerged human system peeps out but fitfully, at exalted moments. He, the peevish and irascible, shy of trodden ways and pretty domesticities, is linked to us by little but his love of melody; but for which saving grace, the hair would soon creep up from thigh to horn of him. At times he will still do us a friendly turn: will lend a helping hand to poor little Psyche, wilfully seeking her own salvation; will stand shoulder to shoulder with us on Marathon plain. But in the main his sympathies are first for the beast: to which his horns are never horrific, but, with his hairy pelt, ever natural and familiar, and his voice (with its talk of help and healing) not harsh or dissonant, but voice of very brother as well as very god.

Pan pipes at Mapledurham or in Hurley backwater; he is, to quote the title of the essay which most concerns him, the Rural Pan, inimical both to fashionable dandy and plebeian pleasure-seeker, to be sought neither in Piccadilly, or at Ascot or the Guards' Club in Maidenhead. No, his place is by the quiet river-bank, or, as in 'The Rural Pan',

> under the great shadow of Streatley Hill ... or better yet, pushing an explorer's prow up the remote untravelled Thame, till Dorchester's stately roof broods over the quiet fields. In solitudes such as this Pan sits and dabbles, and all the air is full of the music of his piping. ... Out of hearing of all the clamour, the rural Pan may be found stretched on Ranmore Common, loitering under Abinger pines, or prone by the secluded stream of the sinuous Mole, abounding in friendly greetings for his foster-brothers the dab-chick and the water-rat.

Pan avoids high roads and railways, preferring sheep-tracks, and the animal company they afford. He is not unsocial, but 'shy of the company of his more showy brother-deities'; his pleasure is more to go among unpretentious country folk, labourers and shepherds, 'simple cheery sinners'. He is, after all, only half a god, and there is a strong earthy element in him. Like the Scholar Gipsy, he turns up occasionally in remote inns, disguised as a hedger-and-ditcher, and 'strange lore and quaint fancy he will then impart, in the musical Wessex or Mercian he has learned to speak so naturally'—but it is only after he has gone that his identity is discovered. Commercialism, jerry-building, railways are reducing his domain: but there are still commons and sheep-downs where he can hide, though not for many years to come.

Grahame's version of Pan provides a justification for his personal habits by giving them the sanction of a semi-divine myth. But when we examine his portrait more closely, we get the unescapable impression that this Pan was painted with one eye at least on the mirror: that Grahame has not only trimmed his god to suit his fancy, but undergone a considerable degree of self-identification with him. A change of names, and every passage would be accepted, with minor adjustments, as autobiographical: the distrust of Society, the country pottering, the love of animals, the fear of industrial development. The demigod who talks 'musical Wessex' in a country pub and is accepted by the locals as one of themselves at once recalls Grahame's peculiar delight at being mistaken for a Cornish fisherman.

He is, we may guess, all the more pleased because—in Grahame's myth—though *in* the country, he is not *of* it. This is a fact of some importance. Grahame's mythical ruralist—and indeed Grahame himself—never *does* anything in the country; he may be 'addicted to the kindly soil' but not 'to the working thereof'. When ploughing is being done, he is meditating by the furrow. At harvest-time he is gliding past in a canoe or skiff. He is perpetually on holiday; and this is the weakest aspect of his myth. It is a weekend myth: his real work, never acknowledged, lies elsewhere, in the City. Even Rat, we remember, was in the way in a harvest field.

In eliminating the sexual aspect of Pan, Grahame provides evidence that he preserved a pre-pubertal outlook: the child's clear vision, with its characteristic selections and omissions. At the very end of his life he wrote in a letter to the father of a childish admirer that 'she mustn't grow any older, or she will get away from Mole and Rat'. He would, I suspect, have willingly numbered himself amongst the rare souls whom C. E. Maud described as 'those who have kept fresh in their hearts "the everlasting child", whose eyes look out still with wonder on a wondrous world, who ... hear the pipes of Pan among the rushes, and the flowers talking in the forest'.

It is certainly true that many of Grahame's values and insights were almost uncannily similar to those of children or primitive savages: his curious indifference, amounting at times to callousness, over adult relationships; his intense self-liberating imagination; his timelessness, his natural animistic sense, which endowed even lifeless objects with a personality of their own; his tendency to confuse matter and thought, internal and external, dream and reality. All these phenomena can be readily encountered in a book such as Jean Piaget's *The Child's Conception of the World*: Grahame would have at once understood the child who, when asked why bears had four feet, replied: 'Because they've been naughty and God has punished them.' It was half a shrewd and ambitious business-man, half an innocent child who was introduced by Lane to Henry Harland after the publication of *Pagan Papers,* and who became perhaps the most improbable contributor that the newly founded *Yellow Book* ever acquired.

VII

THE GOLDEN YEARS

1894–8

The Yellow Book was first conceived by the expatriate American novelist Henry Harland, on a wet afternoon at his house in the Cromwell Road. Enthusiastically he held forth to the company in the drawing-room about starting a magazine which should represent—ominously familiar phrase—the 'New Movement'. 'New', in fact, was the operative word; everything acquired it as a prefix in the Yellow Decade. There was the 'New Woman', the 'New Morality', and, of course, the 'New Paganism'. Wilde wrote of the 'New Remorse'; H. D. Traill, in an article on the New Fiction, declared that 'not to be *new* is, in these days, to be nothing'. A penny weekly 'with a humanitarian and radical objective' was called *The New Age.* The world of art and literature was in a conscious ferment of re-orientation, and what Harland did was simply to crystallize this new feeling by providing an appropriate vehicle for its expression.

In February 1894, at a riotously tipsy dinner-party in the Devonshire Club, John Lane gave the seal of his approval to the new project. Harland was appointed editor, on the grounds that he was more 'elevated' than anyone else present; Aubrey Beardsley became art editor, and Lane undertook to publish *The Yellow Book* quarterly from the Bodley Head. Unlike many such wine-inspired fancies, this one became reality. The first number appeared two months later, in April, with a list of contributors that included Henry James, Richard Le Gallienne, Saintsbury, Gosse, Richard Garnett, George Moore, Arthur Symons, and A. C. Benson. Max Beerbohm supplied an undergraduate essay called 'A Defence of Cosmetics', while Harland himself reminisced about the white mice he had kept in childhood. Mr Evelyn Waugh's father went so far along the path of respectability as to criticize lady novelists for describing childbirth—'this freedom of speech', he wrote, 'is degenerating into a license which some of us cannot but view with regret and apprehension.' Could anything have been more modest and respectable?

Yet as soon as *The Yellow Book* appeared it was greeted with a howl of anger and derision by conservative critics, who were particularly upset by Beardsley's satirical drawings and Beerbohm's light-hearted irony, which they took (or affected to take) *au pied de la lettre.* This must have alarmed Harland, who for all his desperate attempts at unconventionality—the goatee beard, the unkempt hair, the

John Lane.
Lane was Kenneth Grahame's publisher at the Bodley Head.
He was also publisher of *The Yellow Book* to which
Grahame contributed.

Henry Harland
sketched by Aubrey Beardsley.
Harland was appointed editor of
The Yellow Book by John Lane.

stories composed in dressing-gown and pyjamas—was at heart a conventional bourgeois, shocked to the core by the least suggestion of irregularity or real vice. Nevertheless, he persisted in his plan; the second number appeared towards the end of July, while the critical rumpus was still going on. It contained, *inter alia,* Grahame's first contribution, 'The Roman Road', perhaps the best of all the stories which compose *The Golden Age.*

Harland must have got in touch with Grahame, probably at Lane's suggestion, as soon as the first number had appeared. At all events, Grahame had the galley-proofs of 'The Roman Road' in May, when Mary Richardson came to visit him in the top-floor flat in Chelsea Gardens; he read the story aloud to her from corrected slips after tea (he had a beautiful reading voice) while she gazed out from his high window over the Thames to the sunlit greenery of Battersea Park. Its moral—that only the artist and the child have a true vision of ultimate reality—agreed very well with the ideals expressed by Harland and his associates. Grahame was promptly invited to submit further stories to the new quarterly. He was, perhaps, all the more ready to comply when the *National Observer*, after a particularly virulent row between Henley and Fitzroy Bell, finally ceased publication in August.

Grahame, as a contributor, was inevitably drawn into the social set which revolved round the Harlands and the Beardsleys. He never felt really at home in this kind of *milieu*: there was a wide gap between his 'new paganism' and theirs, a gap symbolized by the contrasting tone of *Pagan Papers* and the Beardsley sketch which formed its frontispiece. On Saturday evenings he would turn up regularly at Henry and Aline Harland's flat in the Cromwell Road, but always seemed anxious to get into a corner and escape notice if possible. The Harlands, truth to tell, were a little disconcerting. They were liable to invite people to dinner and then forget all about it, so that guests turned up in evening dress to find Henry and Aline sitting down in the kitchen over a pair of chops; they sulked and quarrelled in public; they never bothered to introduce people, or conceal their moods. In general they resembled a pair of completely spoilt children. But worse than their tantrums was the air of conscious 'decadence' cultivated by *The Yellow Book* circle as a whole, the faint flavour of epicenity which Grahame found highly disagreeable. It was certainly a change from the robust atmosphere of Henley's literary imperialism.

Netta Syrett, a fellow contributor, commented specifically on the solid masculinity, the humour, sanity, and normality which distinguished Grahame from the 'Beardsley group', and in particular 'his complete freedom from the affectations which so puzzled me in the other men of the set'. Evelyn Sharp, in her autobiography, recalled his resentment at the famous *Punch* epigram, 'Uncleanliness is next to Bodliness'. Apparently he was so put out that he wanted Lane to take some kind of legal action against *Punch*; but Lane sensibly chose to treat the whole thing as a vast joke. All the evidence suggests that while Grahame had a keen sense of humour, he could not and would not tolerate malice in any form. He was wont to observe, as if for his own self-assurance: 'In *The Yellow Book* itself there is not enough inpropriety to cover a sixpence, and there is no indecency at all'. They were really very respectable socially, these neo-pagans, for all their verbal sensuality and anarchic sentiments.

Evelyn Sharp has left us this picture of Grahame at the Harlands':

> He was, perhaps, shy among strangers, always looked away hastily if he caught you looking at him, simply hated being lionized but liked to talk about his work if he knew you were sympathetic and not likely to gush about it. ... He was very kind and courteous, but had not an ounce of humbug in him. Very sensitive but would die sooner than you let think so if he could help it, and in many ways reminded one of the nicest kind of schoolboy except that he had a fine taste in literature instead of a passion for sport. He had a charming sense of humour and was a great tease. In *The Yellow Book* set we all admired him tremendously, and the appearance of one of his sketches in the Y.B. would be hailed as an event and discussed at length the next Saturday evening. ... He never spoke much, only when he had something to say; he never said anything unkind about anybody, or to anybody, except through inability to say something sincere.

Though Kenneth may have felt distaste for the Decadents' morals, he shared their love of conviviality. He was always to the fore in the Harlands' kitchen, helping over supper; and it was probably after a particularly heavy *Yellow Book* dinner that

KENNETH GRAHAME
shortly before he was appointed Secretary of the Bank of England
in 1898.

the incident of the vegetable cart occurred. Kenneth wandered into Piccadilly late one night, in full evening dress and happy (to say the least) on the Harlands' claret. Here he saw a vegetable cart moving eastwards towards Covent Garden. He ran after it, swung himself aboard among the cabbages, and promptly fell asleep. When he woke it was broad daylight. He was still in the cart; but now it was empty, and moving down Piccadilly in the opposite direction. As Alan Lidderdale, who tells the story, observed, 'it was one of the regrets of Kenneth's life that he never knew what happened in the interval.'

I have always thought this episode an apt symbol of Grahame's uneasy flirtation with the Beardsley group. He joined them in a fit of literary intoxication and woke up to a childhood morning without being quite sure how he had got there; he only knew he had a moral hangover. There were some things better forgotten, and he forgot them as quickly as he could. But the two years before Oscar Wilde's trial went deeper into his emotional make-up than he suspected, and left a queer literary legacy behind.

The ethical dilemma in which Grahame found himself was largely, of course, due to his education. One of the perennial problems which the monastic humanists of the Middle Ages were forced to face was the reconciliation of the Christian faith with a non-Christian tradition of literature and scholarship. By the nineteenth century this paradox had lost its sting: classics, cricket, and Christianity formed a holy trinity sanctified by upper-class usage. Thus when the post-Arnold aesthetic rebellion took place, the rebels found ready-made symbols waiting for them, symbols which they had learnt at school.

One result of this common symbolism drawn from the classical world was to give a superficial appearance of unanimity to what was in fact a most diverse opposition. Henley, Morris, Beardsley, and Grahame (to take a random cross-section) were united by one thing only: anti-authoritarianism. In every other way they were deeply divided among themselves. The label of 'neo-pagan' covered a multitude of virtues as well as sins.

Grahame learnt fairly quickly that the ethics of the Decadents did not represent the pagan spirit as he understood it. He was shocked by the cult of perversity and drugs, by Dowson's hashish, by the self-indulgence and self-destruction of James Thomson and Francis Thompson. The sedulous cultivation of vice as a gesture of defiance and despair merely disgusted and repelled him. He chose the only path open to him: the cult of innocence. Everywhere corruption stared him in the face: industrial corruption, social corruption, corruption of the soul among those who should have been his allies in opposition. Only childhood, ever more golden in retrospect, remained untouched, and he fastened hungrily upon it. Between December 1893 and January 1895 the remaining eleven stories in *The Golden Age* were written: and in February 1895 it was published as a book.

Meanwhile Grahame had changed his address once more, and this time in a more radical sense. The days of 'digs' and flats were over. In the autumn of 1894 he and a barrister named Tom Greg took the joint lease of a house: No 5 Kensington Crescent. Greg brought with him his own former housekeeper, Sarah

Bath, an outspoken and strait-laced Somerset martinet who specialized in bachelors. As a magic gesture of ownership Grahame fixed on the front of the house, between the drawing-room windows, the della Robbia plaque he had acquired during his visit to Florence. This, as Annie Grahame observed, 'formed a kind of landmark enabling one to find the house at once; it also served as a shrine for the Italian organ-grinders, who, Kenneth said, used to come and perform their devotions in front of it and then go down into the area and demand alms from Miss Bath, who, however (having travelled in Italy herself), was quite equal to them and sternly refused to give them anything, whereupon they departed muttering curses and shaking their fists at her. ...' The Madonna and Child symbolized many things for Kenneth: simple and sincere faith; the whole atmosphere of the South; perhaps, too, the mother he had lost so early himself.

Why did he choose this particular time to set up house? Partly, in all probability, because he was for a short period appointed Acting Secretary at the Bank, though not yet thirty-five. The great Hammond Chubb, after drafting his epoch-making Report on the reorganizing of Bank administration, had retired: his tenure had lasted fifteen years, and no successor was immediately elected. Grahame filled the post for a few months, till G. F. Glennie's appointment was ratified; and it may well have been intimated to him that an Acting Secretary of the Bank of England could hardly entertain distinguished business guests in a top-floor Chelsea attic. But there was possibly another, rather more subtle, motive. In April 1894 Kenneth's cousin, one A. H. Hawkins, barrister-at-law, who had been a fellow-contributor to the *St James's Gazette*, suddenly woke up to find himself famous. Using his first two names, Anthony Hope, as a pseudonym, he had published a romance entitled *The Prisoner of Zenda.* It made his fortune, and added a new word, Ruritania, to the English language. But its immediate result was that in July Anthony abandoned the Bar and set up as a full-time writer.

The effect of this decision on Kenneth can be only too easily imagined. For nearly fifteen years he had dreamed of just such a release, yet always shrank away from it at the crucial moment, despite the exhortations of Henley and his other friends. The thing remained deliciously impossible, a mirage tempting him with the unattainable; and now Anthony, in very similar circumstances, had actually taken the plunge. Kenneth was both envious and, we may suspect, somewhat iritated: irritated, because his own reactions to Anthony's success forced him to realize consciously that, given the chance of emulating his cousin, he would still refuse. The City owned at least half his soul by now: he needed his cage.

Corruption takes many subtle forms, and in Grahame's case it disguised itself as the security and public esteem conferred by material success. He had had a foretaste of power as Acting Secretary: in five years at the most, since Glennie was already an elderly man, the position would pass to him and be confirmed as a permanency. It was easier to confine one's anarchic whims to paper, and, indeed, this gave them an extra force. Yet some gesture of individualism had to be made to still that small nagging voice of conscience; and the launching out into house-ownership was just sufficient for the purpose.

The bachelor establishment seems to have had a fair measure of success. Under Sarah Bath's sardonic eye Grahame and Greg settled down together amicably enough. Greg was a man of Grahame's own age and, like him, an amateur writer, who contributed occasional pieces to the *Pall Mall Gazette* and *National Observer*. He was for three years Art Critic to the *Manchester Guardian* and *Birmingham Daily Post,* during which time he wrote on practically every exhibition of importance in London. He was a connoisseur of wines, on which he wrote rather whimsical little essays, and sponsored a magnificent edition of the works of Sir Richard Burton. As an undergraduate at Oriel he first developed a mania for collecting pottery, and later wrote a monograph on the subject.

It is plain that he influenced Grahame a good deal during the year they spent together at the house in Kensington Crescent before Greg's marriage. Over some things they disagreed; Walter Grahame noted Grahame's 'annoyance at Mr Greg's insistence on hanging the pictures in their house in obedience to the dictates of what Kenneth called the Manchester School,' for instance. But in general they were temperamentally congenial to a degree, as can be seen not only from Greg's interests but also from the essays he wrote, which occasionally give us a glimpse into that bachelor household, so snug and well-ordered, so pleasantly littered with *objets d'art* and collector's treasure-trove.

He rhapsodizes over the special treasures he can display to visiting friends: the Grès de Flandres tankards, the salt glaze teapot, the two-volume first edition of Grimm's *Fairy Tales* 'with Cruikshank's plates, bound in their resplendent morocco, handiwork of Zahnsdorf, that Poole of book-clothiers'. It was an atmosphere that Grahame was quick to share and absorb; for the rest of his life there were always first editions and Continental pottery somewhere in the background.

While *The Golden Age* stories were accumulating, Grahame found time to complete a somewhat different work, first roughed out in MS as early as 1890. This was *The Headswoman*, the only story he wrote which dealt entirely with adult characters, and much less well known than it deserves to be. It may therefore be worthwhile to give a brief outline of the plot. Jeanne, the daughter of the executioner in a small French town, succeeds to the office despite the council's objections to her as a woman. She proves to be highly efficient until called upon to execute an attractive young stranger (in fact heir to a nearby château). He is rescued at the last minute and Jeanne finally succumbs to the rescuer and marries him. She leaves the office of executioner vacant for her cousin.

In one sense, of course, *The Headswoman* is, as the *Star's* reviewer pointed out, a squib on feminism. Jeanne trots out all the popular arguments for Women's Rights, and the young nobleman is an intellectual Radical who talks airily about 'the way of the bloated capitalist'. The satire is delicate and well-aimed, but Jeanne is by no means the victim of it: it is the Mayor, the pettifogging lawyer, the local bureaucracy who are really made to look foolish. Jeanne herself is drawn with great sympathy; and we remember that many of Grahame's friends at the time shared her aims—women such as Evelyn Sharp, Beatrice Harraden, and, later, Constance

Smedley. What Grahame is really attacking is entrenched masculine prejudice: the feminist's weakness for being *plus royale que le roi* comes off very lightly by comparison.

But what strikes a modern reader most forcibly is the prolonged joke about execution as such. It is somewhat morbid gallows-humour at its best, and only Grahame's feather-light touch prevents it from being downright unpleasant.

The Headswoman hints at the line Grahame might have taken if the world of childhood had not claimed him: satirical fantasy not unlike that practised by Voltaire. But this would have meant coming to grips more or less directly with all those vast unpleasant problems confronting Victorian society towards the turn of the century. It was useless for Grahame to call his story a fantasy and set it in the sixteenth century: his satirical eye was too acute, and the contemporary world would keep breaking in. If he had been a romantic fantasist (in the strict sense of the words) he could have happily turned out novels which bore no relation to reality, as so many of his contemporaries in fact did. Unfortunately he was a realist by natural endowment: once he chose a subject he treated it with exhaustive honesty.

This may go far to explain why *The Headswoman* remains his nearest approach to 'adult' fiction. Direct engagement stimulated his satirical sense, but put too great a strain on his delicate sensibilities.

The Headswoman was published in October 1894, in a number of *The Yellow Book* which also included John Davidson's 'Ballad of a Nun' and Beardsley's two famous satirical drawings, 'Lady Gold's Escort' and 'The Wagnerites', not to mention an authentic whiff of the Celtic Fringe from Nora Hopper. (It is difficult to guess whether the presence of Beardsley or Miss Hopper embarrassed Grahame more.) By now America was interesting itself in the author of *Pagan Papers*; one Golden Age story, 'The Blue Room', first appeared in *Phil May's Illustrated Winter Annual*, another, 'The Secret Drawer', in the *Chicago Chapbook*. By now, too, Henley's *New Review* had begun publication, and Grahame, loyal as ever to his old editor, let him print 'A Harvesting' and '*Lusisti Satis*' in the March 1895 number, about the same time as *The Golden Age* appeared in book form.

This time Grahame (and Lane) had no cause to complain of the reviewers. Swinburne set the tone with a two-column eulogy in the *Daily Chronicle*, where he described the book as 'well-nigh too praiseworthy for praise', and in accordance with his own dictum spent the bulk of his space in lavish quotations. He was supported by Richard Le Gallienne in the *Star;* Israel Zangwill in the *Pall Mall Gazette*; and a host of women's magazines, which declared, in varying terms, that the work should become compulsory reading for English parents—'they will understand their own children the better for doing so'. The reservations when they came, were all in the intellectual periodicals, the *Bookman*, the *Fortnightly Review*, the *Spectator*; and what they objected to, with some unanimity, was the ambiguous status of the narrator, fluctuating in viewpoint between child and adult.

Professor Sully in the *Fortnightly Review* loses control of himself completely, and begins snarling about 'a dishonour done to the sacred cause of childhood ... merely

'A HARVESTING'.
E. H. Shepard's drawing as it appeared in *The Golden Age*.

the exaggeration of a tone of cynical superiority which runs through the volume'. Here we recognize the voice of a sentimental Olympian hit at his most vulnerable point. The child-cult of the later nineteenth century was not based on a sympathy for, or consideration of, children as they really were, on their own terms. It had far more selfish motives: relief of guilt, gratification of the ego. Children became the ideal symbol of their elders' glutinous yearning for purity. There was no question of communication or understanding: the traffic of sentiment all went one way. Children were regarded as *objects*—dolls, pets, almost mythic symbols, which reflected nothing but the magnanimity and tenderness of their elders.

Now Grahame, with his incurable realism, had stripped off this fulsome facade and drawn the relationship between upper-middle-class adult and child as it really was. The complacent Professor Sully, author of a monstrously patronizing book called *Children's Ways,* was disconcerted for two obvious reasons. The unflattering and only too accurate portrait of the Olympians shattered his self-esteem; but worse, the thought of children summing up their elders with such cool and precocious contempt struck at the very heart of the Victorian child-myth. Children were supposed to be innocent, unthinking, all-adoring, uncritical; grateful acolytes sunning themselves in the benevolence of an omniscient father-figure. Grahame destroyed the whole myth at one stroke. He scaled adult pretensions and sentimentalities down to life-size; he showed that children not only possessed a private life of their own (which was romantic) but a mordant eye for the weaknesses of their elders (which was highly embarrassing).

The very word 'Olympians' was diabolically well-chosen. It suggested simultaneously pompous self-elevation, arbitrary thunderbolts, and faintly ridiculous claims to divine infallibility. Those who knew their Homer as Grahame did would also remember that, for all their dignity, the original Olympians behaved in a singularly ungodlike way, quarrelling, scheming, full of jealously and petty spite, activated by the lowest human motives. Most 'Olympian' reviewers had received the benefits of a Victorian grounding in the classics; they would not be slow to take the hint. Broadminded people sometimes enjoy being attacked; but few are tolerant enough to survive the puncturing of their personal myths. Hence Professor Sully's incoherent rage.

But the majority of readers found the delicate satire very much to their taste: they too had suffered under Olympian tutelage. As the critic of the *Academy* remarked of *The Golden Age* children: 'So typical are their thoughts and actions, misgivings and ambitions, that *The Golden Age* is to some extent every reader's biography.' A copy found its way to Miss Bradley's uncle, the Dean of St Paul's, who was laid up at the time with an attack of bronchitis. His taste in secular literature was rather for Blue Books than pure romance; but he was found absorbed in the pages of *The Golden Age*, and even a little tearful. When asked the reason for such unwonted emotion and told that the book was only meant to amuse him, the octogenarian shook his head sadly and said: 'You see, I also was brought up by an Aunt. ...'

The Golden Age was published in February, and Grahame found himself famous overnight. The first edition quickly sold out, and Lane, with his usual acumen, reprinted at once. Invitations began to pour in to Kensington Crescent, not only now from literary friends but Society hostesses as well. The satirist of childhood was taken up as a literary lion—a process which he endured with mixed delight and embarrassment. But despite a constant round of dinner-parties, and his duties at the Bank, he continued to write. The creative impulse which had produced *The Golden Age* was by no means yet exhausted: about half the stories later collected as *Dream Days* were composed during 1895.

In the spring, however, fortified by steadily accumulating royalties, Grahame was able to gratify his annual migratory urge. Southward he went, following the swallows, till he fetched up at Alassio on the Italian Riviera—a place to which he was to return at least twice during the next three years, and which made a lasting impression on him.

At that time Alassio had not yet become the fashionable resort it is today. It was still a picturesque, undisturbed fishing-port, and Grahame stayed, not in a

Alassio, Italy.
Grahame visited Alassio several times during the years following 1895.
The unspoilt fishing village made a great impression on him and
his experiences contributed to his description of Mole End and to
the adventures of the Wayfaring Rat in *The Wind in the Willows*.

smart hotel but with a private family, in their old-fashioned Ligurian home. Idiosyncratic features such as box-bunks and bowling-alley caught his fancy so strongly that later he transferred most of them to Mole End:

> On the walls hung wire baskets with ferns in them, alternating with brackets carrying plaster statuary—Garibaldi and the infant Samuel, and Queen Victoria, and other heroes of modern Italy. Down one side of the fore-court ran a skittle-alley, with benches along it and little wooden tables marked with rings that hinted at beer-mugs.

Mole End
by E. H. Shepard.

Grahame has made only the most perfunctory attempt to integrate these memories into an English setting. Wine, indeed, has been nationalized into beer, and *boccìe* into our more familiar skittles; but what on earth is Garibaldi doing in Mole End? Yet such is Grahame's skill at creating a *mise en scène* depending solely on its own private logic and imagery, that these oddly-flavoured incongruities strengthen rather than destroy the illusion. In the same way we never notice the physical difficulties presented by Mole End—an open-air residence if ever there was one—existing at the bottom of a tunnel.

We catch a glimpse of Grahame's life at Alassio in 'Wayfarers All', where he puts some of his own experiences into the mouth of the Seafaring Rat:

> Then the crew took to the boats and rowed shorewards, singing as they went, and drawing after them the long bobbing procession of casks, like a mile of porpoises. On the sands they had horses waiting, which dragged the casks up the steep street of the little town with a fine rush and clatter and scramble. When the last cask was in, we went and refreshed and rested, and sat late into the night, drinking with our friends; and the next morning I was off to the great olive-woods for a spell and a rest. ... I led a lazy life among the peasants, lying and watching them work, or stretched high on the hill-side with the blue Mediterranean far below me.

From the same passage (and a reference in his correspondence) it seems probable that Grahame made his way home by way of Marseilles, where he characteristically developed an inordinate passion for the local cuisine.

Back in England life seemed stable, assured, and tranquil. There was £40,000,000 worth of bullion in the Bank—the highest figure yet recorded—and the wholesale price of English gold showing a steady upward trend. Against this solid background the literary aesthetes—and *The Yellow Book*—continued to flourish; Grahame contributed esays to the April, July, and October numbers. But there was an undercurrent of depression, boredom, and disillusionment in the air. This was the year in which Max Nordau published *Degeneration:*

> The prevalent feeling is that of imminent perdition and extinction. *Fin de siècle* is at once a confession and a complaint. The old northern faith contained the fearsome doctrine of the Dusk of the Gods. In our days there have arisen in more highly developed minds vague qualms of the Dusk of the Nations, in which all suns and all stars are gradually waning, and mankind with all its institutions and creations is perishing in the midst of a dying world.

The symptoms are characteristic of a post-industrial society that has staggered through its religious crisis; and it was in an effort to stem the consequent tide of materialism that the aesthetic movement had developed. But in the autumn of 1895 this movement—fragile and artificial enough at the best of times—received its death-blow.

Oscar Wilde, though in point of fact he never contributed to *The Yellow Book,* had come to typify, in the public mind, the ethics for which *The Yellow Book* stood. His trial and condemnation for homosexual practices came as a horrible revelation to English society, and effectively prevented the aesthetic myth from taking general root. Those who had dabbled innocently in these fashionable literary waters extricated themselves with some speed; it is interesting to note that Grahame's only contribution to *The Yellow Book* after this date (apart from 'Dies Irae', which was almost certainly commissioned before the débâcle) is a short and indifferent poem. Evelyn Sharp, in her autobiography, recorded that

> the Oscar Wilde trial shocked society into an extreme of prudishness never exceeded in the earliest days of the good Queen, and one London daily started a shilling cricket fund to which panic-stricken citizens hastened to contribute lest their sexual normality should be doubted—the connection was subtle, but felt at the time to be real.

It seems highly improbable that any of the mud flung was aimed at, let alone stuck to, Grahame. His subtle withdrawal from the extremes of aesthetic social intercourse was often remarked upon, and the subject-matter of his stories alone more or less guaranteed his immunity. But he cannot in any case have failed to be deeply struck by the brilliant, flamboyant playwright and after-dinner wit being subjected to cruel public ignominy, and consigned to a common gaol. Wilde's fate sank deep into his impressionable mind; and twelve years were to pass before the core of that terrible episode re-emerged, transmuted and scaled down to animal fantasy in the misfortunes of Mr Toad.

Grahame spent the Christmas of 1895 in Brussels, together with Evelyn Sharp and the Harlands, who were probably glad to be abroad during the worst period of scandal. As Editor of *The Yellow Book* Harland had naturally come in for a fair share of public abuse. Grahame, apparently, enjoyed himself in his own idiosyncratic way and he returned to work, unperturbed, in the New Year. 'Dies Irae' appeared in January; 'Saturnia Regna' in March, as a contribution to Henley's *New Review*, which also printed 'Mutabile Semper' a month later. Then there followed a break till December, when 'The Magic Ring' was published in *Scribner's Magazine*.

During the summer Grahame was once more drawn into the social round. We find him dining on 5 July with Gosse in a company that included the Harlands, Yeats, Lionel Johnson, Hardy, Ernest Rhys, George Moore, and Andrew Lang. There were Saturday evenings in the Cromwell Road, and luncheon parties such as that at which he first met Helen Dunham, 'at Mrs Crawshay's—where there were also Ethel Arnold and Lady Horner, and Professor Butcher, and Mr Goschen—and much good talk'. The combination of scholarship, high finance, and high society tells its own tale.

The aftermath of the Wilde scandal brought an atmosphere of exhausted futility, which is clearly reflected in *The Yellow Book*. The grand concept of protest had ended in public ignominy: the forces of bourgeois convention were stronger than ever. 'Castle Ennui', Harland wrote in July, 'is the Bastille of modern life. ... You can only escape from it at the risk of breaking your social neck, or remaining a fugitive from social justice to the end of your days.' Less than a year later *The Yellow Book* itself had succumbed: the last issue appeared in January 1897. William

OSCAR WILDE'S IMPRISONMENT
during his trial in 1895 for homosexuality received prominent coverage
in *The Illustrated Police Budget*.

Morris died in October, after completing the Kelmscott Chaucer; Stevenson was already dead, far away in Samoa. The New Age had failed and the old order was breaking up.

A new plutocracy, enriched by the South African diamond mines, had established itself in Park Lane. These *nouveaux riches* had their own ideas about progress and culture. 1896 saw the foundation of something revolutionary in the history of journalism—the *Daily Mail*. It also saw the appearance of that strange, noisy, lethal object, the Horseless Carriage. Nothing, perhaps, better symbolized the rising dominance of the Industrial Age: and motoring enthusiasts had to struggle against violent, almost hysterical, opposition. Till 14 November 1896 there was a ban on the monsters in England; and even after this ban was lifted, a 12mph speed limit was imposed. It was generally held that the motor-car was noisy, dangerous, ridiculous, and a source of terror to horses. Even more than the railways, motor-cars, it was clear, would disrupt the peace of the countryside: trains at least stuck to their rails, but the 'petrol-piddling monster' (as Kipling called it) could reach the most remote village.

It is not hard to imagine how Grahame reacted to this invasion: he still felt strongly on the subject in 1907, though by then the novelty had been more or less assimilated, if not accepted, as far as the general public were concerned. *Punch*,

Programme of the First Legal Run of the New Automotor Carriages in England.

AN ILLUSTRATED SOUVENIR OF THE EVENT, PUBLISHED BY

THE AUTOMOTOR AND HORSELESS VEHICLE JOURNAL

A RECORD AND REVIEW OF APPLIED AUTOMATIC LOCOMOTION.

Circulates amongst Makers and Users of Autocars, Cycles, etc., in the United Kingdom, the Colonies, and the Continent.

SOUVENIR NUMBER. NOVEMBER 14, 1896. PRICE ONE PENNY.

REVIVAL OF A STATUTE-STRANGLED INDUSTRY.

TO-DAY—the 14th of November—should be hereafter an eventful one in the commercial history of this country, marking as it does the birth of a new industry, and the creation of a fresh field for the mechanical genius and enterprise of all interested in engineering carriage building. By the passing of the Light Locomotives Act, 1896, the Legislature removed the stumbling block which has until now practically prevented any power other than horse or similar animal being used to draw or propel any ordinary vehicle in the streets.

By an arbitrary straining of the law, rules which might by some show of justice be applied to a heavy lumbering traction engine weighing many tons, to the user of which speed was of no consequence, were made to cover every form of road conveyance. Thus a rider of a tricycle which weighed some 80 lbs. using an oil motor to act as an auxiliary in climbing hills, has been repeatedly summoned and fined for the threefold offence of travelling at a greater speed than four miles an hour, not having an advance guard in front carrying a red flag, and of not being licensed by the particular local authority through whose district the hapless traveller journeyed. Whether the vehicle weighed 80 lbs. or 80 tons, the same law was held to refer to both so long as the motive power was self-contained. In some countries ridicule would have killed such a legal anomaly—had it existed, say in China, our writers would have levelled yet another shaft tipped with wit and wisdom at the foibles of the "heathen Chinee"—but as it was good law in this most perfect of countries, but few were found to question its justice. All that perverse ingenuity could do to fetter any possible growth of noiseless vehicles was done, until the state of affairs which existed until yesterday may be well described in the following words* :—

"Among the legal restrictions may be mentioned :—Firstly, that such engines have been held to be a nuisance at common law ; secondly, that in nearly every case the owner is obliged to obtain a license from a Court of Quarter Sessions before he can travel with his engine on any highway, and that he may have to wait nearly three months before such license can be granted to him ; that his license, although it is evidence that his engine is constructed in accordance with the requirements of the Act of Parliament, affords the owner no protection against any person or public body raising the most frivolous objections to the passage of his engine. Thirdly, that in country districts, though there may be no other traffic on the road, the speed of the engine is limited to four miles an hour, and a man is required to walk in front at a distance of not less than 20 yards. Fourthly, that the road authorities have an almost arbitrary power to forbid the use of certain bridges by such engines, though the bridges themselves may be of ample strength to carry the weight without danger ; and, further, that although the damage done to a bridge by the passage of heavy weights drawn by horses is made good at the public expense, such damage must be made good by the engine-owner in case the same load should be drawn by a traction engine. Fifthly, that certain urban authorities have been allowed to embody in their local Acts clauses by which they are able to prohibit the use of road locomotives on any street or road within their jurisdiction."

This chaotic state of tyranny might have prevailed for all time had not our Continental friends—the French in particular—and our American cousins taken up the question of automotor carriages, and by constructing and running some hundreds of them, demonstrated that they could be safely driven through crowded streets at considerable speeds, and at a cost which was considerably lower than is involved in the use of horses. When our trade rivals had thus got the start, a few of the more intelligent observers of things of interest abroad began to ask the pertinent question—why should Great Britain be left behind in any matter relating to locomotion? The folly of the necessity for a state of things which rendered such a query possible was well shown in the history of early horseless vehicles which appeared in the last issue of the AUTOMOTOR AND HORSELESS VEHICLE JOURNAL. In that article it was shown clearly that in the first half of the century practical steam vehicles were in frequent use on our highways, and had they been given fair play they would without any doubt long before this have been improved and perfected in common with every other piece of mechanism which has been produced in the last fifty years. The interested opponents of progress in those days, however, burked the vehicles by the rude but effective means of blocking the roads with stones and raising the toll dues to prohibitive rates; while their successors, in a more ingenious but quite as certain process, stopped the way with a judge's dictum upholding an absurdity.

* McLaren "Steam on Common Roads."

THE SOUVENIR ISSUE OF THE AUTOMOTOR AND HORSELESS VEHICLES JOURNAL commemorates the lifting of the ban on motor vehicles on 14 November 1896. The speed limit was raised to 12 mph. Grahame saw this decision as a major threat to the countryside and his views are made clear in *The Wind in the Willows* when Toad's 'canary coloured vessel [is] driven on a shoal by the reckless jockeying of rival mariners'.

always fairly reliable as a weather-gauge in matters of this sort, suggests that at first opinion was contemptuous of the new device, and only later came to fear it. An 1896 cartoon has this caption: 'Decidedly Uncomfortable: Awkward position of Mr Newfangle, who, when halfway up a steep hill, discovers by the sudden retrograde movement of the Autocar that the Motor has become exhausted'. By 1904 the tone has changed:

> *Motorist* (cheerfully—to fellow-guest in house-party): 'What luck? Killed anything?'
> *Angler* (bitterly): 'No. Have you?'

It is this later, more bitter, mood which is enshrined in 'The Open Road' in *The Wind in the Willows*.

By the end of 1898 Kenneth Grahame was an established success both in his profession and in the world of letters. He succeeded G.F. Glennie as Secretary of the Bank at the age of thirty-nine—one of the youngest Secretaries on record. At this period the Secretary, whose office dated back to 1694, was at one and the same time the Secretary to the Company and Secretary to the Governor. In the former capacity he was largely concerned with the constitutional side of the Bank's administration: he was present at meetings of the Court of Directors to take minutes, and it was his duty to see that the decisions made were subsequently carried out. He dealt also with all those duties which did not fall within the scope of the two other senior officials, the Chief Cashier and the Chief Accountant: he dealt with visitors and he organized staff. As Secretary to the Governor his position was rather more vaguely defined: he was not primarily concerned with implementing banking policy but was, ideally, not so much a banker as a lay adviser: the Governor's conscience, so to speak.

His elevation does not seem to have gone to Kenneth's head. When Evelyn Sharp wrote to congratulate him,

> and supposed flippantly that he would now dress in red and gold and ride in the Lord Mayor's Show, he wrote back to say that he should do nothing of the kind, not because he hadn't a right to, if he liked, but because he couldn't ride. He was at the same time, he added, having gold braid put on the collar of his frock-coat and round his silk hat. I feel sure that this was not the Kenneth Grahame known to his colleagues at the Bank of England.

Nevertheless he could not keep his literary *alter ego* a complete secret, even from the moguls of Threadneedle Street. His fame had spread too far. Old Dr Kingdon, the Consultant Physician to the Bank, who had sympathized with Kenneth in his relationship to Uncle John the Parliamentary Agent, was now somewhat more down-to-earth:

> Kenneth's a dear boy, a *very* dear boy, but he doesn't think half enough of his position in the Bank and in the City. They tell me that he *writes tales.* So did Charles Lamb—but what of that? Maybe Charles Lamb didn't think much of his position at East India House, but what after all *was* his position in the City to Kenneth's? Kenneth should think *less* of books and *more* of being what he has come to be in the City.

KENNETH GRAHAME AS SECRETARY OF THE BANK OF ENGLAND.
This portrait is a newspaper sketch of 1898.

But if the new Secretary was a little odd by Dr Kingdon's standards, he had in his own terms reached a most effective compromise. The nightmare terror of galley-slave and hireling, the bureaucratic blue pencil chasing death down the centuries—these had receded into what Grahame described as the back-kitchen of his consciousness.

The literary world, too, had given him its accolade. He was a household name, and his royalties mounted steadily. In its issue of 4 December 1897 the *Academy* included him among those selected for literary profiling and assessment under the heading 'Some Younger Reputations'. Others so honoured were Yeats, Gissing, Quiller-Couch, Wells, Beerbohm, W. W. Jacobs, Robert Hichens, and Anthony Hope. The article on Grahame is extremely enthusiastic; it ends with these uncompromising words: 'It matters very little whether or not Mr Grahame writes any more. In *The Golden Age* he has given us a book, a four-square piece of literature complete in itself. Many a literary man writes hard all his life, and never a book—in the best sense of the word—is forthcoming. Mr Grahame made one the first time.'

In March 1898 Kenneth went down with one of his recurrent bouts of influenza. On the 10th he wrote to Grace Dunham, Helen Dunham's sister, enclosing a specially bound copy of Blake's *Songs of Innocence* as a wedding present, and adding at the end: 'I am shaking with influenza myself, and feel like Shem or Japhet out of the Ark—left by a careless child on the carpet—trodden on by a heavy-footed housemaid—and badly mended with very inferior glue.' However, he was well enough in April to lunch his visiting American publisher, Charles Scribner, at the Hyde Park Club. Perhaps as a result of this meeting, 'A Saga of the Seas' was published in the August issue of *Scribner's Magazine.* By now six of the stories that were to appear in *Dream Days* had been composed and published: the rate of production was noticeably slower than for *The Golden Age*. Two more—'A

Departure' and 'The Reluctant Dragon'—were written during that summer, but never issued in any periodical. *Dream Days*, the long awaited sequel to *The Golden Age*, was published in December 1898.

The reviews were, if anything, more enthusiastic even than those Grahame had already received; but behind the chorus of praise we can once again discern the irritated complaints of a few Olympian reviewers. The *Athenaeum,* with greater perception than some reviewers, decided that *Dream Days* was not so much a children's book as a collection of stories about children for grown-up people. But by now Grahame had reached the point where he could afford to ignore minority critics. The book became, first a best-seller, then a classic.

The originality, if not the creative achievement, of Kenneth Grahame's short stories about children is often under-rated today. A post-Freudian epoch has accustomed us to the child's-eye view of things; we are prepared to accept the unpalatable truth that children of a certain age dislike and despise adult concepts. In *The Golden Age* he made children live as they were, not as their elders would wish them to be. This was a completely new achievement; and it soon caught on. The year after *Dream Days* was published Kipling did for the adolescent schoolboy what Grahame had done for his younger brother: and the result was *Stalky and Co.*

We have already seen something of Grahame's skill in characterizing adults but his two volumes of short stories must stand or fall, in the last resort, by the childish family quartet round whom they are built: Charlotte, Harold, Edward, Selina, with the personality of the narrator omnipresent in the background. His success may be gauged from the fact that these prototypes have left their mark on almost every subsequent fictional family of the kind, from E. Nesbit's *The Railway Children* to Arthur Ransome's *Swallows and Amazons*. This is all the odder since we know practically nothing about them in the way of external detail: they are never physically described, and their background is of the sketchiest. Our visual impression of them is almost entirely derived from E. H. Shepard's evocative drawings and silhouettes.

This was clever of Grahame. He saw very clearly that any writer who wishes to give his characters permanence must work from inner, rather than external, characteristics; and in seizing on those perennial traits which embody the whole essence of childhood, he created two minor classics.

In *The Golden Age* we begin with the children's minuscule world unbreached by disillusion: but story by story reality breaks in a little further, the magic pictures begin to fade, the sandcastle to crumble before the advancing tide, till 'finally we found ourselves sitting silent on an upturned wheelbarrow, our chins on our fists, staring haggardly into the raw new conditions of our changed life, the ruins of a past behind our backs'. With *Dream Days* the development of the pattern is not so clear; but this is hardly surprising. It is a sequel only in the most superficial sense: the stories it contains are later additions to an already complete creative pattern. But the final story, 'A Departure', forms a logical conclusion to the whole sequence. It was, in point of fact, the last thing of its kind which Grahame ever wrote, and seems designed as a conscious valediction to his dream-children.

'The Reluctant Dragon.'
Maxfield Parrish's etching for *Dream Days*.

In this story, you will remember, the Olympians—always open, as Grahame remarks, to sentiment of a treacly, woodcut order—have, without warning, parcelled up the children's toys 'for dispatch to London, to gladden the lives and bring light into the eyes of London waifs and Poplar Annies'. The children—growing too old for toys, yet still inarticulately resentful of this outrage to their private, familiar world—steal the parcel before it goes, and bury the toys by moonlight. (They are being neither selfish nor snobbish—no more snobbish, at

DREAM DAYS.
One of E. H. Shepard's silhouettes.

least, than all children—but they do instinctively condemn the gesture of their elders as not only arbitrary but false.) We leave the dolls in the care of the Man in the Moon:

> He was going to see after them, it was evident; for he was always there, more or less, and it was no trouble to him at all, and he would tell them how things were still going, up here, and throw in a story or two of his own whenever they seemed a trifle dull.

It is, of course, not only the dolls—symbol of childishness—that are being buried; it is Harold, Edward, Selina, and Charlotte themselves. Time moves inexorably on, and these dream-children pass into the keeping of the Man in the Moon, the artist, the story-teller. For him they never change or grow old; and only he—'a good fellow too, cheery, comforting, with a fund of anecdote; a man in whom one had every confidence—can by his magic preserve them unchanged for ever.

Grahame spent the Christmas of 1898 in Essex with Roland and his wife. Roland, like Kenneth, had been a frequent visitor on week-ends to the Feilings at Amwell Bury. In 1895 Joan Feiling was left a widow with two small sons, Tony and Keith, who had already unwittingly contributed material to *The Golden Age*, as we have seen. In 1897 she and Roland were married; and it is possible that the happy atmosphere of that family Christmas made Kenneth reconsider his ambition to be 'the felowe that goes alone'. After all, in a month or two he would be forty: middle-aged bachelorhood was a by no means unmixed blessing. Still, things were turning out excellently for him. He had reached the top of his profession (whatever his private feelings about it) with uncommon speed and no great exertion. He had—what undoubtedly pleased him more—made a considerable name for himself as a writer. Best of all, perhaps for the first time in his life, he knew real financial security. He looked forward to the New Year with cheerful confidence.

VIII

MR GRAHAME AND MISS THOMSON

1899

To judge from the evidence offered by his published work, Kenneth Grahame was not a marrying man. *Amo* is the dreariest of verbs; women are irrational creatures; marriage is a deadly and soul-destroying institution. Girls are by definition an inferior breed who kick shins, gossip about trivialities, and use their feminine armoury in order to dominate, tease, and devour. The most sheerly happy moments in Grahame's work come when he—or his *alter ego* the narrator—is utterly alone, savouring the subtle magic of solitude, 'the world forgetting, by the world forgot'.

On the other hand, it is plain that behind this rejection lies not basic aversion but immature romantic idealism. It is not the *concept* of love which fails to touch Grahame's sympathies: the fairy-tale convention of Finding the Princess, the courtly love absorbed from Malory and the Troubadours, these he prized above almost everything else. What he hated and feared were the all-too-imperfect manifestations of love's power as observed in the adult world. The Olympians married, not for an intangible ideal, but for money, or dull social reasons, or driven by the blind impulses of the sexual urge. Sex, of course, and more particularly the onset of puberty, is one of the great enemies in Grahame's world. It disrupts the timelessness, wreaks appalling metamorphoses in hitherto right-minded children, breaks up the entire ideal pattern. One of Grahame's deliberate motives in writing *The Wind in the Willows* was 'by simply using the animal, to get away ... from weary sex-problems'; in the blurb he wrote for his publishers the book is described as 'clean of the clash of sex'.

This kind of emotional make-up, especially when combined with normal, healthy, physical instincts, can have peculiarly disastrous effects. The 'I' of Grahame's early books loses his heart three times; and the three objects of his affections might have been selected as text-book illustrations of delayed adolescence. There is the baker's wife, symbolizing maternal affection; the star-spangled circus equestrienne, who is the Unattainable Ideal in her magic ring; and the all-too-human, pert, teasing girl of 'Mutabile Semper':

> In later life it is to her sex that the wee (but very wise) folk sometimes delegate their power of torment. Such understudies are found to play the part exceedingly well; and

> many a time the infatuated youth believes he sees in the depth of one sole pair of eyes ... the authentic fairy wicket standing ajar; many a time must he hear the quaint old formula, 'I'm sure, if I've ever done anything to lead you to think', etc. (runs it not so?), ere he shall realize that here is the gate upon no magic pleasance but on a cheap suburban villa, banging behind the wrathful rate-collector or hurled open to speed the pallid householder to the Registrar's Office.

The implication could hardly be clearer. Grahame, in his own way, was extremely susceptible; but every time he tried to incorporate the object of his affections into that charmed, illusory, childish, sexless world of ideals, trouble was sure to follow. In most cases, luckily, once the girl got some inkling of what she was up against, that would be that. The real danger would be a woman who, superficially at any rate, shared Grahame's dream-world herself.

Since Grahame's diary has not survived, and any intimate letters connected with his early life have long since vanished, it is almost impossible to reconstruct this side of his life during the years before his marriage. Yet there are tantalizing hints of an earlier affair in some of Grahame's poems. The mysterious relationship that was ended long before Grahame's marriage was almost certainly with the girl whom he first met at Drayton Gardens, and holidayed with at Pitlochry and in Italy; the girl who joined the New Shakespere Society with him and shared all his private literary devotions: his cousin, Annie Grahame. 'I had been reared on old Scotch ballads and stories and folk-lore,' she wrote, 'which appealed to Kenneth also and later on at any rate formed a bond of union between us,' and of the holiday at the Villino Landau:

> We made some very pleasant expeditions—notably one to the Madonna del Sarso—a little church on a hillside some miles at the back of Fiesole where on the second Sunday in May a festival is held annually. ... We got back at about 7 p.m., none the worse for the long day, which Kenneth had beguiled with delightful fairy tales. ...

Poor Annie: she never married, and Elspeth Grahame, though using her information to supply background material for Chalmers' labours, carefully saw to it that he should not mention her once in his finished book. Arguments *ex silentio* are notoriously unreliable; but this one seems more suggestive than most.

It is plain from the whole episode that Grahame failed to achieve, and probably did not desire, a normal adult relationship. After all, most men taking their girl-friend for a long walk in the Florentine hills do not beguile the time with fairy tales, delightful or otherwise, whatever else they may talk about. Grahame's confession to Helen Dunham, in 1896, that he did not feel in the least grown up, and did not anticipate any immediate change in that direction, simply confirms the diagnosis. In all probability he would have gone to his grave a gentle, fantastic bachelor (like Lear, Carroll, and Hans Andersen) if fate, having a taste for irony, had not thrown Elspeth Thomson in his path.

Elspeth, like her future husband, was born in Edinburgh, on 3 January 1862. She was the second in the family of four, the youngest of whom was later to become Lord Courtauld-Thomson, the owner of Dorneywood. Her father,

ELSPETH THOMSON
by Sir Frank Dicksee RA.

Robert William Thomson, was a remarkable inventor, who took out patents on, *inter alia,* the pneumatic tyre, and a special type of fountain pen with a glass nib: he also produced a steam-driven road vehicle, and designed the first floating dock. Her mother, Clara, whose maiden name was Hertz, was of a literary and artistic bent, and a constant stream of distinguished visitors frequented the house in Moray Place. From her earliest years Elspeth was accustomed to such company. When Mark Twain arrived, to find her parents out and only the children at home, in the nursery,

> Elspeth received the visitor and offered him tea. He replied that he drank only whisky. Undaunted, and with rare social sense, the little girl ran down with a teapot and persuaded the butler to fill it with whisky, which the guest drank neat.

And at the age of ten—shortly after her father's death—Elspeth, on holiday at Pontresina with the rest of the family, struck up a precocious friendship with

Tennyson. All her life she was to feed on the personalities of artistic celebrities, and use their genius as a prop for her own lack of creative talent.

Furthermore, she not only cultivated a particularly sentimental brand of fairy-tale fantasy (which contrasts sharply with Grahame's own private world), but had a strong enough personality to impose her own terms on many of her distinguished correspondents. In 1890 Justin McCarthy, the leader of the Irish Party, was writing lyrically to the twenty-eight-year-old Elspeth about his love for 'Rivers—and poets who love Rivers and painters who give us pictures of them'. Old Sir John Tenniel bombarded her till the end of his life with coyly gallant Valentines and sub-Carrollian fantasies, such as his invention of a flying machine called the Furious Flycycle.

In 1875, three years after Robert Thomson's death, and when Elspeth was thirteen, her mother married again. Her second husband was a penniless barrister named John Fletcher Moulton, who, sustained by Clara's income, rose rapidly in his profession, and finally became a Lord of Appeal. The family moved from Edinburgh to London, and set up house at 57 Onslow Square. Here they lost no time in establishing themselves:

> They were both keenly interested in literature, science, and art, and their circle included practically all the mid-Victorian leaders in these subjects, notably Swinburne, Browning, Oscar Wilde, Lord Kelvin, Spottiswoode, Lord Leighton, Frank Dicksee and Tenniel, as well as many visitors of great interest from continental countries, since Mrs Fletcher Moulton as well as her husband spoke French and German perfectly.

Their elder daughter was given a cosmopolitan education as it was then understood: her sister Winnie, too, was an excellent amateur musician and artist. Elspeth spent some time as a pupil in a French convent: here she exercised her undoubted talent for languages (she spoke fluent Flemish as well as French), and acquired a superficially 'Continental' outlook on life to offset those gloomy Calvinist Sundays remembered from Moray Place.

By the time Elspeth Thomson met Kenneth Grahame she was nearly thirty-seven, and had reached a critical period in her life. For almost twenty years she had lived in the house at Onslow Square, first as Fletcher Moulton's stepdaughter, and after 1888 (the year of her mother's death) as his hostess and housekeeper also. She entertained the world of literature and art, filled her days with luncheons, tea-parties, soirées. When Fletcher Moulton went into politics, Elspeth was there to support him. His was a stormy passage; elected for Clapham in 1885 as a Liberal, he lost his seat the following year, and did not regain it till 1894. 1895 saw him back in the wilderness, and it was not till August 1898 that he found a safe constituency at Launceston in Cornwall. All this time Elspeth was at hand to discuss his campaigns, often in letters to him in his constituency, and give him unfailing support.

The trouble was that Elspeth had achieved little in her own right—unless we count a curious little penny novelette about a virtuous working-class girl, issued in 1888 over the pseudonym of 'Clarence Onslow', and entitled *Amelia Jane's*

Ambition. Bachelors perhaps fought shy of this strong-minded, strong-featured girl, with intellectual pretensions and an inexhaustible fund of conversational gambits. She was both a blue-stocking and an aesthete, simultaneously clever and fey: not particularly pretty, and verging on middle age. In later life acquaintances remembered her as 'a superficial and twilight woman' who 'talked stridently and interminably, laying down the law about her preferences in literature and art, and never taking much heed of what anybody else had to say'.

There cannot be any doubt that she regarded Kenneth Grahame as an ideal potential catch. He was Secretary of the Bank of England, and therefore both respectable and a man of substance; he was also the author of *The Golden Age*, a factor which appealed to the sentimental child-fantasist in her. The two attractions in combination proved irresistible; and Elspeth set about playing her fish with dogged ruthlessness. It seems likely that their acquaintance dates from some time in the second half of 1897. There is a story of Kenneth's having gone to see Fletcher Moulton on banking business, finding him out, and being entertained instead by his elder step-daughter.

The announcement of the engagement caused considerable surprise; and from 1898 onwards a curious change of tone is observable in much of Grahame's writing. A soft, false, dreamy sentimentality begins to intrude, utterly out of key with the tough, satirical note struck in *The Golden Age*. Grahame begins to behave as though he were an ordinary romantic children's writer, and seems to find the role uncomfortable.

Elspeth had a remarkable talent for imposing her own beliefs, habits and wish-fulfilments on other people. She was a woman of dominant, almost obsessional personality, which could absorb even so canny a politician as Justin McCarthy: there is no reason to suppose that Kenneth Grahame was any more immune from her hypnotic self-projection.

Elspeth firmly convinced herself in a very short time that here was a man who shared her own private world of childish sentimentalism: more disastrously, she convinced Grahame as well. He was not only a potential husband but an ideal romantic fairy-tale soul-mate. Once she got an idea of this sort into her head, the facts were simply made to fit in. After a while Grahame slipped into his allotted rôle. He fell in with her whimsies conscientiously. He attempted to incorporate her as a childish dream-princess in his story 'A Saga of the Seas', and the result was a page or two of frightful mawkishness. He even took to writing her coyly mis-spelt little *billets-doux*. Then, in the early spring of 1899, he played right into her hands by falling seriously ill.

As usual, it was his chest that proved his undoing. At first he seemed to be suffering from nothing worse than a tiresome, debilitating cold and cough. On Easter Sunday he wrote to Elspeth, who was similarly laid up, the first of a series of baby-talk letters:

> Darlin Minkie Ope youre makin steddy progress & beginnin ter think of oppin outer your nest & avin a short fly round. I ad nuther good nite & avnt ardly corfd torl

terday—but it aint so nice a day, & doesnt tempt one out. ... Feel orfle slack still but am wearin down the cold grajjly. Wish the sun wood cum out fer a bit. Im very dull & bored ere. Spose youre a bit dull'n bored were *you* are, aint you? But you've got a maid, & a poodle, (tho they're bicyclin most of the time) & your friends do drop in sumtimes. Easter is always detestable. Your whale-books a rippin good book, [almost certainly this refers to Melville's *Moby Dick*] wif lots of reedin in it, & it sor me froo Good Friday triumphantly. Spose youve got a sort o mudie box spred out on *your* quilt.

This aint much uv a letter my deer but aint got no spirits & dont take no interest nor no *notice* just yet. But Im wishing you elth & appiness my deer & a speedy recuvry & peece & quiet. Goodbye darlin from your own luvin Dino

Grahame got up the same afternoon, and returned to work in the City the next day, Monday 3 April. In the evening he attended a dinner of the Court of Directors, which he mentioned to Elspeth in a letter on Tuesday afternoon. At this point the correspondence ceases abruptly for some time. Grahame's confident diagnosis of recovery had been sadly mistaken. A bad relapse set in, with pneumonia and empyema. Grahame underwent an operation involving section of the ribs and returned to Kensington Crescent to be nursed by his sister Helen and his devoted housekeeper, Sarah Bath. His convalescence was difficult and prolonged.

This situation suited Elspeth very well. She was a constant visitor, with carnations and grapes: she persuaded her step-father—who was still in ignorance of her precise relationship to Grahame—to send the young Secretary gifts from his ample cellar.

I am not suggesting that Elspeth, like any coolly scheming middle-aged woman, deliberately set out to compromise Grahame: there is no doubt that she was genuinely in love with him at this point. She had by now convinced herself that Grahame exactly fitted her own dream ideal: all that remained was the mechanical process of making the dream come true. Relentlessly Elspeth took the initiative; and such were her persuasive powers that for just long enough she convinced Grahame as well. By the time he began to have doubts it was too late.

By 21 May Grahame was fit enough to 'crawl about with a stick'. Fletcher Moulton continued to supply him with 'ancient port' and offered him the use of a carriage. His position *vis-à-vis* Elspeth was still a secret: Fletcher Moulton might have raised his eyebrows at the note which Grahame had sent her on May 26: 'Darling—come when you can, tomorrow afternoon—I rather think my sister's going out about 3.30 or so, for the rest of the afternoon—anyhow come. Your lovin own Dino.' By now he was deeply compromised; and Elspeth, while perhaps uneasy about her stepfather's possible reactions, knew that Kenneth himself was sure. The etiquette governing a relationship of this kind was far stricter in 1899 than it is now, and any infringement of the rules (such as unchaperoned visits) provoked much more stringent social reprisals. And even if this had not been so, Grahame's sense of decency was only too easy to work on.

Kenneth and Helen travelled down to the west country together. The first ten days of Kenneth's convalescence were spent at Torquay; and from the moment of

BODINNICK, CORNWALL, 1904.
The village of Bodinnick faces Fowey across the River Fowey. Kenneth Grahame's regular visits provided some of the inspiration for *The Wind in the Willows.*

their arrival Kenneth wrote to Elspeth at least once a day. His letters—but not Elspeth's replies—have all survived. Unlike any of his other surviving correspondence, they are all scribbled in pencil, and use the curious baby-spelling which he had first adopted while an invalid in London.

The caged Bohemian is chafing a little: he dislikes the idea of being looked after and organized; his mind is straying wistfully towards beer and—characteristically—chambermaids. Elspeth equally was apparently already beginning to find Grahame's emotional elusiveness a little trying. The following day Grahame and his sister moved to Fowey, the little Cornish fishing port later to be incorporated in *The Wind in the Willows*. 'As the river mouth came in view larst nite with the boats & the little grey town I felt summow 'sif I was coming *'ome'*, Grahame wrote, 'from boardin-school at Torquay.' He found the Fowey Hotel a charming place, '& bed a nice *narrer* sorft one insted of a broard ard one that leadeth to destruckshin'—which seems to suggest which way his mind was subconsciously turning about the future.

But his side was healing well, and the exercises to inflate his damaged lung were proceeding successfully, and there were the harbour and the valerian-smothered lanes to explore. The only drawback seems to have been Helen, who was always urging him, unsuccessfully, into more 'social' activities. She seems, too, to have been curiously devoid of a sense of humour:

> My sister went along the cliffs & climed down to a little cove & as she sat there a big rat cum out & sat bside er & ett winkles! I sed did ee buy them orf of a barrer & drop em in is at but she looked puzzled & seriouse & sed no ee only scraped in the seaweed wif is little pors & fetcht em out. Then I began agin was it a *black* pin—but by this time she evdently thort I was *ravin* so I dropt the subjick.

Presents continued to arrive: not only toilet water, bundles of magazines, and good advice from Elspeth ('Dont *you* get sittin up too late & doin too much neither my deer cos it weekins the fect of your preechin to me') but also the *Contes drolatiques* from Fletcher Moulton, who still, apparently, thought of Grahame as no more than a close friend.

Clearly this situation was an impossible one; and for once Elspeth's nerve seems to have failed her. At any rate, it was Grahame now who took the initiative. He had been showing some concern at the endless calling, dinner-parties and good works with which her life was filled; and on 22 June he wrote: 'My darlin, this is orlso to say that I'm ritin to your farver today cos I think it wos time you was "brort to your bearins" & got a chance of actin for your own future & not rampagin bout for uvver peeple.' Helen had decided to move on to friends at the Lizard, and Grahame was hoping, among other things, to get Elspeth down to Fowey, which probably sharpened his resolve.

The effect on Fletcher Moulton seems to have been, at first, disastrous. He was a strong-willed, egotistic man, and had got used to Elspeth running the Onslow Square house for him. All the evidence suggests that he put up the most violent opposition to her proposed marriage. On 24 June Grahame is thanking Elspeth for a long letter 'ritten midst the shouts & the crash o battle soterspeak'. Though Fletcher Moulton was persuaded to give his consent, it is unlikely that he viewed the affair with any great favour—especially since it had been conducted behind his back. But the essential practical nature of his objection is suggested by the fact that hardly was Elspeth off his hands before he himself married again.

Nor was Elspeth's attitude, once her stepfather knew how things lay, calculated to sooth Grahame's strained nerves. Now the position was clear to all concerned, she seems to have changed her tack and become infuriatingly casual and unpractical. By the 25th Grahame himself was talking about a possible elopement; he had had no reply from Fletcher Moulton, and was in a highly nervous state. But on the 26th Fletcher Moulton wrote a stiff and grudging letter of capitulation, and the tension eased a little. The marriage was fixed for 22 July in Fowey.

There can be little doubt that what helped Grahame through this crisis more than any other single factor was his incipient friendship with Quiller-Couch. Q had settled permanently in Fowey eight years previously, at a pleasant house called The Haven, looking out over the harbour; and he soon developed an interest in the convalescent writer whose tastes for literature and sailing were so identical with his own. He took Grahame out on yachting-parties, introduced him to Fowey society,

SIR ARTHUR QUILLER-COUCH.
Q was one of Kenneth Grahame's few friends and was often his host during Grahame's frequent stays in Fowey.

and lent him a little skiff, the *Richard and Emily,* to go exploring in on his own up the creeks and backwaters. Q went out of his way to charm Helen Grahame with expeditions and river-picnics: as a result Grahame wrote, 'sister as bin distinckly more amiable & reely I fink it is ony er sort o' "awkwardness".' She went off to the Lizard on the 27th, but firmly announced, to Grahame's dismay, that she was coming back.

Meanwhile arrangements for the wedding got, rather creakily, under way:

> I see you wos thinkin orl the time bout close [clothes] wile poor me was ony angshus to fulfil the requirements of the lor! Fowey'd be orl rite, for a wemmick-marriage [Wemmick was the lawyer's clerk in *Great Expectations* who suddenly got married one

morning on the spur of the moment]—but I wish you'd tell me *ow much* of a wemmick-marriage its got ter be. [June 29]

The following day Grahame and Q ran down a 'tame curate' in the billiard-room and got him to put up the banns; and Grahame contemplated wearing 'a blue serge soot & a soft at, & ee [Courtauld Thomson, Elspeth's brother] mite liketer do same'—an improbable hope. From internal hints it looks as though Elspeth's friends and relations took much the same line about the whole thing as Fletcher Moulton.

Helen returned to Fowey sooner than Grahame expected; and the first knowledge she had of the official engagement was the announcement in the *Morning Post* on Saturday 1 July. 'She's just sed she'd seen it, & that was abslootly orl. There must be sumfin at the bottom of er sullen sort o silence wot I ain't got at yet' There was: she detested Elspeth, of whom she had seen quite enough while looking after Kenneth in Kensington Crescent. There is a by no means improbable tradition that she asked Grahame, after reading the news in the *Morning Post*, whether he was *really* going to marry Elspeth; whereat he replied, in an infinitely despondent voice: 'I suppose so; I suppose so.' At this Helen 'sed she was goin ome on Toosday wereat I bowed my edd in silence, saying nuffin'. But there was always Q to cheer Kenneth up with 'messing about in boats'; as Kenneth himself admitted to his fiancée, she was a martyr to tides ('but mustnt complane its the moon wot dus it'), and letters had to wait.

As July drew on more and more practical details pressed in on Grahame. There was accommodation to be arranged (he left his room in the hotel and stayed with Quiller-Couch), the honeymoon site to be chosen, invitations to be agreed on. Elspeth shocked conventional opinion by refusing to wear an engagement ring; so Grahame sent one to Miss Bradley instead. 'I respect unconventionality of any kind too much to even protest', he wrote. 'But I do feel strongly that there ought to be a ring in the business *somewhere*—to appease the gods.' (Elspeth's attitude to jewellery of any kind was a little odd: Grahame described it, accurately, as 'non-conformist', and the nearest they came to an open row was when he sent her a pendant.) The machinery of society had taken over, and the private fantasy was being dragged to its public, conventional, irrevocable conclusion.

Something of this conflict is reflected in an odd note Grahame sent Elspeth on 7 July, in the course of which he wrote:

> Mrs Q ses larst nite wy dont we jus go way ter Newquay 'from the Satty till the Mundy' wich I fort a most immoril sjeschin—Wensdy to Friday wd a bin orlrite not bein a 'week-end'. Darlin, ow'd you like ter go on livin at Ons: Sq: & cum away wif me fer week-ends? Then [several words illegible] and you needn't rite no notes & it wood be so nice & immoril & yet nobody coodnt find no forlt not even arnts.

Nice and immoral—yet safe from aunts: nothing could so vividly have summed up. Grahame's simultaneous desire, fear, and emotional childishness. The tempo of his letters, stimulated by improving health and mental anticipation, quickens considerably towards the end. He is worked up into an unmistakable state of passion which he can hardly understand, let alone keep in proportion. His last letter of all, posted on Thursday 13 July, ends: 'Goodbye sweetie & dont sorst yourself cos its a long journey down & *I* want ter do the sorstin of you wen you gets ere—so you've goter save up fer your luver my pretty oos awatin of you ere & is your lovin own Dino'. This enforced separation, filled by constant letters, was perhaps the worst thing that could have happened to both fo them. It projected the actuality of their relationship—and emotional capacities—on an inflated, imaginary scale. It excited Grahame to a tension he could not sustain, and led Elspeth to believe all the more firmly that he was the passionate lover of her dreams. They were both to be cruelly disappointed.

All the time congratulatory notes poured in to off-set what Grahame described as the 'shock-and-blow' letters. There was old Sir John Tenniel ('I am bold to offer you the very respectfully *affectionate* congratulations of a venerable *fossil*'); Sir Frank Dicksee, who had painted Elspeth; the Lidderdales; and many others. To Elspeth, Beatrice Roberts wrote: 'If Mr Grahame is as nice as his books, you are very much to be congratulated', a compliment which sets the general tone, and nicely balances Sir Martin Conway's remarks to Kenneth: 'You are going to marry a very charming and very clever lady, and you will never be bored again as long as you live.' In his reply Kenneth declared (presumably with Onslow Square week-ends still at the back of his mind): 'My beastly virtue has been my enemy through life, but once married I will try & be frankly depraved, and then all will go well.'

The wedding finally took place on Saturday 22 July 1899, at St. Fimbarrus's Church, Fowey. Fletcher Moulton, together with Elspeth herself and Courtauld, Harold and Winnie Thomson had arrived before the week-end. Elspeth had thrown Grahame into a last-minute panic by turning up (as we might expect) in very un-Wemmicky finery, complete with poodle and lady's maid. Anthony Hope Hawkins, the novelist, who was also Grahame's cousin, had agreed to be best man, and took his duties in a spirited way: he hired a hurdy-gurdy man to grind his organ outside The Haven at crack of dawn, and make sure the household woke up in time. At the Fowey Hotel Elspeth (in one of her more exhibitionistic back-to-nature moods) went out before breakfast to admire the view from the Castle, and broke into the dining-room when the meal was nearly over, still in her old muslin, and with a daisy-chain strung round her neck. Wemmick won after all: Elspeth decided to get married as she was, and the expensive wedding-dress remained unpacked.

Elspeth Thomson, that *habituée* of dinner-table and salon, was no more; Mrs Kenneth Grahame had made her first characteristic gesture, before the ring was even on her finger.

St Ives c1900.
Kenneth and Elspeth Grahame honeymooned here briefly in 1899 before returning to Kenneth's beloved Fowey.

Edward Atkinson and his Devoted Housekeeper Miss Marsden.
Grahame found 'Atky' highly congenial and was a regular visitor to his home on the River Fowey.

IX

THE WILD WOOD AND THE WIDE WORLD

1900–07

Elspeth did not have her husband to herself for long. Three days of the honeymoon were spent at St Ives; but when the coast was clear of relatives the Grahames soon returned to Fowey, and the congenial company of the Quiller-Couches. Once again Elspeth became a martyr to tides, but this time in a more physical sense. Nothing—not even marriage—could keep Grahame for long from his beloved boats, or the uninvolved male companionship, free of emotional stress, which he came more and more to rely upon. Q was a great yachtsman, and the rest of July was spent afloat, in yawl or dinghy. It was not, we may surmise, Elspeth's kind of world; Fowey and Onslow Square had little in common, and the London hostess probably felt somewhat out of things in this bracing atmosphere.

From the start she and Q failed to hit it off: each saw the other as a dangerous influence, and Q, one suspects, made short work of her literary pretentiousness. Nor did she feel any natural sympathy, with Grahame's other great Fowey friend, Edward Atkinson. 'Atky', as he was universally known, represented the extreme of all those characteristics which Elspeth learnt to distrust in her husband. He was a sixty-two-year-old bachelor of private means, who owned thirty boats and—though an indifferent sailor—was Commodore of the Fowey Yacht Club. He was also an obsessional collector of *objets d'art,* and his beautiful riverside house up the Fowey estuary was filled to overflowing with knick-knacks of every description: the surplus went into forming a Fowey art gallery. He had drawerfuls of mechanical toys (which delighted Grahame) and a rope-ladder in lieu of a staircase. His neat grey beard and aquiline features were a familiar sight in the Fowey streets—generally crowned by an exquisite and idiosyncratic hat ordered specially from Paris. He lived alone with his devoted housekeeper, Miss Marsden, but occasionally took undergraduate friends on canoeing trips in the South of France. Grahame found him highly congenial; Elspeth saw him as a subtle menace to her marriage. It probably never occurred to her, then or later, that Atky's influence would play a large part in the crystallization of *The Wind in the Willows*.

Grahame had been away from the Bank for nearly four months now, and it was essential that he should get settled back into his duties before September. The honeymoon was cut short (by Grahame's standards of leisure, at any rate) and the

Grahames returned to London. Sarah Bath, Grahame's old housekeeper at Kensington Crescent, had declined to continue in office after his marriage—she had probably formed her own opinion of Elspeth during the carnations-and-grapes period—and Kenneth shows some embarrassment in his letter to Elspeth on the subject:

> Bout, *Sarah, I* aint conshuns-stricken, & ony rote er a sivvil note sayin if she cared ter stay wif me I shd be very glad, *cos* you arst me to, afore I left, sayin it wd save so much trubble. But in many respex she aint kwite the person for us, and she *as* got 'erself' on the brane—those people of the *pessant* clars orfin ave. Aint erd from her gain.

One of Sarah's predominant characteristics was a certain blunt outspokenness; it is likely that she gave Master Kenneth her unvarnished opinion of his prospective wife. Poor Grahame: in this episode perhaps most of all we sense the embarrassed falseness of his relationship with Elspeth—the artificial baby-talk; the nervous self-justification; the incompatability of her world and his, however ignored or disguised; the pathetic effort at compromise.

Worst of all, after months of exacerbated anticipation, their physical relationship proved a bitter disappointment—to Elspeth at any rate. She was hardly married before she sent a desperate *cri de coeur* to Mrs Thomas Hardy at Max Gate, which elicited, *inter alia*, the following remarks:

> It is really too early days with you to be benefited by advice from one who has just come to the twenty-fifth year of matrimony. ... I can scarcely think that love proper, and enduring, is in the nature of men—as a rule—perhaps there is no woman 'whom custom will not stale'. There is ever a desire to give but little in return for our devotion, and affection—theirs being akin to children's, a sort of easy affectionateness. ... Keeping separate a good deal is a wise plan in crises—and being both free—and expecting little, neither gratitude, nor affections, love, nor *justice*, nor anything you may set your heart on—Love interest,—adoration, and all that kind of thing is usually a failure—complete—someone comes by and upsets your pail of milk in the end—If he belongs to the public in any way, years of devotion count for nothing—Influence can seldom be retained as years go by, and *hundreds* of wives go through a phase of disillusion—it is really a pity to have any ideals in the first place.

After which Mrs Hardy (remembering the politeness due to a bride, however distraught) congratulates Elspeth in due form, and invites them both to look in if they are ever in the neighbourhood of Dorchester.

Elspeth's reactions were only what we might expect in the circumstances. Both she and Grahame were living in a dream-world, but it was not the same dream-world. As in the case of the Golden City, imagination was vastly more romantic than physical reality. Besides, neither of them was young; both were totally inexperienced; and Grahame was still convalescing from a very serious operation. If they had possessed the wisdom of maturity they would have been patient; but all they could understand was that life had failed to measure up to their private fantasies.

Mrs Hardy's letter, taken in combination both with what we know of

Grahame's temperament, and some very odd poems written by Elspeth after her marriage, suggests an additional difficulty. Elspeth was clearly by nature a passionate woman: it is she who makes all the real running in the engagement correspondence, and talks of nocturnal delights. She had been discreetly chaste for thirty-seven years; and Grahame's initial burst of ardour must have roused all her dormant instincts. But it seems all too clear that this ardour—as far as Grahame was concerned—had been artificially stimulated, and vanished almost at once, leaving Elspeth bitter and frustrated. 'My first touch of the earth,' declared Keats's Endymion, 'came nigh to kill': and so it was, in all probability, with Grahame. Shattered and repelled by this adult relationship, he retreated even further than before into his safe, private world—a world, this time, not of children but of animals. *The Wind in the Willows,* you will remember, was, in Grahame's thrice-emphasized words, clean of the clash of sex.

It is at this point that Elspeth most clearly earns our sympathy. Pretentious, shallow, and domineering she may have been; but she was also desperately unhappy. She had pursued a dream, and it had shattered in her hands. Soured by disappointment, she let herself go; and as though in some horrible fairy-tale, each of her virtues gradually turned into the corresponding weakness. Her cleverness became glib arrogance, her conversational powers degenerated into opinionated loquaciousness, her gift for household management into close-fisted thrift. From a smart hostess she turned, within a very few years, into something very little short of a slattern; and her unconventional tricks ripened equally fast into plain eccentricity. Both she and Grahame are equally to be pitied; perhaps hers was the harder lot of the two. He had preserved his dream-world inviolate: hers was irreparably destroyed, for love was its cornerstone—sentimental, romantic, ideal love—and love she had found wanting.

Nevertheless, Elspeth had one consolation. As if subconsciously sensing that her first opportunity would also be her last, she became pregnant immediately after her marriage.

Grahame had taken a long lease of a house in Campden Hill—16 Durham Villas—which was to be their home for the next six years. He was at once plunged back into City life, to the exclusion of more literary pursuits—though his uncreativity during those early years of marriage must be attributed in part at least to more personal causes. He had suffered a severe shock, and it would be some time before his mechanism readjusted itself. Nor were his duties as Secretary especially arduous: and Kenneth, as he himself confesses, was indolent by nature.

'An accomplished, but, it would appear, not an assertive Secretary': that is Sir John Clapham's opinion, and one that commands general agreement. Mr H. A. Siepmann, a distinguished banker himself, is somewhat more severe: 'The tradition is that he was a very dilatory and lackadaisical Secretary. Perhaps that is the reason why so little has been said about his activities in the City. I rather think that, in quite a few ways, he fell short of the Bank's standards—such as they were.' After Grahame's death his brother-in-law Courtauld Thomson (that astute businessman) wrote to the then Governor of the Bank, with wry irony: 'Though possibly these books were not all written during banking hours, his duties as Secretary may have suggested the titles *Golden Age* and *Dream Days*.'

Furthermore, there is evidence of a rather exotic sort that Grahame continued after his marriage as a reader and adviser for John Lane. During the latter half of 1900 he was conducting a curious correspondence with Frederick Rolfe—Baron Corvo himself—and from Corvo's letters it is clear that Grahame exerted considerable influence in the publishing world of his day. The first is dated 16 August:

> Dear Sir: I believe you read the MS of Toto Maidalchini's Folk Lore which I am publishing with Lane and calling A Sensational Atomist; and have earned my gratitude by generous praise.
>
> Will you allow me to ask whether you have influence to use to get for me permanent and regular literary work, so that I may be delivered from desperate and restless circumstances, and also freed to realize some literary plans which I have made. To prevent misconception, may I sternly state that what I have said here is a 'necessary proposition', unsuggested by another, *entirely confidential,* and a liberty for which I apologise.
>
> Yours faithfully, Frederick Baron Corvo.

Grahame must have replied encouragingly; almost by return of post Corvo sent him a vast list of projected works, somewhat akin to the experiments performed by the Laputan scientists in *Gulliver's Travels.* Finally Grahame obtained Corvo an introduction to Smith, Elder & Co., and the correspondence lapsed.

At the beginning of her married life—till the birth of her child at least—Elspeth attempted to reproduce in Durham Villas the atmosphere of Onslow Square. There were dinner-parties and soirées; but Kenneth (like Badger) was awkward in her sort of 'society'. Miss Bradley, a frequent guest, later wrote that 'the easy informal hospitality at the Grahames' house on Campden Hill will be remembered with peculiar pleasure by many of their intimate circle', but she added:

> Kenneth's mind was not ruled by the ordinary conventions. He made little attempt at small-talk but his silences were curiously companionable; & presently the thought would flow. ... He was a good—sympathetic—conversationalist because he was as genuinely interested in the person he was talking to & in the latter's views as in his own—he was entirely without pretensions or affectations of any description. Never a great talker in a mixed company, he would sometimes give utterance to his least conventional sentiments with genial but unhesitating conviction.

Kenneth was far more at ease in the company of Graham Robertson, the artist and playwright, who designed the original frontispiece for *The Wind in the Willows.* Robertson at this period lived just round the corner in Argyll Road, and the two became close friends. Robertson was an Old Etonian bachelor, who believed in fairies and owned a houseful of dogs: whether he was a close friend of Elspeth's we do not know. Certainly some of the details he has recorded about Grahame are

THE WIND IN THE WILLOWS.
The Wind in the Willows was published in 1908. Graham Robertson's frontispiece was the only illustration to appear in the first edition.

more revealing and vivid than almost any other single source. In particular, he analyses the exact impression given by Grahame's withdrawn 'otherness':

> Oddly enough (for he was a most attractive man) Kenneth had few friends. He simply didn't want them. He would say rather wonderingly to his wife: 'You *like* people. They interest you. But I am interested in *places*!'

And in his memoir of Grahame he wrote:

> He had a marvellous gift of silence. ... He would slowly become part of the landscape and a word from him would come as unexpectedly as a sudden remark from an oak or a beech.

Another fact on which Robertson sheds some light is Grahame's increasing passion for toys:

> His special room in No. 16 was most characteristic; it looked like a nursery. Books there were certainly, but they were outnumbered by toys. Toys were everywhere—intriguing, fascinating toys which could hardly have been conducive to study.

Clearly the buried dolls were having a resurrection; it looks as though the result of marriage was to accelerate Grahame's childish reversion. Yet already the subject had cropped up regularly in his letters to Elspeth from Fowey. While she wove coy little fantasies about a private Love-Post, he rummaged in playboxes. 'By the way,' he enquires disconcertingly, 'oos lookin arter my drorful o dolls at ome & givin em seed & water & grounsle?' Later he recounts how Q took him up-river to 'Rosebank', Atky's house, where 'we found a drore full of toys wot wound up, and we ad a great race tween a fish, a snaik, a beetle wot flapped is wings, & a rabbit'. The split between Grahame's public and private selves, apparently healed at the time of 'The Reluctant Dragon', now began to widen once more under the stress of an intolerable personal relationship.

The birth of a son to the Grahames clearly eased their domestic tension. But—as so often in such a case—the child did not solve its parents' problems: it merely enabled them to ignore what could not be undone. Each projected on to it the image of their disappointed dreams; and the result, inevitably, was tragic.

Alastair Grahame was born, prematurely, on 12 May 1900; and to his parents' intense distress, proved to have congenital cataract of the right eye, which was completely blind, together with a pronounced squint in the left—which was also 'oversighted'. He was to be their only child: the reasons for this we can only surmise. Kenneth's retreat from passion would not account for it entirely: we must remember that at the time of Alastair's birth Elspeth was thirty-eight, and that during the next few years she was to be constantly ill, or hypochondriacal, or both. It is possible that the Grahames refrained from increasing their family on medical advice, or even for fear of producing a second child with worse physical defects

'Mouse'—Alastair Grahame. Elspeth Grahame.

These two miniatures are by Elspeth's sister—Winifred Hope Thomson.

than the first: there are some indications that Alastair's semi-blindness may have been hereditary.

Whatever the reason, the inevitable result was that Alastair (or 'Mouse', as everyone called him) became the recipient of both his parents' thwarted emotions. To say that he was chronically spoilt (which of course he was) is to over-simplify the problem. Kenneth wrote *The Wind in the Willows* for him; Elspeth fed him with fantasy of another sort. He was a sickly, physically handicapped, sensitive but not over-bright child: and throughout his life he had to struggle with the image of himself which his mother created and steadfastly believed. Elspeth managed to convince herself—and did her best to convince everyone else—that Alastair was, in every respect, whether physical or mental, not only normal but brilliant. The boy's whole life became a struggle to live up to the impossible ideal she set him: and in the end the strain proved too great. But all this lay in the future. For the time being it was enough that Mouse's nursery had become the focus of life in 16 Durham Villas.

In other respects Kenneth, at least, was marking time during this period. He only came into the public eye once: but this was in a peculiarly bizarre way. On 24 November 1903, at about eleven in the morning, a respectably dressed stranger presented himself at one of the offices in the Secretary's department, and asked to see 'the Governor, Sir Augustus Prevost'. Now Prevost was no longer Governor; but the messenger, finding nothing amiss, asked the stranger (who had given his name as George F. Robinson) if he would care to speak with the Secretary, as Sir Augustus was out of town. Mr Robinson agreed, and was taken to a waiting-room, where Grahame presently arrived to interview him.

The visitor at once repeated his original question: were Sir Augustus Prevost, or Mr Morley (the then Governor) at the Bank? No, Grahame said, somewhat puzzled, they were not. 'I suppose you're in charge, then,' said Robinson, and thrust a large roll of manuscript towards him, tied with ribbon at each end. As Grahame hesitated, Robinson peremptorily ordered him to read it. Grahame, by now thoroughly annoyed, declined the privilege, and asked Robinson to state his business briefly. The answer was unexpected and startling. Remarking 'well, if you won't, then—' and something else which Grahame failed to hear, Robinson suddenly produced a large Service revolver. The Secretary retreated rapidly outside the door, just in time to stop one of the Directors who was about to come in. At the same time Robinson fired his first shot, and followed it up with two more.

Grahame quickly took charge of the situation. The police were fetched, and the Governor and the Directors warned of the danger. Robinson came out of the waiting-room and fired another shot at a messenger in the corridor; then, tiring of this sport, wandered into the Directors' Library, where the Head Doorkeeper, with great presence of mind, turned the key on him. As he threatened to shoot anyone who came near, he was left alone until a powerful fire-hose could be brought to bear on him. This knocked him off his feet, and after a tremendous struggle he was carted away by the police, tied up in an ambulance.

At Cloak Lane police station he was charged with 'Wandering in Threadneedle

NO MORE "SHOTS IN THE LOCKER."

Suggestions for Precautionary Measures at the Bank of England.

["EASY ACCESS.—We confess to some surprise at the ease with which a wandering lunatic, without apparently stating any very definite business, can obtain access to high officials at the Bank."—*Pall Mall Gazette.*]

THIS CARTOON IN PUNCH
appeared following newspaper reports of a madman attempting to shoot Kenneth Grahame within the portals of the Bank of England.

Street: deemed to be a lunatic', and harangued the police in a way that is only chastely hinted at by the brief report in *The Times*: 'From statements made by him at the station he appears to hold Socialistic views.' The following day, at the Mansion House, Sir Alfred Newton, judging him unfit to plead, adjourned the case *sine die,* and he was committed to Broadmoor—but not before he had delivered himself of a remarkable pronouncement:

> The prisoner pleaded that his rolled documents had been tied at one end with a black ribbon, at the other with a white. These documents had been presented to Mr Grahame lengthwise. It had therefore been open to Mr Grahame to grasp either one of the two ends. Instead of the innocuous white end Mr Grahame had preferred to take the end bound by the black ribbon, thus proving that Fate demanded his immediate demise. Mr Robinson looked upon himself as a mere instrument in the matter and quite without prejudice or guile.

Letters of sympathy and congratulation poured in: not only from friends and relatives, but complete strangers as far afield as Nova Scotia, panic-stricken at the thought of any danger befalling the author of *The Golden Age*. From Onslow Square Fletcher Moulton wrote to Elspeth:

> We both send you our deepest sympathy in the shock and anxiety which you have had today. Nothing but the promptness and presence of mind of your husband could

have avoided a terrible calamity and you must be very proud of his having shewn himself so cool and courageous. But don't let yourself brood over it—such an outrage cannot occur again. It was an accident that he was the one in danger & it is not possible that such carelessness will be allowed in future on the part of the Bank servants.

This touched on the really important significance of the affair. 'Mr Kenneth Grahame,' observed an anonymous wag in *Punch* the following year, 'is wondering what is the meaning of the expression, "As safe as the Bank of England".'

Over the years—and especially since his appointment as Secretary—Grahame's attitude to the Bank had been slowly changing. From a prison it had changed insensibly into something of an ivory tower. It represented tradition, continuity, solid values, a firm structure of society. Outside, cads and Radicals might snarl: it made no difference. But now, in an hour, the whole fabric had been torn from top to bottom. A lunatic—and not only a lunatic, but a *Socialist* lunatic, the equivalent of those dreadful bomb-throwing anarchists—had wandered into the sacred precincts and assaulted the person of the *Old Lady*. The whole episode, for all his fortitude at the time, must have shocked Grahame in a deep and indefinable way. He was not to forget it.

Otherwise his existence remained unruffled. Peter Pan had arrived in Kensington Gardens; Anthony Hope was married at St Bride's; Henley died—another link with the old days gone—and Grahame was a mourner at his funeral. The Wright Brothers made their famous flight, and the speed limit for motor-cars—poop! poop!—was raised to 20mph.

Elspeth's health had been deteriorating in a way that hints at nervous origins—she spent nearly all day on a sofa, sipping hot water—and in May 1904 she left London, alone, for a long cure at Woodhall Spa in Lincolnshire. In a letter to Mrs. Ward, a day or two before Elspeth's departure, Grahame wrote: 'He (Mouse) had a bad crying fit on the night of his birthday, and I had to tell him stories about moles, giraffes & water-rats (he selected these as subjects) till after 12.' In the same month the Grahame's maid, a Wiltshire girl named Louise, being asked by Elspeth why the master was late (they were going out to dinner, and Kenneth was supposed to be changing) replied: 'He's with Master Mouse, Madam, he's telling him some ditty or other about a Toad.' So, three years before Grahame set pen to paper again, the first germ of *The Wind in the Willows* was being evolved in bed-time stories for a small child. The major characters were all assembled (perhaps it is just as well that the giraffe dropped out along the road); now they only needed a background and shaping motif. Grahame's spring of creative imagination, all the more powerful for its long confinement underground, was once more slowly forcing its way towards the surface: and this time it brought with it an unprecedently well-stocked sub-conscious mind.

Meanwhile occasional reminders of Grahame's past literary activities continued to reach him. In October 1904 a young lady in San Francisco, having been tickled by the essay 'Marginalia' in *Pagan Papers*, decided on a highly original *réplique*. 'When,' Grahame had asked rhetorically, 'shall that true poet arise who, disdaining the trivialities of text, shall give the world a book of verse consisting entirely of margin?' Miss Josephine Hoveed obligingly supplied it. *Margin,* which she sent to Grahame with her letter of appreciation, was, like the Bellman's Chart, a perfect and absolute blank.

Two months later (for reasons which will be apparent in a moment) Grahame replied. The following is his pencilled draft:

> Dear Madam: Please accept my sincere thanks for the beautiful copy wh. has reached me of your new work 'Margin'—a copy which I understand exhausts the Edition & baffles the clamorous Public. Nothing cd be more charming, or more acceptable, than the binding, lettering, and general bodily format of
>
> But the format must give place to the pleasure the contents have given me. For your verse has a limpid spaciousness, a clarity, & a breadth, wh. soothes while it satisfied, and throughout there is a haunting suggestion of broad heaths, moonlight, wind-swept spaces & the OPEN ROAD. To these positive virtues one must add the negative qualities—an absence of all that frets or jars—the superior English of the Printer's Reader—the Celtic Twilight or the Split Infinitive. Such verse as yours must it seems to me go far—it must arrive. Indeed it has done both. Hence this line.

It is an amusing letter; and it has an added interest from the incidental light it sheds on Grahame's preoccupations at the time—including the Open Road.

In September Kenneth decided to go abroad alone, to Spain. Mouse, who had been playing up his German governess (he used to lie dreamily in the middle of the road when motor-cars were approaching), was sent off to Broadstairs. At the time, despite his eye-trouble, he seemed in good general health. Elspeth was still taking her cure; there is no evidence that Kenneth suggested her accompanying him to Spain, and much which inclines one to believe he was glad of the chance to get away.

He had only got as far as the Pyrenees when a telegram reached him—rather miraculously for the Spain of 1904—summoning him home at once. Mouse had gone down with a sudden attack of peritonitis; and Elspeth, galvanized out of her sickly lassitude, had at once left Woodhall and joined him in Broadstairs. Here she stayed during the operation and subsequent crisis; and here Kenneth found her. By the end of the year Alastair was on the mend, though still not well enough to be moved from Broadstairs. On 3 January 1905 he was able to write to Q as follows:

> Very many thanks for the beautiful Christmas book you have sent to poor Mouse. He is devoted to picture-books and they are most useful now that he is mentally active again & has such long hours to get through each day. I am glad to say that since the wound healed entirely, he has forgotten his pains and terrors, and 'rots' everybody all round as before. The other day when the doctor arrived he cocked his eye at his nurses whom he knew to be modest and shamefaced women beyond the ordinary, & began cheerily: 'Hullo doctor! Are your bowels open to-day?' One of the women stupidly begged him not to refer to such things—'it wasn't *nice*'. This gave him the opening he wished for. 'Not *nice*?' he said furiously, 'then what does he say it to me for? I didn't

begin it, he said it first!' And thenceforth he chanted the enquiry in plainsong, till the doctor was hustled out of the room.

E. is still down there, & I don't know when she will return. All regards & good wishes to all four of you.

In August the whole family went to Scotland for a summer holiday, and stayed at what Elspeth described as 'a famous old Scottish castle', though she does not name it: it *may* have been Inveraray. Kenneth does not appear to have enjoyed himself; it was a stupid idea, he told Q, and Scotland 'had gone down-hill considerably since I was there last—anyhow I didn't care about it'. But this distaste for his surroundings did not stop the nightly development of his bed-time stories for Alastair. A guest who arrived late for tea one day and wanted to meet Kenneth, was directed upstairs to the night-nursery, where she eavesdropped, fascinated, outside the door. Kenneth was telling his story, and Alastair interrupting from time to time—'sometimes asking for an explanation, sometimes arguing a point, at others laughing'. When asked what the story had been *about*, the guest replied: 'I know there was a Badger in it, a Mole, a Toad, and a Water-rat, and the places they lived in and were surrounded by.' Badger had now arrived; the pattern was developing.

In the autumn of 1905 it was decided that Alastair's nurse should be replaced by a governess. Already he was showing those unmistakable symptoms peculiar to a spoilt only child of educated parents: pertness, precociousness, a trick of mimicking his elders' aphorisms without understanding them. Elspeth kept him largely segregated from other children, and dressed him in girlish or *outré* clothes. She was moreover, only too ready to encourage his premature signs of 'brilliance' or sophistication: nothing is more pathetic than the way in which she preserves his childish sayings. For her they obviously enhance his nature; the unprejudiced reader will find them irksome at first, and, finally tragic. Elspeth was a tremendous snob, among other things: so Alastair's childish desire to have the sweep in for tea (what child is ever conscious of social distinctions?) she magnifies into a 'complete understanding of, and sympathy with, human beings of every class in life, from the highest to the lowest'.

Miss Naomi Stott, the governess, clearly did her best to counter-balance the fantasy and pseudo-sophistication which Elspeth injected daily into her son; in the memoir she wrote of him for Chalmers she emphasizes other, more likeable, qualities—his fearlessness, hatred of suffering, charming manners, sensitivity. But even she tells some unconsciously devastating anecdotes about Alastair:

> I am told that, at the age of three and on a railway journey he was continually urged by his nurse to 'see the pretty lambs' or other objects of the flying landscape. Presently the travellers caught sight of the sea and Nannie made haste to call attention to the 'pretty ships'. Alastair said, 'Oh, Nannie, do leave the boats in the water, they look very well there'.

At four he was complaining primly of 'vulgar eating and arms on the table'. (His precocious vocabulary caused an older girl to say, with more truth than perhaps she knew, 'You are only a baby who has swallowed a dictionary'.) One thinks of Macaulay's famous *réplique* at the same age—'Thank you, Madam, the agony has abated'—but Alastair never showed any degree of Macaulay's stamina: even though Kenneth could write to Q that winter saying Mouse had 'become most bookish'. In that household it would have been surprising if he had not.

The Christmas of 1905 was remarkable for a double visit—from Anstey Guthrie (better known as F. Anstey, the author of *Vice Versa*) and old Sir John Tenniel, who still kept up a playful correspondence with Elspeth, and sent her a verse Valentine every year. Guthrie, too, was an old friend—he first met Elspeth in 1889—and she occasionally told him off to 'chaperon' Kenneth at City dinners. On this occasion he chased Alastair up to bed, growling like a wolf; but later, under Elspeth's prodding, and after several revisions, sent her a stiff little memoir for publication in which he said that meeting Alastair 'was rather like being presented to a young prince'.

In May 1906 Kenneth Grahame and his family moved house: after thirty years and more of London life he returned to the country at last. The change may have been partly dictated by medical considerations: neither Elspeth, Alastair, nor Grahame himself were in anything like good health. What is interesting and infinitely revealing is the place they chose. With the whole of the Home Counties to pick from, Grahame went back to the very centre of his childhood: Cookham Dene. As he wrote a year or two later of Mole, 'the wafts from his old home pleaded, whispered, conjured, and finally claimed him imperiously'. The pattern was now nearly complete. Lingering on a summer evening by the same chalk-pit which had obsessed and fascinated him so as a child, which symbolized for him the burial-ground of all his youthful dreams and ambitions, Grahame may well have recalled what he wrote on the subject so long before, in 'A Funeral':

> The sun is low by this time and strikes athwart: a cool wind wanders up the valley; the rabbits are dotting the neighbour field, intent on their evening meal; and—did somebody mention beer? or did I only dream it with the rest? It is time to have done with fancies and get back to the world of facts. If only one could! But that cry of the Portuguese Nun wails ever in the mind's ear: 'I defy you to forget me utterly.'

How—in that place of all places—could he ever forget?

X

THE WIND IN THE WILLOWS

The Background

Just as the characters which populate *The Wind in the Willows* are (as we shall later see) composite portraits drawn partly from life and partly from literature, so the general background and thematic material of the book has similar antecedents. It will perhaps be easier to discuss the background first. In both cases Grahame adds to the core of reality he employs: the final product differs essentially from its models. His inner purpose throughout was threefold: to satirize contemporary society, to sublimate his personal fears, and to construct an ideal model of the Good Life. His treatment of the River Bank offers a good example of the process at work.

The core of reality, in this case, is that stretch of the Thames which runs, roughly, from Marlow to Pangbourne; and in particular the area round Cookham Dene. This had the most powerful and emotive associations for him. He had known it during his most impressionable period as a child; he had returned to it in middle age, drawn by compulsive and no longer to be neglected memories. Here he had spent—and still spent—long hours in backwater or eyot, watching water-rats, moles, otters, and toads go about their private business. This was the still centre about which the book evolved.

But—as we have come to recognize—Grahame never drew straight from life, but borrowed piecemeal. His various models were absorbed like those snips of coloured paper which combine to form a pattern under the kaleidoscope. For this reason it is a task as pointless as it is fascinating to press any topographical identifications too closely. Toad Hall, for example, contains elements from Harleyford Manor, Mapledurham House and Cliveden—each supplied part of its *mise en scène*. Elements from a dozen river-islands, weirs, and backwaters have been blended in 'The Piper at the Gates'; elsewhere Cookham merges into Cornwall, and the Thames flows seaward to Fowey.

The River is perhaps the most all-persuasive symbol running through the book; and it is interesting to measure the degree of idealization which Graham imposed on his Thames-side setting in order to achieve that timeless, drowsy beatitude. The River acts as a boundary, to begin with; beyond it lie the Wild Wood and the Wide World, with which it is several times contrasted. It is a symbol of rural

Mapledurham House c1890.

Harleyford Manor c1875.

Cliveden c1883.

Each of these houses on the River Thames contributed some of the elements of Toad Hall. All three were within a few miles of Cookham and Pangbourne.

traditionalism, faithful, steady-going, reliable; and though the railways may have killed out the pleasant life of the road (as Grahame had observed as early as 1892) 'many of its best conditions still linger round these old toll-gates, free from dust and clatter, on the silent liquid Highway to the West'. Water stands for purity, natural life, lushness, the slow, peaceful, primitive tempo of existence; the river-god's rhythm, as Mr T. S. Eliot aptly reminds us, was present in the nursery bedroom. There is a hint of mysticism in its whispering reeds, so closely connected with the pipes of Pan. It is the perfect background for a reaffirmation of all Grahame's values.

The actual river, of course, whether at Cookham or Fowey, was not like that at all, and Grahame, as a keenly observant naturalist, knew it perfectly well. His symbolism demanded that animals should show themselves as more natural, more peaceable, and (oddest of all) less concerned with sex than humankind; and therefore the whole Nature-red-in-the-tooth-and-claw concept, not to mention the mating season, had to be rejected. Furthermore, since the River Bank was to stand for idyllic peacefulness, another very material element had to be suppressed. Richard Jefferies was complaining bitterly in the eighties that the Thames otter, the water-rat, the moorhen, and indeed the whole riverbank population, were in danger of being exterminated by sheer senseless slaughter. In *The Open Air* he wrote:

> The result is that the osier-beds on the eyots and by the backwaters—the copses of the rivers—are almost devoid of life. A few moorhens creep under the aquatic grasses and conceal themselves beneath the bushes, water-voles hide among the flags, but the once extensive host of water-fowl and river life has been reduced to the small limits. ... The shameless way in which every otter that dares to show itself is shot, trapped, beaten to death, and literally battered out of existence, should arouse the indignation of every sportsman and every lover of nature.

Nothing of this appears in *The Wind in the Willows:* the terrors lie elsewhere, and this is Arcadia. Grahame was no longer willing to see—as Jefferies always saw—the skeleton exposed in the stream among the buttercups, and tall grasses, and flowers, and summer happiness. There was a time when his attitude to nature had been more realistic; when he had accepted the decaying hedgehog or murdered chaffinch with cheerful aplomb. But now Death had been ousted from his summer idyll altogether; sex was not the only exile.

Yet Jefferies' books had a considerable influence on the shaping of *The Wind in the Willows*. There is a striking similarity between his and Grahame's descriptions of the 'pageant of summer' and the whole variegated picture of river life. In *Bevis* and *Wood Magic* the resemblances become more specific still. Here we find whispering reeds and river-talk which recall the final paragraphs of 'The Piper at the Gates', there are also, for good measure, a talking Weasel, Mouse, and Rat who may well have been in Grahame's mind when he wrote his own fable.

This idealization of the River Bank had very deep roots in Grahame's past. All his life he had fought with nostalgic doggedness to preserve his faith in a pre-industrial, agricultural, essentially aristocratic society. But as early as 1890 it was becoming uncomfortably clear that the rural squirearchy was collapsing (or at least being profoundly modified) under economic pressure from the Machine Age and slowly increasing political infiltration by Radicals. In 1906, with the Liberal landslide, fifty-three Labour MPs were carried into Parliament; and the same year saw the first public appearance of that hearty, flamboyant, gabby vulgarian, Horatio Bottomley, who 'perceived that the moment had come for the exploitation of ... a sort of jolly-good-fellowship all round'. He also, without being aware of it, supplied a good deal of colour to the character of Mr Toad.

HORATIO BOTTOMLEY.
This hearty, flamboyant, gabby vulgarian, without being aware of it, supplied a good deal of colour to the character of Mr Toad.

The result of this social upheaval was a violent, often unformulated nostalgic urge for 'escape', which—oddly enough—cut across political denominations: even the early Radicals yearned for lost rural innocence, as a glance into William Morris or Blatchford's *Merrie England* at once makes plain. It took many forms, from the 'simple life' to a preoccupation with childhood, but all of them were basically a protest against urbanism; and many identified urbanism with political anarchy of a vaguely proletarian sort. This produced an impalpable but widely diffused atmosphere of unease, described by Esmé Wingfield Stratford in *Victorian Aftermath:*

Little Grey Seatown.
Fowey, Cornwall, seen from Polruan on the opposite bank of the River Fowey.
The Fowey Hotel is at the far left and St Fimbarrus's Church, at which
the Grahames were married, is at the far right.

Fowey.
'... you look down flights of
stone steps, overhung by great pink tufts
of valerian and ending in a patch of
sparkling blue water.'
The Wind in the Willows

River Fowey.
Kenneth Grahame's walks from Fowey took
him upstream and along the many
tidal creeks.

St Catherine's Down, Fowey.
'The Wayfaring Rat' was probably conceived on a walk across the Downs to the cliffs beyond.

Kynance Cove, Cornwall.
Trolling off the cove was one of the memories that Grahame gathered into his private world of release and romance.

'SHOVE THAT UNDER YOUR FEET.'
Arthur Rackham's plate illustrates 'The River Bank'. This chapter of *The Wind in the Willows* is believed to have been written after a boat trip that Kenneth Grahame took up-river from Fowey to Golant.

'IT WAS A GOLDEN AFTERNOON; THE SMELL OF THE DUST THEY KICKED UP WAS RICH AND SATISFYING.'
Kenneth Grahame invited Arthur Rackham to illustrate *The Wind in the Willows* but the colour plates that he produced for the book were as a result of a commission which came after Grahame's death. Earlier attempts at illustrating *The Wind in the Willows* in colour by artists such as Nancy Barnhart, Wyndham Payne and Paul Bransom were completely inappropriate.

> No one, surely, who remembers that time, can have forgotten, unless he is abnormally insensitive, the apprehension, never very far below the threshold, of some approaching peril—it might be German, it might be Red or even Yellow, but in any case destined to break the continuity of the safe and prosperous life of those who could afford to live it.

There is no reason to suppose that Grahame was immune from this infectious emotional apprehensiveness; and a good deal which indicates that *The Wind in the Willows* was, *inter alia,* a subconscious defence against it, a fantasy in which country gentlemen finally triumphed over the unprincipled radical *canaille.* This general terror had, in Grahame's case, been made extremely personal and specific by the attack on him by Mr Robinson, the Socialist lunatic, some four or five years before. The episode reappears in the exchange between Toad and the trigger-happy ferret sentry; but its effects went much deeper. The lurking lawless terror of the Wild Wood, the open anarchy when Toad Hall is usurped by stoats and weasels—all this is Grahame's minuscule projection of his own social fears.

Graham's attitude to Socialism was very much that of Henley—who must have influenced him considerably—or of Cobbett before him. He was all for individual freedom to the point of eccentricity as long as it was contained 'within the fabric of a firm but self-reformative social structure'—as long, that is, as the rural *status quo* was preserved, complete with its attendant class-structure. Anything that threatened this he regarded as destructive Philistinism. His attitude, like Cobbett's was semipatriarchal; he had the same characteristic distaste for the education of the lower orders.

This static rural traditionalism which Grahame idealized was, of course, in many ways a product of ardent wish-fulfilment. Village life was visibly breaking up, and no one was more acutely aware of the changes going on—especially in his early essays—than Grahame himself. Nor, indeed, did he have any illusions about the crimes, brutality, violence, and poverty, which characterized the earlier England of Fielding. The social picture which *The Wind in the Willows* presents is not life as Grahame thought it was, or once had been: it is his ideal vision of what it *should* be, his dream of the true Golden Age. It is precisely because he knew at heart that the dream was lost beyond any hope of realization that his imaginary world acquired such compulsive fascination for him. The contrast is brought out sharply when Grahame's attitude is compared with that of the actual villagers in Cookham Dene, who 'were ever child-like admirers of Progressive Stunts—and not given to nostalgia'. Again, of course, something of this local addiction to the newfangled has been gently satirized in the character of Toad.

Throughout the whole book there runs the *leitmotif* which may be roughly described as the conflict between Us and Them—or more specifically, the attempts made by Grahame's ideal rural society to defend itself against encroachment. (The curious thing is that though Grahame set out to create a trouble-free Arcadia he could not stifle his private anxieties: the Wild Wood loomed menacingly across the River, stoats and weasels lurked ready to invade Toad's ancestral home.) This society is specifically identified with the River-Bankers: Rat, Mole, Badger, Otter, and their friends form a close-knit community of leisured landowners who observe an extremely strict code of responsible behaviour.

The paramount virtue in this code, emphasized over and over again, is loyalty to one's own caste: and in this, of course, the animals come very close to their human counterparts. The whole moral and ethical point about Toad's behaviour is that he has let the side down. He has been corrupted by modern gadgets: he has made a public fool of himself; he is conceited and irresponsible and a spendthrift; he has disgraced his friends by being imprisoned. The stoats and weasels are enabled to gain possession of Toad Hall precisely because Toad has neglected his property and gone gallivanting on unbecoming picaresque adventures. The one thing that can bring Badger out of his cosy retirement is this threat to River-Bank society; he and Rat lecture Toad with the inflexible moral fervour of Alchoholics Anonymous:

> 'You knew it must come to this, sooner or later, Toad,' the Badger explained severely. 'You've disregarded all the warnings we've given you, you've gone on squandering the money your father left you, and you're getting us animals a bad name in the district by your furious driving and your smashes and your rows with the police. Independence is all very well, but we animals never allow our friends to make fools of themselves beyond a certain limit; and that limit you've reached.'

Toad, of course, stands for a figure who was becoming increasingly prevalent after the turn of the century: the landed *rentier* squandering his capital on riotous pleasures. This kind of irresponsibility provided the best possible propaganda for radicals who wanted to bring the whole system of inherited wealth and traditional class-values crashing down. In this sense the Adventures of Toad constitute a social object-lesson. If you neglect your responsibilities, Grahame proclaims in effect you are letting in the enemy and betraying your own friends. And what happens as a result? You are 'handcuffed, imprisoned, starved, chased, terrified out of your life, insulted, jeered at, and ignominously flung into the water—by a woman too!' You return home to find your country house occupied by insolent riff-raff. Only the loyalty of your friends finally contrives to restore the traditional *status quo*.

Examined from this point of view, the whole business of the Wild Wood and Toad Hall's capture takes on an unmistakable social symbolism. The Wild Wooders, stoats, weasels, and the rest, are clearly identified in Grahame's mind with the stunted, malevolent proletariat of contemporary upper-middle-class caricature. They have 'little evil wedge-shaped faces ... all fixing on him [Mole] glances of malice and hatred: all hard-eyed and evil and sharp'. They are carefully contrasted with the rural community; and their main delight is to crow over a member of the privileged classes who has infringed his own social code. Toad's imprisonment gives them peculiar pleasure.

Again, like the urban mob-anarchist of every Edwardian upper-middle-class nightmare, they have no notion of how to behave: they are lazy, messy, and ill-organized:

> 'And the Wild Wooders have been living in Toad Hall ever since', continued the Rat; 'and going on simply anyhow! Lying in bed half the day, and breakfast at all

hours, and the place in such a mess (I'm told) it's not fit to be seen. ... And they're telling the tradespeople and everybody that they've come to stay for good.'

Nothing could be more evocative of that nervous mood, half-contemptuous, half-terrified, which ran through the English bourgeoisie with increasing insistence from about the turn of the century. Toad Hall, its dignity destroyed, the prey of ignorant *sans-culottes*, typifies the entire myth; and one's mind travels forward, with a certain ironical relish, to contemplate those other Stately Homes which today house Civil Servants or delinquent adolescents.

It is a characteristic touch of Grahame's that when the invaders are finally ousted, the first thing they are made to do is sweep under the beds, change the sheets, and supply each room with 'a can of hot water, and clean towels, and fresh cakes of soap'. What could better symbolize the triumph of the *ancien régime* over the upstart Unwashed (who of course kept coal in their baths)? And that triumph itself is in accordance with the stock caricature, according to which the proletariat always show themselves vicious but spineless, miserable cowards when confronted with a tough and united front. (Weasels, ferrets, and stoats are admirably chosen creatures to support such a picture.) Their mistaken aggressiveness is soon dissipated by a little gentlemanly strong-arm work, and they revert to forelock-pulling obsequiousness with comforting rapidity. Pathetically eager to be of service to the gentry, they fulfil the last detail of the legend by blaming their leaders for leading them astray.

Thus the nagging terror of the mob—as Grahame had known it, for example, in the Pall Mall riots—has been exorcized by the most time-honoured reactionary's recipe of them all—physical violence. The paternal squirearchy is restored in triumph, and Wild Wooders gaze in respectful admiration as the Old Order, safely restored to its traditional authority and privilege, goes swaggering by on the last page. In this sense *The Wind in the Willows* was provoked by Grahame's need to combat his ever-increasing fear (shared by many of his class and period) that the structure of society might be destroyed through social revolution.

This also, of course, suggests one reason why *The Wind in the Willows* had no sequel. In 1908 the rural myth, though tottering, could still be maintained with some plausibility. There was yet hope that the squirearchy might triumph if it managed to curb its more irresponsible members. A few years later—even before 1914—it was plain that the old order was irretrievably doomed, and no amount of wishful thinking could ever bring it back. The Motor-car no less than Labour had come to stay; the power of the Unions grew steadily; gentlemen of private means, far from going back to the land, took up speed-boats and aeroplanes. and urban industrialism finally got a stranglehold over the entire country. It is appropriate that Grahame, asked what became of Toad's good resolutions for the future, replied: 'Of course Toad never really reformed; he was by nature incapable of it.'

This hint of things to come, the ultimate triumph of mechanical progress over rural traditionalism, is sounded very early in *The Wind in the Willows*—'The Open Road' deals with it in unmistakable terms. The destruction of the caravan—which

Grahame associated symbolically with untrammelled country Bohemianism—by the inhuman and somehow monstrous motor-car: this is the core of the matter. Into that chapter Grahame packed a whole social revolution, focused and scaled down into an episode at once fabulous and beguilingly familiar.

The most interesting thing about Grahame's animal society is that it has more in common with the rich bourgeoisie than the aristocracy. All the River-Bankers are of apparently independent means; their life seems to be one unending holiday, boating, tramping round the countryside, eating enormous meals, and getting caught up in occasional adventures. They don't run farms or administer big estates; Toad is blamed, not for neglecting his duties as a landlord, but for behaving badly. What Grahame has done, of course, is to project his own private dream on to a social pattern which he admired, but to which he did not belong.

Nothing brings this home so sharply as Grahame's attitude to money. At first one suspects that, like so many rural Utopians, he wants to dispense with it altogether, or has left it out for the benefit of his childish audience. Then comes a revealing little episode which aligns Grahame more nearly to his middle-class banking forebears than to the aristocratic ideal he so admired. Toad at the booking-office in his washerwoman's disguise, without a penny to his name, is a bourgeois anxiety-dream incarnate:

> To his horror he recollected that he had left both coat and waistcoat behind him in his cell, and with them his pocketbook, money, keys, watch, matches—pencil-case—all that makes life worth living, all that distinguishes the many-pocketed animal, the lord of creation, from the inferior one-pocketed or no-pocketed productions that hop or trip about permissively, unequipped for the real contest.

Miserably he tries to carry the thing off with upper-class panache, and fails in the most ludicrous fashion. Toad's father may have been an admirable animal, as Badger says; but he almost certainly made his pile in copper-mines or tea-broking.

This incident suggests what one of the underlying emotional driving-forces of *The Wind in the Willows* may have been. For all his Scottish pedigree, Grahame felt 'rather mere' about his lack of inherited wealth. When Fletcher Moulton sent him presents of port, he made embarrassed references to 'the humble "four-ale"—which more properly belongs to my lot in life'. By 1900 wealth rather than breeding had become the criterion of acceptance; a lifetime spent in banking can only have added to Grahame's self-consciousness on the subject.

To this self-consciousness was added a deep self-distrust, what Grahame described to Elspeth as 'much natral "gaucherie" wot as never been strove gainst'. Grahame seems to have been constantly afraid that his colleagues and employers, and society at large in the authoritarian sense, were sneering at him, condemning him, ready to pursue and punish him for his shortcomings. This anxiety-state is confirmed only too accurately by the dream which Grahame (with pre-Freudian candour) incorporated in 'Bertie's Escapade':

> Mr Grahame's night was a very disturbed one, owing to agitating dreams. He dreamt that the house was broken into by burglars, and he wanted to get up and down

> and catch them, but he could not move hand or foot. He heard them ransacking his pantry, stealing his cold chicken and things [? 'trifles'], and plundering his wine-cellar, and still he could not move a muscle. Then he dreamt that he was at one of the great City Banquets that he used to go to, and he heard the Chairman propose the health of 'The King' and there was great cheering. And he thought of a most excellent speech to make in reply—a really clever speech. And he tried to make it, but they held him down in his chair and wouldn't let him. And then he dreamt that the Chairman actually proposed his own health—the health of Mr Grahame! and he got up to reply, and he couldn't think of anything to say! And he stood there, for hours and hours it seemed, in a dead silence, the glittering eyes of the guests—there were hundreds and hundreds of guests—all fixed on him, and still he couldn't think of anything to say! Till at last the Chairman rose, 'He can't think of anything to say! *Turn him out!*' Then the waiters fell on him and dragged him from the room, and threw him into the street, and flung his hat and coat after him; and as he was shot out he heard the whole company singing wildly 'For he's a jolly good fellow ...!''

This dream suggests several compulsive fears. First, there is the terror of losing property, which reminds us of that scene in the booking office. This again brings us back to the bourgeois nightmare of revolution and expropriation. (Significantly, what Grahame most fears to lose is food—that well-known substitute for emotional satisfaction.) Next we find the generalized fear of impotence—not specifically in a sexual sense. Grahame can't move, can't speak, can't think of anything. Lastly there is the terror of disgrace or ridicule as a result of this or some other shortcoming, and in particular of *public* disgrace. Some of this anxiety may stem from Grahame's indifferent capacity as Secretary of the Bank; but the dream also provides a link between the repressed bohemian of his earlier work and Toad's curious behaviour in *The Wind in the Willows.*

We have seen how Grahame compounded more and more with respectability as he grew older; but the public figure, though it might overshadow the anarchic Id, could not wholly destroy it. What provided the tension, I suspect, was the new *persona's* terror that at any moment the old Adam might disgrace it. There was a time when Grahame had wanted nothing so much as to contract out of Society into Epicurean idleness: and deep down this was what he still wanted. But he had learnt—from Wilde's example above all—how mercilessly Society dealt with any infringement of the unwritten laws. Taken in this context Toad's adventures make considerably more sense; they represent Society's ruthless pursuit of the nonconformist, the heterodox, the *déclassé.*

Grahame's attitude to Toad is extremely ambivalent. He is ostensibly on the side of the angels, yet shows very little sympathy for Authority as such. While condemning Toad's excesses, he has, one suspects, a sneaking urge to behave in exactly the same way: Toad, in fact, is a sublimation of all his own unrecognized desires, and is harried by all the forces which Grahame himself found particularly terrifying. There is no one so congenitally scared of a magistrate as your thoroughgoing romantic Bohemian: he has nightmares about prisons, pursuit, disgrace, the ineluctable hand of the law.

This kind of compulsive terror permeates all Toad's adventures. The pursuit-motif is repeated again and again: most strikingly, perhaps, in the railway chase:

> 'They are gaining on us fast!' cried the engine-driver. 'And the engine is crowded with the queerest lot of people! Men like ancient warders, waving halberds; policemen in their helmets, waving truncheons; and shabbily dressed men in pot-hats, obvious and unmistakable plain-clothes detectives even at this distance, waving revolvers and walking-sticks; all waving, and all shouting the same thing— "Stop, stop, stop!"'

These authoritarian pursuers can be linked not only with the Olympians, and the villagers in 'The Reluctant Dragon' and the *They* of Lear's Limericks; but, beyond these, with the whole ugly apparatus which in 1895 represented England's condemnation of Wilde and everything his decade stood for. Grahame still felt the urge towards Bohemianism; but now he was haunted by those fearful Furies which outraged Orthodoxy had let loose when the arch-Bohemian went too far.

We have now traced the main motifs behind *The Wind in the Willows* against their personal and historical impulses in Grahame's mind. There is the idealized river-landscape with its peaceful Epicurean inhabitants; the menace, finally destroyed, of the Wild Wood; the conflict between a paternalist society and the hubristic Bohemian individual, as exemplified by Toad; and the stabilization of the traditional *status quo* by the realization of a completely self-contained and self-sufficient myth. We have seen how this myth was constructed from diverse elements in Grahame's life and background, and enriched by constant associative allusions. There remain for consideration the two most personal and idiosyncratic chapters, both of which lie outside the book's overall structure: 'The Piper at the Gates' and 'Wayfarers All'.

What these chapters have in common is an overwhelmingly violent emotional experience, which in both cases can be related with some confidence to Grahame's own life. If, at one level, *The Wind in the Willows* subsumes the totality of its author's life—his fears, passions, pleasures, disappointments and beliefs—into a timeless myth, 'The Piper at the Gates' and 'Wayfarers All' crystallize, mythically, the most intimate and intensely felt experiences that Grahame ever sustained. The first forms a mystical testament to his *fin de siècle* faith in the beneficent, personalized powers of Nature; the second enshrines what he felt—and had felt for many years—to be his betrayal of that gleaming sunlit dream, and hints fairly clearly at the compromise he finally settled on.

The vision of Pan may perhaps stand as the supreme example of nineteenth-century neo-pagan mysticism: intensely felt, flawlessly written, with an exquisite, balance between chaste simplicity of style and the rich, colourful, almost sensuous atmosphere which the words themselves evoke. Yet this said, it must be admitted that Grahame's achievement here succeeded only by a hair's-breadth, and could never be repeated. As Mr MacNeice remarked, apostrophizing his hypothetical Communist, 'this poise is perfect, but maintained for one day only'. The 'kindly demigod' whom Grahame presents has been transformed: desexualized, paternalized, the Friend and Helper of Victorian iconography. He contains in his pagan body something of those Christian traits which Grahame sought for so long and never found—or dared to accept. This Pan is an extraordinary syncretic compromise, a project of Edwardian ruralism, post-Beardsley social opposition, wistful yearning for conformity, an urge towards some replacement for Arnold's God as a comforting Father Figure. It is significant that this Pan's last and most welcome gift (which he never had in antiquity, and which seems to be a creation of Grahame's own) is forgetfulness. The awe of that ultimate revelation was too much for the small creatures who inhabited Grahame's fantasy-world: it may have been too much for Grahame himself—or he may have shrunk from the recognition of its transience.

But there were other things, too, that he wished to forget: all his lost aspirations, the life he might (or dreamed he had) have led if things had turned out differently.

'The Piper at the Gates' celebrates a vision; but in the very *O altitudo* of participation Grahame is already begging for the release which oblivion brings. What he cannot bear to remember is his own denial of the light. Like Edmund, he had the white vision in the meadow, but he compromised and was lost. And for that he never quite forgave himself.

'Wayfarers All' deals with the same essential problem in slightly different terms. This time the symbol is the Southern *mystique* of sun and wine and warm Mediterranean shores, the anti-Puritan Good Life; the call to adventure:

> Restlessly the Rat ... lay looking out towards the great ring of Downs that barred his vision further southwards—his simple horizon hitherto, his Mountains of the Moon, his limit behind which lay nothing he had cared to see or to know. Today, to him gazing south with a new-born need stirring in his heart, the clear sky over their long, low outline seemed to pulsate with promise; today, the unseen was everything, the unknown the only real fact of life. On this side of the hills was now the real blank, on the other lay the crowded and coloured panorama that his inner eye was seeing so clearly.

At this critical moment comes the seductive propaganda of the Sea Rat; in a hypnotic trance Rat prepares to go South with the rest of them; but at the door he runs into Mole. Mole stops him (as they had both earlier restrained Toad) by sheer physical violence—'grappling with him strongly he dragged him inside, threw him down, and held him'—and sits by him till the hysteria has worn off. Then slyly, he slips him a pencil and some sheets of paper, and suggests poetry as a therapeutic. The Rat swallows this elementary bait:

> The Rat pushed the paper away from him wearily, but the discreet Mole took occasion to leave the room, and when he peeped in again some time later, the Rat was absorbed and deaf to the world; alternately scribbling and sucking the top of his pencil. It is true that he sucked a good deal more than he scribbled; but it was joy to the Mole to know that the cure had at least begun.

Clearly, in this private drama, all three participants represent aspects of Grahame's own personality. Rat is the repressed Bohemian Ulysses, fretting in London and at

Cookham Dene, feeling an unformulated migrant urge in the blood. The Sea Rat speaks with the inner voice of the self-tempter: every voyage, each landfall from Corsica to Alassio and Marseilles was one Grahame had already made himself. Mole here is the respectable, conformist side of Grahame: conscientious, practical and loyal, he stands for all the domestic and public virtues.

It almost looks as though in 1907 Grahame was on the edge of leaving Elspeth. We remember the long period of separation: had not Grahame's father, forty years earlier, vanished in precisely the same footloose way? The Sea Rat's motives for emigration are interesting: 'Family troubles, as usual, began it. The domestic storm-cone was hoisted, and I shipped myself on board a small trading-vessel bound for Constantinople. ...' The voice that lured Grahame to the untrammelled life of an Italian beachcomber was persuasively insistent: 'Take the Adventure, heed the call, now ere the irrevocable moment passes! 'Tis but a banging of the door behind you, a blithesome step forward, and you are out of the old life and into the new!'

But the step was never taken. The struggle may have been an internal one: its reality and agonizing force cannot be in doubt. The entranced, spellbound Rat was defeated: once again, and for the last time, Grahame compromised. The dream of the solitary traveller was abandoned for ever. There would be no escape now, no enchanted and lonely pursuit of the warm, elusive Southern mirage, no miraculous new life. It was over and finished. And yet not quite finished: for one outlet still remained through which Grahame could obtain the emotional release he so desperately needed. Like Rat, he took a pencil and a few sheets of paper; he sucked and he scribbled; and out of his despair and yearning a classic was born.

The Wind in the Willows was finally published in October 1908, with a jacket and frontispiece by Graham Robertson that delighted the author. 'It's as windy and willowy as they make 'em,' he wrote, 'and we are critics of willows down here, and of wind too.' Neither publishers nor critics, however, at first realized the windfall that had landed in their laps. The Bodley Head turned *The Wind in the Reeds* (as it was then entitled) down flat, and it was eventually taken on, with some misgivings, by Methuen. A long time had elapsed since *Dream Days*; and there was the danger that the public might be disappointed at not getting something along the same lines.

Elspeth was justifiably nervous of the reception that the book might get. In *Punch* the anonymous reviewer described the book as 'a sort of irresponsible holiday story in which the chief characters are woodland animals, who are represented as enjoying most of the advantages of civilisation'. 'His rat, toad and mole,' declared the *Saturday Review of Literature*, 'are very human in their behaviour, and remind us of undergraduates of sporting proclivities.' H. W. Nevinson in the *Nation* took a similar line: 'All the animals had a very stirring time, and but for their peculiar shapes they would well pass for first-rate human boys.' This reviewer ran the book eleventh in a mixed bag of thirteen. And *The Times* made the inevitable comment: 'For ourselves we lay *The Wind in the Willows* reverently aside and again, for the hundredth time, take up *The Golden Age*.'

THE TIMES LITERARY SUPPLEMENT, THURSDAY, OCTOBER 22, 1908.

UNIVERSITY PRESS

lassical Scholarship. By
D., Fellow of St. John's College, and Public
ity of Cambridge.

e Revival of Learning to the End of th
(in Italy, France, England and the Nether

hteenth Century in Germany, and the Nine.
urope and the United States of America.

volumes now published include a survey of
s and works of the leading scholars from the
ith to the nineteenth century. Each of the
embraced in these volumes opens with a
ogical conspectus of the scholars of that period,
he dates of their births and deaths, and, in
four centuries, grouping them under the
to which they belong. The two volumes
sixty-four portraits and other illustrations.

iplomatist in the Fifties.
SIR ERNEST SATOW, G.C.M.G.

rnest Satow's subject is Hübner, the distin-
Austrian diplomatist who was attached to
rt of Paris during the years from 1849 to
Hübner's period of residence there included
events of first-rate importance—the coup
f December 2, 1851, and the proclamation of
pire; the Crimean War; and the outbreak of
for the liberation of Italy.

re. By WILLIAM OSLER, M.D.,
sor of Medicine in the University of Oxford.

Linacre Lecture for 1908, delivered at St.
College, Cambridge. The first chapter con-
an Introduction and Life, and the second and
eal with Linacre as Medical Humanist and
arian respectively, and the fourth and last is
to the Linacre Foundations. The plates, of
there are eleven, include the portraits of
at Windsor and the British Museum.

ional History of England.
e delivered by F. W. MAITLAND, LL.D., late
f the Laws of England in the University of

simplicity, lucidity, and directness of ex-
, these expositions of the true meaning of

FICTION.

"The Wind in the Willows."

The author of "The Golden Age" and of "Dream Days," the historian of the immortal Harold, has disappointed us. There is no getting away from that melancholy fact. He has written in THE WIND IN THE WILLOWS (Methuen, 6s.) a book with hardly a smile in it, through which we wander in a haze of perplexity, uninterested by the story itself and at a loss to understand its deeper purpose. The chief character is a mole, whom the reader plumps upon on the first page whitewashing his house. Here is an initial nut to crack; a mole whitewashing. No doubt moles like their abodes to be clean; but whitewashing? Are we very stupid, or is this joke really inferior? However, let it pass. Then enters a water rat, on his way to a river picnic, in a skiff, with a hamper of provisions, including cold tongue, cold ham, French rolls, and soda water. Nut number two; for obviously a water rat is of all animals the one that would never use a boat with which to navigate a stream. Again, are we very stupid, or is this nonsense of poor quality? Later we meet a wealthy toad, who, after a tour of England in a caravan, drawn by a horse, becomes a rabid motorist. He is also an inveterate public speaker. We meet also a variety of animals whose foibles doubtless are borrowed from mankind, and so the book goes on until the end. Beneath the allegory ordinary life is depicted more or less closely, but certainly not very amusingly or searchingly; while as a contribution to natural history the work is negligible. There are neat and fanciful passages; but they do not convince. The puzzle is, for whom is the book intended? Grown up readers will find it monotonous and elusive; children will hope in vain for more fun. The materials for an English "Uncle Remus" are here, but without the animating spirit. For ourselves, we lay "The Wind in the Willows" reverently aside, and again, for the hundredth time, take up "The Golden Age." Perhaps that is the real inner purpose of the new work—to send readers to its deathless forerunners—to "The Golden Age" and "Dream Days." So be it.

"A Room with a View."

Mr. E. M. Forster's title A ROOM WITH A VIEW

crowd into 406 pages. With all its f
effective. The short sentences bri
of it like the small bones of a fish's
backbone. Sometimes long waves o
the whole structure like some Atlantic
the chops of the Channel. The h
strip of a midshipman, with a girl's
courage, who finds himself suddenl
to kidnap Nelson off Beachy Head.
thick indeed; the lure, we gather, is
Hamilton; the agent a flashing sabr
(enter the Gentleman), with privat
special service company of the guar
—still more dangerous and insidious
gang of grizzly traitors at his back!
Sussex coast from Lewes to Peve
guards it, but it is a coast line with v
Somehow, all the historians, and M
omitted to depict the terrible stat
Eastbourne in 1805, helpless, if the re
in the hands of the "Black Gap Ga
it up to the neck," sighs poor old Di
the sloop Tremendous, as after such
ne'er again shall be, he lies dying in
Beachy Head. And already the
station has been sacked and burnt wi
whit the wiser); a French ship rides
the Gentleman revels in peril with
guards about him. Don't ask ques
not answer them); just read, and yo
the only Union Jack flying for miles
up through the chimney of a fortifie
wherein Kit finds himself in compan
and one or two more of the warrior
loves. To the horrified garrison
reveal a portentous list of Kent and
are *à nous*—" magistrates, squires, a
a deputy lieutenant, and small fry
and the like— by the score." Afte
find Nelson saved by a miracle fron
powder magazines, on his own quart
of fighting with quite impossibly f
weaker side, there is one battle pict
Tremendous, which for naked r

CRITICAL REACTION TO THE WIND IN THE WILLOWS
on its publication was generally unfavourable. *The Times Literary Supplement*
was particularly scornful.

It was *The Times*, too, which (together with *T.P.'s Weekly*) levelled a criticism at Grahame's method which strikes most oddly on modern ears. 'As a contribution to natural history,' proclaimed the anonymous pundit in Printing House Square, 'the work is negligible.' And *T.P.'s Weekly* referred to numerous incidents 'which (I am sorry to say) will win no credence from the very best authorities on biology'. The Olympian critics were having a field-day.

One of the longest and most thoughtful notices was that composed by Mr Arthur Ransome for *The Bookman*. Having analysed, with some penetration, the 'horrible chasm between dream and reality' which characterized Grahame's earlier works, he went on:

> *The Wind in the Willows* is an attempt to write for children instead of about them. But Mr Grahame's past has been too strong for him. Instead of writing about children for grown-up people, he has written about animals for children. The difference is only in the names. He writes of the animals with the same wistfulness with which he wrote of children, and, in his attitude towards his audience, he is quite unable to resist that appeal from dreamland to a knowledge of the world that makes the charm of all his

> books, and separates them from children's literature. The poems in the book are the only things really written for the nursery, and the poems are very bad.
>
> If we judge the book by its aim, it is a failure, like a speech to Hottentots made in Chinese. And yet, for the Chinese, if by any accident there should happen to be one or two of them among the audience, the speech might be quite a success.

Now this review has a good deal of cogency. Mr Ransome only goes badly wrong over two points: the assumption that Grahame was aiming at the nursery, and its corollary that children would not understand the result. Like so many adult critics, Mr Ransome was worried about Grahame's shifting planes of reality; but here his author knew rather better than he did the psychology of the child's mind. As Grahame wrote, years later, to a friendly schoolmaster: 'It is the special charm of the child's point of view that the dual nature of these characters does not present the slightest difficulty to them. It is only the old fogies who are apt to begin "Well, but..." and so on. To the child it is all entirely natural and as it should be.'

Several reviewers at once suspected, as Graham Robertson had feared, that the book was some kind of allegory or satire. 'Some grown-up readers,' *Punch* declared, 'may find in the story a satirical purpose which its author would probably disclaim.' 'Grown-up readers,' *The Times* pronounced uneasily, 'will find it monotonous and elusive'—a queer pair of epithets—and went on: 'Beneath the allegory ordinary life is depicted more or less closely.' But it was Arnold Bennett—one of the few serious writers and critics who thought the book worth their attention—who went straight to the heart of the matter:

> The book is fairly certain to be misunderstood of the people. The publishers' own announcement describes it as 'perhaps chiefly for youth', a description with which I disagree. [It is interesting to recall that Grahame had written this blurb himself.] The obtuse are capable of seeing in it nothing save a bread-and-butter imitation of *The Jungle Book*. ... The author may call his chief characters the Rat, the Mole, the Toad—they are human beings, and they are meant to be nothing but human beings. ... The book is an urbane exercise in irony at the expense of the English character and of mankind. It is entirely successful.

Bennett, of course, only penetrated to one level of *The Wind in the Willows;* but among so much jejune and wrong-headed criticism, we may well be grateful that he achieved so much.

The most broadly based and perceptive notice, however, was beyond doubt that written by Richard Middleton in *Vanity Fair.* He accepted the allegory in the spirit (conscious or unconscious) which had directed the author's creative processes:

> The book for me is notable for its intimate sympathy with Nature and for its delicate expression of emotions which I, probably in common with most people, had previously believed to be my exclusive property. When all is said the boastful, unstable Toad, the hospitable Water Rat, the shy, wise, childlike Badger, and the Mole with his pleasant habit of brave boyish impulse, are neither animals nor men, but are types of that deeper humanity which sways us all. To be wise, an allegory must admit of a wide application, and the man has read his *Pilgrim's Progress* in vain who does not realise that not merely

> Christian but Ignorance, Talkative and Justice Hategood himself, are crying for mastery in the heart of us all. And if I may venture to describe as an allegory a work which, critics, who ought to have known better, have dismissed as a fairy-story, it is certain that *The Wind in the Willows* is a wise book.

Grahame himself, we may well suppose, approved this generous and far-sighted appraisal.

The critics would, perhaps, have been better employed even on their own terms if they had used some of their space to point out Grahame's literary influences, and the strange way he contrived to transmute them for his own purposes. It is true that direct allusions were far less frequent in *The Wind in the Willows* than in Grahame's earlier books but even so no one seems to have noticed that Toad's dealings with the gypsy are a hilarious parody of *Lavengro*, while the Sea Rat's historical musings on Constantinople are lifted direct from William Morris's *Sigurd the Volsung*. Even more remarkable is Grahame's *penchant* for parodying Homer.

Most of Toad's adventures bear a certain ludicrous resemblance to Ulysses' exploits in the *Odyssey;* and the resemblance becomes detailed and explicit in the last chapter, which parodies the hero's return and the slaying of the suitors. (Its very title—'The Return of Ulysses'—offers the broadest of hints as to what Grahame had in mind.) There is an irreverent take-off of the stock Homeric arming ceremony:

> First, there was a belt to go round each animal, and then a sword to be stuck into each belt, and then a cutlass on the other side to balance it. Then a pair of pistols, a policeman's truncheon, several sets of handcuffs, some bandages and sticking-plaster, and a flask and a swandwich-case.

'Rat ... Proceeded to Dress Them up for the Coming Expedition'. Drawing by E. H. Shepard.

Yet Grahame is quite capable of turning a Homeric simile to striking and serious use when he chooses: there is an excellent example in 'The Piper at the Gates':

> As one awakened suddenly from a beautiful dream, who struggles to recall it, and can recapture nothing but a dim sense of the beauty of it, the beauty! Till that, too, fades away in its turn, and the dreamer bitterly accepts the hard cold waking and all its penalties; so Mole, after struggling with his memory for a brief space, shook his head sadly and followed the Rat.

Clearly, as always, Grahame derived Toad's adventures from many sources, not Homer only; Mlle Fyrth suggests, with some plausibility, that he may also have drawn on mediaeval romances and ballads, to which we may add the early English picaresque novels by authors such as Fielding, and the Falstaff of *The Merry Wives of Windsor,* who likewise had embarrassing dealings with laundry and was disguised as someone else's aunt. But in any case this rich alluvial deposit of parody and imitation must have its effect on the reader, whose enjoyment is deepened—perhaps without his being consciously aware of it—by the associations such a technique evokes.

The general question of Grahame's reading in English literature is a complicated one, and bedevilled by his admitted habit of making up his own quotations when he could not find one to fit the occasion. His favourite authors seem to have been Shakespeare, Malory, Sir Thomas Browne, Tennyson, Browning, Matthew Arnold, and (as we might expect) Lewis Carroll.

Grahame's work reveals a major debt to Ruskin and to William Morris. Ruskin supplied both his passion for the Gothic revival and admiration of the Italian Primitives and also caused him 'to rely more and more on impressions derived from art and the imaginative life which were quite inconsistent with the Bible Protestantism of his childhood'.

Grahame shared, very strongly, William Morris's dream of a rural, non-industrial Earthly Paradise: the return of the lost Golden Age. What is more, he knew the works of Morris very well: not only the beautifully illustrated mediaeval folios that issued from the Kelmscott Press (and which are clearly referred to in 'Its Walls were as of Jasper') but also such books as *The Earthly Paradise* or *News from Nowhere,* with their more specifically social content. He had made a personal pilgrimage to Kelmscott, and wrote detailed notes of the occasion; his obsession with the New Jerusalem, the Golden City that haunted all Utopians from Augustine to Cobbett and Morris himself, is amply documented in his own writings.

And this leads us to the central reason for the perennial success which *The Wind in the Willows* has enjoyed, and continues to enjoy, with readers of all ages: the reason for its continued sale of about 80,000 copies every year. Its symbolism embodies some of mankind's deepest and most ineradicable yearnings: the pastoral dream, the Golden Age, the search for lost innocence.

Our appreciation of Grahame's work can be deepened and enriched by knowing the elements which went to compose it, personal no less than literary; Grahame himself was to declare—and he spoke truer than perhaps he knew—that his readers 'liked the subject-matter; they did not even notice the source of all the agony, and all the joy. A large amount of what Thoreau called life went into the making of many of those playful pages.' But in the last resort it is the work which endures, on its own merits. The contemporary or ephemeral problems which agitated Grahame's mind so deeply are forgotten today: the vision, the intense personal experience, the myth—it is these that remain.

XI

THE WIND IN THE WILLOWS

The Mosaic of Characters

Three technical stages can be distinguished in the shaping of *The Wind in the Willows*. First, there were the nightly bedtime stories which Grahame told his son Alastair over a period of three years or more, probably beginning early in 1904. Elspeth always believed that she was the inspired fire behind *The Wind in the Willows*—which explains why she denigrated Grahame's earlier work by comparison—and in a tragic sense she was right. If Grahame had never married her it is extremely doubtful whether the book would ever have been written: it needed exactly the emotional shock she provided for the creative flash-point to be reached. Repressed, unhappy, driven in on himself, badly bruised by contact with adult passion, Grahame turned—without being aware for one moment of what he was about—to the world of symbol and myth. In so doing he released the full strength of his genius. His son provided the focal point for its transmutation and eventual release. Next comes the famous series of letters written to Alastair from Fowey and London, which form a skeleton outline of Toad's Adventures. With this stage we may bracket certain elements in 'Bertie's Escapade', the *jeu d'esprit* which Grahame wrote for Alastair's nursery magazine, *The Merry Thought*. Last comes the finished draft, substantially as it appears today.

The genesis of the letters was as follows. In May 1907 Alastair went with his governess, Miss Stott, on a seven weeks' holiday to Littlehampton. At the same time his parents left for the West Country. They spent a few days in Falmouth, and then returned for a prolonged visit to their beloved Fowey. Half-way through June Elspeth returned to Cookham Dene to be with Alastair, whose holiday was now over; but Kenneth, for reasons we can only surmise, went to London—the house in Durham Villas had been kept as a *pied-à-terre*—and remained there at least till September, occasionally coming down to Cookham Dene for week-ends. During this period—from spring to autumn of 1907—he wrote Alastair a series of letters, which Miss Stott, with considerable foresight, preserved. They contain, in embryo, the central narrative theme of *The Wind in the Willows*—Toad's adventures—from the theft of the motor-car to the final banquet.

Now this, as is at once apparent, covers rather less than half the matter in the final draft: it represents the adventures of Mr Toad only. The two chapters, 'The

ALASTAIR GRAHAME.
The nightly bedtime stories which Kenneth Grahame invented for his son contributed to the genesis of *The Wind in the Willows*.

Piper at the Gates of Dawn' and 'Wayfarers All', we know to have been written separately and later inserted in the draft; and the same may possibly be true of the earlier chapters as well.

It may be, however, that Miss Stott only came to realize the unique value of these letters after she had destroyed some of the earlier ones; and in support of this presumption may be mentioned the fact that Rat, Mole, and Badger suddenly appear in the later letters without explanation or introduction. On the other hand, there are two suggestive pieces of evidence which tell a different story. The first is the earliest surviving letter, dated 10 May 1907, which contains this paragraph:

Greenbank Hotel, Falmouth, c1900.
Whilst staying at the hotel, Kenneth Grahame wrote some of his letters in which he described the adventures of Toad to his son.

> Have you heard about the Toad? He was never taken prisoner by brigands at all. It was all a horrid low trick of his. He wrote that letter himself—the letter saying that a hundred pounds must be put in the hollow tree. And he got out of the window early one morning, & went off to a town called Buggleton, & went to the Red Lion Hotel & there he found a party that had just motored down from London, & while they were having breakfast he went into the stable-yard & found their motor-car & went off in it without even saying Poop-poop! And now he has vanished & everyone is looking for him, including the police. I fear he is a bad low animal.

The latter half of this passage is familiar; the opening is not. It suggests a different beginning to Toad's adventures, in which his friends probably did not feature at all.

The second piece of circumstantial evidence concerns 'The River Bank'. While the Grahames were at Fowey in May and June of 1907, they made the acquaintance of an American family also on holiday there—Mr and Mrs Austin Purves of Philadelphia, and their five sons, Dale, Austin Jr, Pierre, Edmund, and John. Kenneth actually stood godfather to Pierre, the youngest, at his Fowey christening, which 'was unusual in that old Cornish customs were carried out, a procession to the Church and the presentation of the Kimbly cake to the first person encountered'. Grahame and Austin Purves continued to correspond regularly until the latter's death in 1915; the two families met again at Fowey just

16, Durham Villas, Campden Hill. W.
21 June 1907.

My dearest Mouse

No doubt you will be interested to hear the further adventures of Mr Toad, after he galloped away across country on the bargee's horse, with the bargee shouting after him in vain. Well presently the horse got tired of galloping so fast, and broke from a gallop into a trot, and then from a trot into a walk, & then he stopped altogether & began to nibble grass. And the toad looked round about him & found he was on a large common. On the common stood a gipsy tent, and a gipsy man was sitting beside it, on a bucket turned upside-down, smoking. In front of the tent a fire of sticks was burning, & over the fire hung an iron pot, and out of the pot came steam, & bubblings, and the most beautiful good smell that ever you smelt.

Mr Toad's Adventures.
One of Kenneth Grahame's letters to Alastair continuing his story.

Golant on the River Fowey 1903.
Evidence from Grahame's friends suggests that 'The River Bank' was prompted by a boat trip from Fowey to Golant.

before the First World War, and after it Grahame entertained the Purves boys on various occasions both in Oxford and in Rome.

All the brothers agree in believing that the general setting of *The Wind in the Willows* is largely derived from Fowey and the Fowey River. This is suggestive and revealing. Hitherto it has generally been supposed that Fowey only contributed 'the little grey sea town' of the Sea Rat's tale, and that the rest was unadulterated Thames-side Berkshire. But it is entirely in key with his Coleridgean methods of composition that Grahame should have added elements from Fowey as well.

More specifically, the Purves brothers confirm that the opening chapter, 'The River Bank', was inspired by a boating trip up the Fowey River, undertaken by Grahame, 'Atky', and their father, 'to a little village called Golant, on the right bank, for tea. They probably hired someone else to row them.' Similarly, the entire open-air sequence of 'Wayfarers All' is supposed to have been directly provoked by a walk Grahame and Austin Purves (or 'Atky') took in the near-by countryside; perhaps 'towards the west of the Fowey side, past Ready Money Cove, to St Catherine's Castle and the hills and sea-coast beyond that'.

Any direct identifications in *The Wind in the Willows* must be handled with extreme caution: Grahame's creative processes were deep, complex, and associative. Nevertheless we have no reason to doubt that the conscious, immediate impulse for these two chapters came about in the way described. This means that they cannot have actually been composed before May or June at the earliest, and probably—if we leave time for subconscious digestion—at least three months later. We can now make a nearer guess at the order of composition. The Toad narrative evolved first; the River Bank sequences came next; and the two set-pieces, 'Wayfarers All' and 'The Piper at the Gates', were composed last of all.

But the external impetus to crystallize the letters and bed-time stories into a book almost certainly came from that extraordinary woman Constance Smedley. Miss Smedley, an arden feminist (she had written a work entitled *Woman: A Few Shrieks)* and co-founder of the International Lyceum Club, was in 1907 living at Bray, within convenient range of Cookham Dene. Among her other activities she was European representative of the American magazine *Everybody's*. The editor, John O'Hara Cosgrave, wrote asking her to try and persuade Grahame to produce a new book. Miss Smedley duly invaded the household at Cookham Dene, and endeared herself to Kenneth by declaring that she was a relation of that other Miss Smedley, the governess in *The Golden Age*. This linking of fantasy and life was a neat psychological stroke: Miss Smedley had sized up her quarry extremely well.

Despite her modernity, her feminism, and the fact that she travelled—unspeakable!—by motor-car, Constance Smedley made closer contact with Grahame than most people. He talked with surprising freedom to her, saying how the return to this scene of his childhood had stimulated his early memories: 'The queer thing is,' he said, 'I can remember everything I felt then, the part of my brain I used from four till about seven can never have altered. Coming back here wakens every recollection.' She approached him, tentatively, about the new book; he told her he hated writing, it was sheer physical torture. Miss Smedley kept her eyes open, observed Grahame's special relationship with Alastair, and saw her way clear:

> He [Alastair] had about him something of his father's remoteness and was perpetually playing games with himself. ... Every evening Mr Grahame told Mouse an unending story, dealing with the adventures of the little animals whom they met in their river journeys. This story was known to him and Mouse alone and was related in a bed-time visit of extreme secrecy. ... Mouse's own tendency to exult in his exploits was gently satirized in Mr Toad, a favourite character who gave the juvenile audience occasion for some slightly self-conscious laughter.

It looks very much as though Miss Smedley managed to gain admission to these secret sessions; at all events she made Grahame talk about the story, and at once exerted all her influence to get him to write it down. No one since Henley had had such an instinctive editorial flair for pushing him in the right direction.

Their meeting took place about the middle of August. Her work accomplished, Miss Smedley extracted an introduction from the Grahames to Thomas Hardy, and drove off, popping and banging, in the direction of Dorchester and Max Gate.

By now the Grahames had moved from their temporary furnished house, Hillyers, to a big sprawling building known as Mayfield, complete with large garden and paddock. Here they remained till the move to Blewbury in 1910; and here, before he drafted *The Wind in the Willows* in its final form, Grahame composed that curious little fragment, 'Bertie's Escapade'. This was a *jeu d'esprit* for domestic consumption, full of private allusions. It involved the Grahames' pig (Bertie himself) and Alastair's pet rabbits, Peter and Benjie, whose names remind us that Beatrix Potter's *Peter Rabbit* had been published in 1904.

Now, at last, the long incubation of Grahame's masterpiece was nearly complete. From all directions and every year of the half-century memories, images, fears, regrets, friends, books, vivid scenes, half-forgotten incidents converged on the single focal point, at last achieved, 'the real, the unmistakable thing, simple, passionate—perfect'. Some of these influences Grahame used consciously and deliberately; others worked themselves in below the threshold of his awareness. Summers of casual Mediterranean wandering; the childhood pattern set by Berkshire meadows and the lazy Thames, the eternal solitary lure of the Ridgeway; paganism, Pan, and *The Yellow Book*; the odd near-eccentric friends who were or had been especially close to him—Furnivall, Henley, Q, 'Atky'; years of political unrest, the collapse of the country squirearchy; the anarchic, proletarian, urban Radicalism which meant strikes and riots; the London Scottish Territorials; the winding creeks and quiet backwaters of Fowey; books by the hundred, known and re-read time and time again—the *Odyssey*, Grimm, Andersen, Æsop, William Morris, Jefferies, Anstey, Wilde, Matthew Arnold; his own life, with its chequered pattern of repressions, disappointments, and compromises; above all, the small child for whom, night after night, he wove the beginnings of the fabric—all these met, mingled, were transformed in the light alembic of that delicate mind.

Why did Grahame choose, at this stage in his career, to write a book in which the main characters were animals? This question was asked by a number of disappointed reviewers who, with the dogged singlemindedness of their kind, had been expecting yet another *Golden Age;* and it is fatally easy to brush it off with a superficial answer. It may be said—and generally is—that the conventions of the bedtime story demanded animals, and that Grahame had plentiful models in the fairy-tales and folklore he knew so well. Both these statements are quite true; but they only scrape the surface of the problem.

Grahame and those who thought as he did both claimed the animal as a brother—thus vindicating Darwin—and at the same time execrated science for taking all the mystery out of life. The traditional English love of animals, which certainly does not pre-date the Romantic Movement, may well stem from the same muddled source, a mixture of evolutionary theory and natural pantheism.

But there are several deeper reasons for the use of animal characters; and they are hinted at, as usual, in Grahame's own work. To begin with, the trend we have observed in his development away from the explicit to the implicit, from statement to symbol, would very much encourage it. He was ripe for unconscious allegory. Secondly, there was his long-dormant satirical *persona,* which needed a mask more effective than that supplied by childhood. Thirdly, there was his growing aversion to humanity as such, which almost certainly had an intimate connection with his unhappy marriage. At this level he turned to the animal world in much the same spirit as Swift, who drew such a telling comparison between Houyhnhnms and Yahoos in *Gulliver's Travels*. He wished both to show the animal's moral superiority to the human species, and at the same time, by an anthropomorphizing trick, to satirize his society in the persons of half-human animals.

The animals of *The Wind in the Willows* are composed from several distinct and separate sources. At one level they are normal creatures of riverside and woodland: moles, water-rats (more accurately water-voles, but Grahame probably wanted to avoid a clash of names), badgers, otters, stoats, and weasels—all were common in the neighbourhood of the Thames round Cookham. We know, too, that Grahame took a keen and direct interest in such creatures. Charis Fairbanks, who stayed at 'Mayfield' about this period, wrote:

> I recall one day, wandering round Cookham and Marlow, his stopping on a wee bridge and endeavouring to call the attention of someone, or something, by a most alluring whistle, as sweet and imperative as any pipe of Pan. I know I'd have gone anywhere it called! But there was no response. After several calls he gave it up, remarking: 'There's a Water Rat down there, at least, it's his home; he's quite a friend of mine. Evidently he's gone on some excursion—I shall hear about it one day.'

This recalls a remark in 'A Funeral': 'the rabbits—I have it from one of themselves—have all gone to an At Home today'. Grahame's affectation to understand animal-talk crops up in several other places (notably his introduction to Billinghurst's *A Hundred Fables of Æsop*, where the Badger puts in a first brief appearance): perhaps he even half-believed it himself.

A similar incident lay behind the creation of Mole. One evening, when Grahame was dressing for dinner, he happened to glance out of his bedroom window (it was late summer, and still light) and saw 'some sort of flurry or disturbance going on' under the trees at the far end of the lawn. Quickly, he stole out in his stockinged feet, and found a robin and a mole fighting for possession of a worm. The robin flew off; but Grahame, with some dexterity, managed to capture the mole, and took it indoors with the intention of showing it to Alastair the following morning. He put it for the night in a small grass-lined hamper on the piano, with a heavy iron weight to hold the lid down. But in the morning the mole had inexplicably vanished—leaving both weight and lid intact. Mrs Blunt, the housekeeper, admitted to having killed what she thought was a 'young rat', by the back door; but she was getting near-sighted in her old age. When Grahame told her what the mole had been for, she said: 'Oh, but, sir, couldn't you just make the mole into a story for Master Alastair?'

The last part of this anecdote may well be apocryphal, since Mole had had his first tentative beginnings some time before; but the little creature's mysterious and somehow symbolic escape from prison would not have been lost on Grahame. It may well have triggered off other more personal and associative details. Grahame

can be more nearly identified with Mole than any other of his characters: the patient, tunnelling, laborious Mole who suddenly bursts through into the sunlight and the leisurely life of the River. Like Grahame, he is tactful, wide-eyed, a little naïve, content to play Watson to Ratty's Holmes; like Grahame again, he develops a violent, aching nostalgia for his old home—and goes back to it. Mole's moments of self-analysis could be applied with equal justice to his creator:

> The Mole saw clearly that he was an animal of tilled field and hedgerow, linked to the ploughed furrow, the frequented pasture, the lane of evening lingerings, the cultivated garden plot. For others the asperities, the stubborn endurance, or the clash of actual conflict, that went with Nature in the rough; he must be wise, must keep to the pleasant places in which his lines were laid and which held adventure enough, in their way, to last for a lifetime.

Thus the Mole has evolved, a being in his own right, rather as crystals accumulate on a thread suspended in solution: he begins with a line in a poem of John Davidson's, gathers up not only subterranean symbolism but also the behaviour of a real live mole in the garden, and is completed with oblique strokes of autobiography and self-analysis. This is Grahame's normal method of composition: and Mole is a comparatively simple example. All the other animals reveal similar constituent elements—natural observation of the beast in question; literary associations; underlying symbolism; a degree of self-portraiture. They also incorporate features borrowed from Grahame's friends.

Rat is more complex altogether. He is a handyman, but also a dreamer; a man (or rat) of action and a poet; cool-headed in a crisis, yet liable to mystical seizures and symptoms indicative of hysteria. In the autobiographical sense he stands for Grahame's emotional extremes—at one end of the scale the practical businessman and freshwater sailor; at the other the volatile, highly imaginative, psychologically disturbed Celt. It may be Rat who supports Mole in his emotional crisis of longing for Mole End; but the rôles are reversed when Rat hears the call of the South and marches out, for all the world like a hypnotized zombie, his eyes no longer brown but a streaked and shifting grey. And the 'seizure', we should note, is cured by—creative writing. There could hardly be a closer parallel.

But other, external, strands went into the Rat's making. There is a touch of Henley in his occasional bursts of blunt dogmatism; and his general habits and appearance derive in large measure from 'Atky', whose riverside bachelor home and passion for 'messing about in boats' struck an immediately responsive chord in Grahame. Further back still, his sculling expeditions and loaded luncheon-hampers recall an older, more eccentric, friend—Dr Furnivall. (Furnivall also provided one aspect of the appearance and *mise en scène* of Pan in 'The Piper at the Gates'. Professor Livingston Lowes describes 'an island in the Thames, where, of a Sunday afternoon, [Furnivall] used to recline against a tree, like a glorious old British river-god with white and curling beard'.) The Downs are his natural horizon; it is that *alter ego* the Sea Rat who tempts him with stories of Sicily and Alassio. Even as early as *Pagan Papers* he appears, momentarily, as the foster-brother of Pan, the rural deity who may be found 'stretched on Ranmore Common, loitering under Abinger pines, or prone by the secluded stream of the sinuous Mole'—an odd verbal coincidence.

There is one very striking literary source for Rat, and that is a story by Oscar Wilde called 'The Devoted Friend', which was published in *The Happy Prince* in 1888. The similarities are obvious and undeniable:

> One morning the old Water-rat put his head out of his hole. He had bright beady eyes and stiff grey whiskers, and his tail was like a long bit of black indiarubber. The little ducks were swimming about in the pond ... and their mother ... was trying to teach them how to stand on their heads in the water.
>
> 'You will never be in the best society unless you can stand on your heads,' she kept saying to them; and every now and then she showed them how it was done. But the little ducks ... were so young that they did not know what an advantage it is to be in society at all.

Grahame must, too, have noted with sympathy how Wilde's Water-rat described himself:

> 'Ah! I know nothing about the feelings of parents,' said the Water-rat; 'I am not a family man. In fact I have never been married, and I never intend to be. Love is all very well in its way, but friendship is much higher. ...'

And that, of course, is one of the unspoken motifs running through *The Wind in the Willows*, where nobody who matters is married, or needs to work, and where the *summum bonum* is loyalty, with creature comforts a close second: an apologia, in fact, for the country bachelor's life.

Badger, again, contains elements of Henley—in particular his weakness for pontifical polysyllables off-set by vernacular slang, and the gruffness which masked a vast benevolent paternalism. He also bears an odd resemblance to old Mr Iden in Richard Jefferies' *Amaryllis at the Fair.*

But, as in Mole's case, the greater part of Badger is autobiographical. It was Grahame—as we remember from those Campden Hill soirées—who felt awkward and out of place in 'Society'; and it was certainly Grahame who turned 'rather low and despondent when he's wanting his victuals'. Slip-shod but well equipped, indifferent to fashions but careful of comfort, Badger represents Grahame's own conception of himself as the rural *ours philanthropique.*

The most attractive feature about him from his creator's point of view, however, was undoubtedly his labyrinthine undergound home, safe from the storms and blizzards of the Wild Wood—yet lying at the very heart of it. This grandiose, earthy catacomb, partly based on Roman ruins (a neat symbolic touch) was a comforting, womb-like, protective concept. It may have been suggested in part by the eccentric activities of the fifth Duke of Portland, who 'had been given to disappearing for weeks; he had avoided the sight of his fellows, and built himself strange underground rooms and passages in his great park at Welbeck'. These facts emerged during the hearing of the Druce case in 1907, about the time Mr Badger's residence was being invented.

One of the most curious (and least commented-on) features of *The Wind in the Willows* is the frequency with which characters indulge in violent, eccentric, and near-pathological emotions or actions. This psychological ferment is in striking contrast to the rural tranquillity of the setting. We would expect Mole and Rat, at least, to behave with 'English self-restraint'; but not a bit of it. Mole goes into hysterical sobs at a whiff of his old home, while Rat is hypnotized into a kind of hysterical trance by the Seafarer. But it is, of course, in Toad that such phenomena reach a peak of intensity; at times his behaviour almost suggests that he is, as it were, the Id personified.

If Toad was partially intended to satirize Alastair himself, then some of his actions can be explained as mere childishness—his wailing and leg-kicking, and refusal to be comforted; the game he plays with chairs when locked up in his bedroom:

> He would arrange bedroom chairs in rude resemblance of a motor-car and would crouch on the foremost of them, bent forward and staring fixedly ahead, making uncouth and ghastly noises, till the climax was reached, when, turning a complete somersault, he would lie prostrate amidst the ruins of the chairs, apparently completely satisfied for the moment.

But this can hardly be used as an over-all explanation; for the most part, indeed, Toad's behaviour is irresistibly suggestive of an adult manic-depressive. His entire life is a series of violent excesses matched by balancing moods of black and lachrymose despair; he shows the classic symptoms of irresponsibility, faddishness, bombastic fantasizing, tearful but impermanent repentance. Even A. A. Milne spotted something of this when he came to write *Toad of Toad Hall*: Alfred the horse remarks to Rat, after one of Toad's more curious outbursts: 'Psychological—that was the word he wanted. Not encyclopaedia. I thought it seemed funny somehow. Psychological.'

Grahame himself hints at such a diagnosis by the language he uses to describe Toad's eccentricities. It is remarkably consistent and revealing. After the smashing of the caravan Toad is in 'a sort of trance', 'spell-bound, sleep-walking'; mention is made of his 'violent paroxysms', his 'painful seizures', his 'possession', in relation to motor-cars. This compulsive urge to steal cars is, on the evidence of the text, purely pathological. As Rat very sensibly asks, why *steal* them? Toad is rich enough to have bought—and to go on buying—cars by the dozen. But when he hears that familiar poop-poop! outside, he has to 'hold on to the leg of the table to conceal his overmastering emotion'. When, compulsively, he drives off in the car, 'as if in a dream, all sense of right and wrong, all fear of obvious consequences, seemed temporarily suspended'. And what goes on in his mind as he tears along the highway suggests the kind of compensation-fantasist for whom fast cars (now as then) symbolize unattained power, potency, or pure irresponsible authority:

> He was only conscious that he was Toad once more, Toad at his best and highest, Toad the terror, the traffic-queller, the Lord of the lone trail, before whom all must give way or be smitten into nothingness and everlasting night. He chanted as he flew,

> and the car responded with sonorous drone; the miles were eaten up under him as he sped he knew not whither, fulfilling his instincts, living his hour, reckless of what might come to him.

What was it gave Grahame the impulse to introduce all these pathological traits of behaviour into *The Wind in the Willows*? In particular, where did he find the model for Toad's extraordinary, and very well-observed, symptoms—the specialized kleptomania, the complex manic-depressive behaviour? This problem remains something of a mystery. Up to a point there can be little doubt that he was describing his own unfulfilled and—in the normal way—firmly repressed urges: letting his anarchic Id out for a fictional romp. The only pathological character we know Grahame to have been on close terms with was old Dr Furnivall, a compulsive but harmless exhibitionist: and while Furnivall may have supplied Toad's hearty insistence on making his friends share his own pleasures, there is no suggestion that he ever indulged in car-stealing.

Other elements are more easily traced. Toad's faddishness probably owed something to the unknown relative who inspired Uncle Thomas of *The Golden Age*; while his flamboyant egotism, his *penchant* for after-dinner speaking, his scandalous downfall and imprisonment—these must surely reflect something of Oscar Wilde's tragedy. Cookham Dene was almost in sight of Reading Gaol.

READING GAOL.
Cookham Dene was almost in sight of the gaol, scene of Wilde's incarceration. Grahame describes Toad's imprisonment: 'under the frowning archway of the grim old castle, whose ancient towers soared high overhead'.

Just as in his earlier books Grahame had achieved a convincing fluidity of viewpoint, which shifted without effort from child to adult, so with *The Wind in the Willows* he takes the process one step further. All the animal characters veer constantly between human and non-human behaviour. Rat lives in a river-bank hole, and also writes poetry. Mole burrows underground, but is capable of rounding up a horse from the paddock. As Guy Pocock intelligently observed, the book is neither a pure animal book, nor 'a fairy tale like *Puss in Boots* in which an animal is simply a human being dressed up; for every now and then, for all its frank anthropomorphism, the story shows an extraordinary insight into the feelings and doings of little wild animals. ... Rat is always a rat, though armed to the teeth; and Mole is always a mole even when he wears goloshes.' Perhaps the oddest instance of this duality is the moment when Toad is recognized for what he is by the bargewoman: instantly he ceases to be a humanized animal capable of driving cars or combing its hair in the middle, and becomes a mere toad, small t, to be thrown overboard in disgust.

This fluidity explains why it has always been so difficult to illustrate *The Wind in the Willows* convincingly. The animals are not conceived in visual terms—or rather, they are never the same for two minutes running: both their size and their nature are constantly changing. Grahame himself was well aware of this problem, and dealt very prettily with queries about it. When asked specifically (apropos the escape on the railway train) whether Toad was life-size or train-size, he answered that he was both and neither: the Toad was train-size, the train was Toad-size, and therefore there could be no illustrations. He later capitulated, and E. H. Shepard came as near as possible to capturing the essence of Rat, Mole, and Toad; but the point remains that the inner eye sees no incongruity in these metamorphoses (and in fact hardly notices them), while visual representation at once pins down Grahame's imagination to a single static concept.

'"Well, I'll Tell You What I'll Do," said the Good Engine Driver.'
Drawing by E. H. Shepard.

An examination of the illustrated editions confirms this point only too well. Again and again Grahame can suggest with words something which visual art, in the programmatic sense, not only fails to capture but renders fatally banal. The classic example is the mystical climax of 'The Piper at the Gates'. Every single attempt to illustrate the scene on Pan's Island is—must be—a disastrous failure. Maxfield Parrish, the American artist and illustrator of *The Golden Age*, writes of this chapter: 'Music might go with it, but nothing else'. Grahame Robertson, too, saw the impossibility of such an illustration: 'In the "appropriately pictured" edition (he begged Elspeth) we won't have a picture of Pan, will we? Perhaps a little bit of his shadow, but no more.'

Pan is a special case, but Grahame's whole imaginative process in *The Wind in the Willows* lies beyond those fixed dimensions which every artist is compelled to impose by the very nature of his medium. There is no stability in Grahame's dream-world, and no incongruity. Human magistrates of a highly contemporary nature try and condemn toads to imprisonment in mediaeval dungeons guarded by halberdiers. The same toad can bargain with a gypsy for a horse, and ride off on it. Most curious of all, a humanized Rat and Mole can walk through a village on a winter's night, and still consider its inhabitants somehow alien—including their dogs and cats. This interchangeability of essential nature is Grahame's hall-mark; and the oddest thing about it is that it still leaves every character sharply defined and psychologically consistent. Perhaps only a writer who combined a satirist's talent with the imperturbable vision of a child could have managed it.

XII

THE VANISHING DREAM

1908–13

While *The Wind in the Willows* was slowly coming to fruition, Grahame continued to perform his not very onerous duties at the Bank of England. He entertained King George V's children to tea, showed them round the vaults, and let them each sign a £1000 bank-note: this visit took place on 23 April 1907. He was popular with junior officials, and seems to have been at some pains, as one of them later wrote, 'to adapt the Queen's English to the purposes of official letters. ... I listened carefully to some advice he once gave me on the subject of punctuation and the construction of sentences.' But, as the same witness remarked of him, he did not fit in with one's preconceived notions of a Bank official; and the literary aura which by now hung round him probably made his colleagues a little uneasy.

From the point of view of the Governor and the Court of Directors, we may surmise, Grahame had certain disabilities as a Secretary. Chief among these,

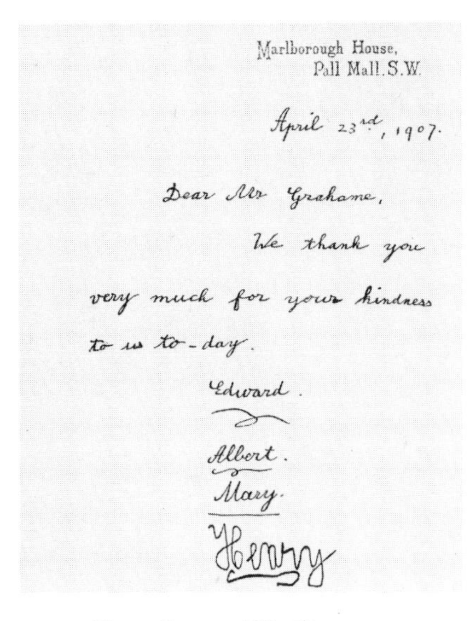
Marlborough House,
Pall Mall. S.W.

April 23rd, 1907.

Dear Mr Grahame,

We thank you very much for your kindness to us to-day.

Edward.

Albert.

Mary.

Henry

King George V's Children
wrote to Kenneth Grahame when he was Secretary of the Bank of England
to thank him for entertaining them to tea at the Bank.

without any doubt, was his frequent absence through illness. He had never been a wholly well man since his dangerous attack of empyema in 1899, and the mental stress under which he had been living thenceforward must have pulled him down physically as well. Consequently he tended to work short hours and take long holidays. A young member of his staff wrote:

> I was too much of a junior to have any personal contact with him in the Bank. My only recollection is of a tall figure striding through the Secretary's outer office shortly before four o'clock, bound for Paddington and Cookham Dene. Even in those more leisurely days it seemed an unconscionably early hour for such an important figure to be leaving for home, but I think the explanation lay in the fact that he had already been warned by his doctors of a decline in health, and he did, in fact, retire very soon afterwards.

Was Grahame's premature retirement exclusively to do with the state of his health? We cannot be certain. Chalmers, indeed, has no doubts on the matter. He speaks of 'an intermittent and virulent form of influenza', and a Harley Street opinion that Grahame must give up his sedentary City life. He further claims that the Court of Directors begged Grahame, instead of retiring, to take a year's holiday with full pay. Though other documents relative to Grahame's resignation were carefully preserved by Elspeth, this one does not appear among them. There is something improbable about the whole story, and one or two hints from external sources suggest an alternative version. To begin with, there is a persistent tradition in banking circles that Grahame did not get on well with William Campbell Middleton, the new Governor appointed in 1907. There is also that curious anxiety-dream which Grahame at this time incorporated into 'Bertie's Escapade'. Some of it, considered in a professional context, is highly interesting: 'At last the Chairman rose, and said "He can't think of anything to say! *Turn him out!*"'

It certainly looks as though Grahame may have been under some kind of official pressure: and if the dream he recorded is any guide at all, this pressure must have been connected with his conduct as Secretary. Inability to speak in a dream generally implies some real or imputed incapacity connected with one's daily life. Grahame could very easily have got off on the wrong foot with Middleton, who had the reputation of being a tough, efficient, go-ahead Governor: a new broom very ready to sweep clean. There is the further point that Grahame resigned in June 1908, four months before *The Wind in the Willows* was published. He was not seriously ill at the time: would it not have been more prudent and more practical to wait till the end of the year, when fresh royalties might well be pouring in? Lastly, the pension granted him by the Court of Directors was no more than £400 p.a.—a surprisingly low figure for a retiring Secretary, even one forced to abdicate early through illness, and hardly consistent with their supposed generous offer of a year's holiday on full pay. The decision, communicated to him on 2nd July, is couched in the coldest of official language; and no personal letters of sympathy or farewell from his colleagues at the Bank survive among his private papers.

If there *was* official disagreement between Grahame and the new Governor, it would suggest yet one more contributory cause to the sense of terror and the motifs of pursuit by Authority which run through *The Wind in the Willows*. It might, too, have had another and at first sight more beneficent effect. Whatever the reason, Grahame's long stint aboard the galley was over. Now, at last, he could see the Good Life within reach: and that prospect may well have spurred him on to capture in words what was shortly to become reality.

Yet here again we sense impending tragedy. He had waited too long and compromised too often; above all he was no longer the 'felowe that goes alone.' Perhaps (with all the experience of his childhood behind him) he guessed that the Good Life, when it came, would fall hopelessly short of the long-cherished dream: if so, what he did—as in *The Golden Age*—was to make the dream immortal before it was destroyed. And he succeeded. Despite its disturbing landscape and deep-rooted symbolism—indeed, Grahame celebrated his release from bondage on the very first page—the book *does* succeed somehow in giving an over-all impression of still, warm peace and tranquillity. The occasionial anachronisms that 'date' it—early motor-cars, references to Kitchener or Garibaldi—fail to make any real impression on our minds: its atmosphere is outside history. It embodies in miniature the whole essence of pre-1914 England—the smooth lawns, the river-picnics, the long, sun-drenched days of idleness, the holidays in Italy, the self-assurance and the stable values. The currents of change and revolution do little more than ruffle the surface of this summer stream: they eddy deep below among the sinuous weeds, unseen, biding their time.

One of Grahame's staunchest admirers was—of all people—Theodore Roosevelt, who wrote asking for autographed copies of *The Golden Age* and *Dream Days*, and invited their author several times, in vain, to come over and stay at the White House. (Another even more improbable fan was Kaiser Wilhelm, who only had two books in his cabin on the royal yacht *Hohenzollern*: the Bible and *The Golden Age*.) In due course Grahame sent Roosevelt a copy of *The Wind in the Willows*; and after the usual initial disappointment at the absence of children, the President became a staunch convert—partly through the prodding of his family.

This turned out very much to Grahame's advantage. Curtis Brown, his literary agent, had experienced (as he tells us in his memoirs) great difficulty in marketing the new book:

> I tried it with magazine editors all over England and America. They thought it too fantastic and wouldn't have it. Then it went to Charles Scribner, father of the present Charles. He said it wouldn't go; but just then he got a letter from Theodore Roosevelt ... saying ... that it was such a beautiful thing that Scribner *must* publish it.

He did. In England Methuen proved equally sceptical at first; he did not even have sufficient faith in the book to pay a guaranteed advance on it. Nevertheless, convinced that he had nothing to lose, he 'agreed to excellent rising royalties, just in case the book *should* fulfil my dreams'. The University of Oxford (to which foundation Grahame's copyright eventually reverted), and in particular the Bodleian Library, have had cause to be grateful for Curtis Brown's optimistic contract.

Grahame was too busy with the completion and publication of *The Wind in the Willows* to celebrate his new-found independence by going abroad at once. He spent much time with Alastair in the woods and lanes round Cookham, teaching him country lore, recapturing something of his own youthful spirit through the child's wonder. Constance Smedley was a regular visitor, and has left us a vivid description of the domestic *mise en scène* at Mayfield:

> I remember the sloe gin poured into tiny cordial glasses ... the ceremony of the salad, served in a great basket with herbs and flasks of condiments and solemnly prepared by Mr Grahame; the rows of tear-bottles of Bristol glass, the peasant toys from all countries, the wonderful collections of old glass and china used, not only looked at. One night I remember being greatly intrigued. Some very tall glasses with a curious convoluted edge were before us through which one saw everything as through the wrong end of an opera glass. They were most fascinating to drink out of: Mr and Mrs Grahame appeared like animated toys miles away across a miniature dining-table. When I left, the housekeeper was waiting in the hall with one of these glasses most beautifully packed up and tied. 'It is the custom', said Mr Grahame, 'to give your guest the cup he has drunk from.'

On 3 November Grahame wrote the first surviving letter in a long correspondence with his American friend Austin Purves. He described his and Elspeth's plans for future travel:

> I am hoping to manage it after the New Year—in Switzerland to begin with, and then perhaps a drop into the northern part of Italy, for colour and anemones and Chianti and so on. If I can get E. sufficiently patched up for the journey. By the way, about her photo. She has not been done for many years, and now absolutely refuses to undergo the process until she is less of a Living Skellington. ...
>
> We have had a beautiful summer here, and now we are having an equally beautiful autumn—still and misty and mild and full of colour. I had a jolly day at Oxford a short time ago. Everything in full swing and the river covered with men doing 'tubbing' practice. The old place was just as beautiful as ever, and I bought some youthful ties and some 'Oxford sausages' in the delightful market—they are a small species without any skins on their poor little persons—and took a walk down Mesopotamia, and explored many old corners.
>
> We can't extract any Fowey news from Q, who is probably mighty busy, and neither Atky nor Miss Marsden have given any sign of life for a long time. I wish we could get down there for a bit before the year closes. Perhaps it may yet be possible.

For some reason, however, he and Elspeth went to Devonshire instead, where he caught influenza yet again. It left him weak and groggy; by mid-December he could still 'only walk a mile or two, and then an armchair and slumber until dinner-time'. The mummers turned up at Mayfield, and disappointed him sadly: 'Hardly any of the good old "St George and the Dragon" play left', he informed Purves, 'Instead, cheap comic songs from the London music halls. But Mouse liked it.' He added drily: 'E. is Christmassing for all she's worth and is not precisely sane at the present season.' There was still no news from Fowey. On the other hand there was a begging-letter from Trant Chambers, who had edited the *St Edward's*

Chronicle with Grahame, and was now a hopeless down-and-out, 'friendless, hungry, penniless, shelterless and without immediate prospect of any kind'. Once again time had shattered the precious yet illusory memories of youth. Grahame sent him a cheque by return, and tried to forget the incident. But he was not to be so easily rid of his former school-fellow; throughout the years this pathetic and destitute drunkard continued to send appeals to Grahame at irregular intervals, turning the knife in old memories, emphasizing the gap between recollection and reality.

By the beginning of 1909 Grahame seems to have withdrawn himself still further into his private world of fantasy. Retirement probably accelerated the process.

In February Kenneth and Elspeth left England on their projected trip to Switzerland and Italy, from which they returned in the spring and in January 1910 Grahame was writing to Purves: 'We are both somewhat stale and rusty and I want to smell foreign smells again and drink wine in the country where it grows; but we feel it would be wiser to get our troubles [house-moving] over first.' This seems reasonable enough till we notice the significant switch from 'we' to 'I'; and again, as if to emphasize the point, Grahame says, '*I* want to go on *my* travels with a light heart.'

Surprisingly but suggestively, there is no evidence that Elspeth had ever been abroad with Grahame since their marriage. (His trip to Spain in 1904, for instance, was made independently.) It is very likely that he would wish to keep his Southern dream-landscape, with all its memories, private and inviolate. The trips he made to Italy were solitary emotional pilgrimages: and it seems infinitely probable that the joint visit with Elspeth was an inner, if not an acknowledged, disaster. Brittany was a compromise; it offered neutral territory, uncharged with associative memories.

There are other hints that some sort of emotional crisis may have taken place on that Italian trip. By July Grahame was deep in the grip of a paralysing indolence with henceforth never entirely left him. Apologizing to Austin Purves for his shortcomings as a correspondent, he reveals his state of mind with fascinating clarity.

> And yet, do you know, I do write you any quantity of magnificent letters. In my armchair of evenings, with closed eyes—strolling in the woods of afternoons—or with head on pillow very late on a thoroughly wet and disagreeable morning. I see my pen covering page after page of cream-laid parchment wove extra antique. Such good stuff, too—witty, anecdotal, pensive, pathetic—I feel myself lick the envelope—I see myself running to the post—I hear the flop of the letter in the box. It's all so real to me—that I was quite surprised to find that you weren't asking me to limit them to, say, three a week. Please believe, that if they never reach you, *it's not my fault.*

Both the indolence and the intensification of Grahame's fantasy life may have been the result of emotional shock, a self-protective defence set up against disappointing reality. The long-dreamed-of release had proved, in the event, a mirage.

This was by no means entirely Elspeth's fault, but was an essential condition of Grahame's character. Elspeth may well have been an irksome travelling companion on a journey to the Hesperides; but, with her or without her, Grahame found that experience was a continual and deepening disappointment. In his late essay, 'Ideals', first published in 1922, he wrote, 'Do we not nearly always find in our past imaginings ... just those two touchstones of the ideal—a fantastic unlikeness to the real thing, together with a special beauty nowhere else to be found?' And so Grahame retreated deeper into his English, as opposed to his Mediterranean, myth: the Cockayne of boating and food and rural seclusion. It was 'Wayfarers All' all over again; and once more Mole had defeated Rat.

Summer that year was miserable, wet and cold, and boating remained out of the question. Elspeth was suffering from inflammation of the optic nerve in one eye, which debarred her from reading; Alastair, as Grahame wrote to Purves, was 'down at his favourite sea-side resort—Littlehampton, a rather horrid little place, which he adores'. Then, as though to anticipate comment, Grahame produces an oddly flimsy pair of excuses for Elspeth and himself not being with the boy: 'I wish our taste in places were similar, so that we could be together; but in any case E. can't take her bad eye to the sea yet, on account of the glare.' And a few lines earlier he had been complaining of July's rainy dismalness! We remember an exactly similar situation in the summer of 1907; it almost looks as though both Kenneth and Elspeth *avoided* having holidays with Alastair.

But there were consolations, for Kenneth at any rate: chief among them two surprise visits from 'Atky', who 'just dropped from the clouds, without notice, ate a hearty lunch, talked a great deal, and flitted away again into the outer darkness'. Kenneth also managed to get away for a flying visit to the Quiller-Couches at Fowey, where he met a young Oxford *littérateur* named Compton Mackenzie. Fan-mail continued to pour in from all over the world: Kenneth's grateful readers included Alfred Deakin, the Prime Minister of Australia; a charming Boston spinster who enquired, 'If you keep writing books that I have to read all the time, how am I ever going to read anything else?'; children of all ages, everywhere; and Margot Asquith, who decided that *The Golden Age* would be good for her German governess.

By autumn the lease of Mayfield was running out, and the area was becoming too thickly populated for the Grahames' taste. They were busy house-hunting, with very little success, till the New Year. Meanwhile Lloyd George had introduced his radical People's Budget, which had repercussions all over the country, dividing friends, and causing tremendous agitation: Lord Rosebery described it as 'Socialism, the end of all—the negation of Faith, of Family, of Monarchy, of Empire'. The stoats and weasels were indeed having a time of it, though today the proposals seem mild enough: a supertax of 6d in the £ over £3000, slight additional duty on spirits and tobacco, and new land taxes.

This Budget was finally passed in November 1909 but thrown out by the Lords, and a General Election loomed ahead. Q, to Grahame's irritation, came out strongly in favour of Lloyd George: 'Q is frightfully busy over the election,' he

The Berkshire Ridgeway on Thurle Down.
The Ridgeway, now designated as one of England's long-distance footpaths, was the route of many of Grahame's walks.

The Berkshire Downs near Compton.
The eastern end of the Berkshire Downs provides wide-open landscapes with easy walking along the length of The Ridgeway.

Blewbury Down.
Kenneth Grahame moved to Blewbury in 1910. With the Downs at his door he hoped for 'some fine walking when I have finished picture-hanging and falling over rolls of carpet'.

THE CHURCH OF ST JAMES THE LESS, PANGBOURNE.
Kenneth Grahame returned to live by the River Thames when, in 1924, he bought Church Cottage. Six years later he died and the funeral took place at the church which lay behind the cottage.

PANGBOURNE.
Pangbourne has developed into a commuter village but traces of the old village remain.

THE RIVER PANG.
This little trout-stream flows through Pangbourne to the Thames.

wrote to Purves, 'propagating his pernicious doctrines throughout the west country'; and to Q himself he declared, perhaps only half-humorously: 'I must not wish you luck in your nefarious designs on our savings, our cellars, and our garden-plots; but I do hope you'll get some fun out of it.' Q did; and three years later he wrote a most entertaining account of his electioneering activities in *News from the Duchy*.

After Christmas Grahame at last found the house he had been looking for, in the village of Blewbury, near Didcot. (He still remained firmly attached to Berkshire.) 'Boham's' was a brick farm-house, with a thatched roof, which dated back to the Tudor period. There were two splendid farm-kitchens, a granary, an apple-loft, and a trout-stream. When eight coats of paint had been removed from the doors they turned out to be three-hundred-years-old linen-folded oak. Grahame wrote loving descriptions of his new property to various friends about a fortnight after moving in. The best, as we should expect, was to Austin Purves:

> Blewbury is perhaps the most beautiful of a string of very pretty and very primitive villages stretched along the northern edge of the Berkshire Downs. It is only about 54 miles from London, but 5400 years remote from it in every way. This is the heart of King Alfred's country, 'Alfred the Great' who beat the Danes close by here; about 860, and nothing has really happened since. True, a tiresome innovator called William the Conqueror came along some years later, and established a thing called the Curfew bell, which still rings here during the winter months, to the annoyance of the more conservative inhabitants, who say they used to get on very well before these new-fangled notions; but this is all that divides us from Saxon times. ...

'A little way off,' he informed Constance Smedley with evident delight, 'there is a farmer whose family has been here for a thousand years. They are real Saxons. They live in a lovely old farm-house with a ghost in it. Indeed all the houses here are very old. They do not build the horrid little red houses that spring up round Cookham.' He was retreating further and further into the protection of the past: not only the pre-Industrial Revolution now, but pre-Conquest. A letter to Alan Lidderdale gives some of the more mundane details:

> We moved into this little old farmhouse a fortnight ago, and have been slaving ever since to get it straight, with very little result—the trouble being that we have got too much stuff for so small a space. I was very sorry to leave Cookham Dene, [*sic*] but there was really nothing there that suited us at all. This is a very beautiful village, in quite a different way, and the Downs are at one's door. I hope for some fine walking when I have finished picture-hanging and falling over rolls of carpet.
>
> Mouse is down at the sea-side, to be out of all this stramash. E. hunts chickens—dead ones—through the village all day, & tries to persuade the farmers wives to part with provisions of any sort, which they refuse to do.

Before the end of May Theodore Roosevelt arrived in Oxford to give the Romanes Lecture. Warren of Magdalen, his host, enquired whether there were any people he particularly wished to meet, and Roosevelt listed Kipling, Andrew Lang, Grahame, Gilbert Murray, and Charles Oman, the historian. Grahame had a long

THEODORE ROOSEVELT.
The *Oxford Illustrated Journal* carried an illustrated report of Dr Roosevelt's Romanes lecture at the Sheldon Theatre. He was one of Grahame's greatest admirers and he requested that he should meet Grahame after the lecture.

talk with Roosevelt after the lecture, and Roosevelt himself later described Grahame in the *Saturday Evening Post* as 'simply charming'. About the same time an American scholar named Clayton Hamilton, who was in London collecting material for a book on Stevenson, managed to get an invitation for a week-end at Boham's, and coaxed a good deal of interesting talk out of his host.

'He was very tall and broad,' Professor Hamilton recollected, 'a massive figure, but with no spare flesh. At that time he was fifty years of age. His hair was white, but his face was almost beatifically young, and he had the clear and roseate complexion of a healthy child. He was dressed in knickerbockers, a soft shirt, and a baggy coat of tweeds.' Grahame seemed to his visitor uneasy indoors: he would lapse into silence for an hour or more. But as soon as the two of them got away for a solitary cross-country walk, Grahame 'would break into an easy current of cheery conversation'. Clearly he had certain inhibitions about letting himself go in Elspeth's presence; and in any case she had a weakness for monopolizing the conversation.

Mr Purves and his wife (but not their children) came over to England in July 1910, and stayed with the Grahames. Grahame had suggested, rather desperately, that Purves might care to 'walk from here, by way of the Downs, to Fowey? Atky says six weeks would do it quite comfortably.' (Atky was now roaming between

Corsica and Sardinia; each year, as Grahame put it, 'his St Anthony's fever seems to agitate his lean limbs more violently'.) But Purves prudently declined: he and his wife spent their time photographing local beauty-spots, and keeping an astonished eye on their host and hostess:

> I remember clearly [writes Mr Austin Purves, Jr] my mother's amusement, or consternation, or both, at the fact that Mr and Mrs Grahame lived in separate parts of the house. My parents were very connubial and the Grahames simply expected their guests to enjoy the same household and sleeping arrangements as they themselves did. ... Anyway, at breakfast after this nocturnal separation of the sexes there was tea and toast and one egg. Mrs Grahame said: The egg is for Kenneth.

There was no doubt that by now the Grahames were becoming mildly eccentric recluses. Andrew Lang and Edmund Gosse both lamented the fact that they never saw Kenneth any more, and that he only came to London once in a blue moon. Guests were warned against bringing evening clothes; and Grahame seems to have spoken no less than the truth when he told R. E. Moody, the artist: 'We live here in a state of primitive simplicity which is almost shocking.' Elspeth was determined that the whole village should revolve about her; she stumped round with a stick (and in clattering sabots after her Brittany expedition) laying down the law and getting laughed at behind her back. She seldom got up before eleven, often went to bed in her clothes, and kept rolls of silk and satin dresses upstairs which she never wore: she preferred an ancient navy-blue serge coat and skirt, with a frayed cardigan and hand-knitted stockings. Much of the time she spent on her divan, sipping hot water. She ate practically nothing, and mouse-nests proliferated in the larder; she put Kenneth into special underwear which was only changed once a year. It is perhaps not surprising that he took a long solitary walk on the Ridgeway every day.

Publishers were still busy dangling baits for him, however. On 27 July he received a letter from Gordon Home of A. & C. Black, asking him to write a 40,000 word book called *Highways and Hedges,* which was to give the reader a breath of country life as seen from the hedgerow and suggest any ideas that such scenes conjure up. It could, said Home, warming to his theme, contain 'anecdotes, folk-lore, philosophy, political economy, botany, ornithology, and references to anything and everything that rambles in beautiful English country are likely to bring to mind'. Grahame found the idea attractive, and persuaded Home to grant him the right to publish in serial form; but the whole thing foundered when Home proposed a £50 fee for the whole rights in lieu of royalties. Not unnaturally, Grahame refused. We may regret Home's shortsightedness: this is a book which Grahame would have done superbly.

Autumn and winter passed in a country round of sheep-fairs, circuses, and village gossip. At East Ilsley sheep-fair 'Mouse was soon in the thick of it, but when I sought him out and discovered him bidding at the auction for pedigree rams [Grahame wrote] I had to haul him out of action'. It was all very rural and back-to-nature; but there is a certain wistfulness in Grahame's complaint to Q, that

Christmas, of missing all the chief events and pageants of life. But he was down with another attack of bronchitis at the time, which must have depressed him; and he was saddened by the premature death of Roland's wife, Joan, after an unexpected heart attack.

In February of 1911 the whole family, Alastair now included, began a prolonged holiday, first at the Lizard, then at Fowey, which continued till the end of April. 'I want Mouse to make the acquaintance of my Cornish haunts, and friends, before he goes to school,' Grahame told Purves; and on the whole this holiday seems to have been a success. Alastair enjoyed himself in the wild scenery round the Lizard; at Fowey there were the Quiller-Couches, and Atky, who provided magnificent lunches ('mostly fancy hors-d'oeuvres and every sort of sausage') and let the boy browse among his books and records.

But Alastair was now eleven; and it was high time for him to be sent to school, whatever misgivings his parents may have had. (Kenneth had supplemented the teaching of Miss Stott with his own general knowledge papers: his idiosyncratic questions were only matched by Alastair's pseudo-adult—and often highly amusing—answers. Example: *What do you know about the Phoenix?* 'The Phenix is an inshurance co. There is only *one* at a time. Before it dies it lights a bonfire and roosts on it and when it is dead a new Phenix pops out of the ashes—but is it a new one? peradventure it is the same old bird all the time?? tut-tut! a strange bird it lives 100 years.') The school chosen was The Old Malthouse, at Langton Matravers, near Wareham, on the Dorset coast, and Mouse went there soon after Easter, 1911.

The Old Malthouse, in fact, turned out to be the only school where the boy was happy and relaxed: it seems to have been a cheerful, friendly, permissive place, very far from the harsh discipline and narrow ethics of the typical contemporary prep school.

Alastair's letters from The Old Malthouse shed as much incidental light on his parents as they do on his own activities. 'My dear Madame,' he writes to Elspeth on 21 May, 'your humble servant is glad to hear that improvements are coming up like bulbs and that Inferiority is doing some work *at last*!' A pencilled note in Elspeth's handwriting informs us that 'Inferiority was his whimsical [*sic*] name for his father at that time'. Comment would be superfluous. The 'improvements' were to Boham's: we do not know their exact nature. Nor do we know what Grahame was supposed to be working at; whatever it was came to nothing.

In September an unhappy tragedy occurred. 'Atky' was drowned while out yachting with Bevil Quiller-Couch, despite the younger man's gallant attempts to rescue him. Grahame wrote to Purves:

> Again and again in imagination I get into my boat at Whitehouse Steps and scull up the river by the grey old sea-wall, under the screaming gulls, past the tall Russian and Norwegian ships at their moorings, and so into Mixton Pill, and ship my oars at the little stone pier, and find Atky waiting on the steps, thin, in blue serge, with his Elizabethan head; and stroll up the pathway you know, to the little house above it, and

be talking all the time and always some fresh whimsicality. ... I feel as if we had all suddenly grown much older. All, that is, except Atky. He couldn't do it; he didn't know how.

The old familiar faces were going, the timeless myth slowly being destroyed; the creative spark was nearly dead. As Bardolph told Pistol, 'the fuel is gone that maintained that fire'. Only country solitude now remained for comfort.

Alastair was returned to school on 28 September, and Kenneth and Elspeth went for a few weeks to Pont-Aven in Southern Brittany, 'because', as Grahame put it to Curtis Brown, 'we want something fairly cheap—and not too far—and yet proper foreign. ... It has been a beautiful summer here—but I want a change of diet and a change of smells—and I believe the smells of some of the Brittany ports are very rich and satisfying.' Yet on his return he wrote to Purves: 'We had rather an interesting time in Brittany in the late autumn—saw a lot of new country and new things. But to me that is not the *South* and therefore—nothing. You've got to have the Alps to the north of you before the air begins to have the right feel in it.' Then why, we may ask, did he not go South? The plea of poverty was absurd: by now he was affluent—though Elspeth watched every penny. It looks inescapably as though he was unwilling to cross the Alps at this period other than alone.

All the same, he had a pleasant enough time at Pont-Aven. He was addressed (appropriately enough, considering his semi-military appearance) as 'Mon Colonel', and invited to take part in a full-dress Breton wedding. Elspeth recounts

ALASTAIR GRAHAME
at Blewbury
in 1912.

an interesting, if improbable, anecdote of his compulsive effect on small children: as soon as he arrived at his hotel, she says, he was surrounded by a group of Breton urchins, all demanding a story—in a language they could not understand. Those with experience of small Breton children outside hotels might surmise that they were offering to shine the English milord's shoes, or simply begging for coppers—Elspeth never missed an opportunity of making events square with her preconceptions.

They returned to a vile winter of storms and high winds: 'I hardly get out at all now,' Grahame wrote to Curtis Brown: 'When this sea of mud abates, I will go forth once more on the Downs, and give it prayerful consideration among my friends the hares and plovers.'

But about his writing he said nothing, for there was nothing to say. He had a sufficient income; he had lost his dream; there was now no driving impulse for him to go on writing. Instead, he sat by the fire and read Milton, or tramped for hours (the old, well-tried anodyne) over the Berkshire Downs.

He had tried to recapture his own youth through Alastair; but Elspeth monopolized the boy. From the tone of Alastair's letters it even looks as though she encouraged him to disparage Kenneth: certainly there was a sense of rivalry between them for the boy's affections, and at this time Mouse himself obviously inclined towards his mother. 'I also enclose a warning to Inferiority,' he wrote to Elspeth on 10 December 1911: *could* he have coined that nickname himself? 'If he does not take me to the Pantomime, and to Monte Carlo, and give me three helpings of Christmas pudding, and mince-pies, and otherwise show his paternal affection, [*sic*] well—I'll let him know it.'

In March 1912 Grahame made one of his rare visits to London to see a trial performance, in a small theatre, of a dramatized version of 'The Roman Road'. ('I find it difficult to think that so undramatic a bit of writing can possibly appeal from the boards,' he wrote, and he was right; though perhaps for the wrong reasons.) The moving spirit behind this venture was an American entertainer and children's writer called Kitty Cheatham, who had already visited the Grahames at Blewbury. Grahame hated publicity of any kind, but felt it was only fair to attend: Miss Cheatham was rounding off the evening with other dramatic readings from *The Golden Age*. Curtis Brown was also there, and describes the scene backstage:

> After it was over, we went around to the artist's reception-room. Kitty was surrounded by a congratulatory throng, but when she saw that beautiful head, she literally leaped through the crowd and landed with both arms round K. G's neck, exclaiming: 'You Angel Lamb!' Not even pistol shots could have been more startling to his grave dignity; but there was nothing in his attitude to indicate it.

That year the notion of going abroad was not repeated. The Grahames spent a fortnight in Lyme Regis, and then moved on—inevitably—to Fowey, where Grahame was saddened by the bare and desolate state of Atky's magical house up the estuary. The wonderful collection of clocks and barometers, the curious, faded,

KENNETH GRAHAME
selling baskets at the Blewbury Church Feast.

damp-speckled water-colours had no attraction for the dealers. Atky was dead, and his Arabian Nights atmosphere dissipated: nothing remained but a houseful of old junk. 'The place is for sale,' Grahame told Purves unhappily, 'not to be let, and I don't think it will sell in a hurry—it's not everybody's house.' He hankered after buying it himself; but the various snags and drawbacks proved too great, and they returned to Boham's. Once again August brought cold and incessant rain: vague plans for a trip to Scotland had to be abandoned.

In January 1913 Quiller-Couch accepted a Professorship in English Literature at Cambridge (he had been knighted the previous June) and on Thursday 15 May of that year Grahame was his guest at the Rustat Audit Feast in Jesus. Q had a second guest, A. E. Housman: one would dearly like to know how Grahame and Housman reacted to each other. Sir Sydney Cockerell, to whose rooms the party afterwards moved on, remembered that they sat talking till midnight: but added (in a letter to Elspeth nearly twenty years later) 'alas that I cannot recall any word of what must certainly have been a very interesting conversation!' Indeed it must: Housman, the scholar who had conquered poverty—and worse than poverty—to fight his way to the top of the academic ladder; Housman, the poet-fantasist with his dream of rural Shropshire—who could better have personified all that Grahame himself had desired and failed to achieve? There is only one hint of the effect that their meeting may have had on Grahame; and that is uncertain. Two months later he broke his long literary silence with 'The Felowe that Goes Alone'. Was it possible that he had Housman's example in mind?

Grahame (like A. A. Milne, who admitted it) was uneasy with children except in very special circumstances, and tended to ignore them, through shyness or conventionality, in public. C. L. Hinds records a meeting on a station, with Grahame as host, 'watchful, a little fussy, bothering about wraps and a carriage, ignoring two children who were of the party, but studiously polite to their parents'. His talent was for silent companionship: when Dale and Austin Purves rowed him up the coast to Lantick Bay, not more than fifty words were exchanged during several hours. 'Nor,' writes Dale, 'was there any need for words: communication was either needless or unrestrained—I don't know which. I think we all regarded it as time excellently spent.'

In August the long-projected trip to Scotland came off at last; and once again Alastair was included in the party. He seems have enjoyed himself vastly: enough, at any rate, for Grahame to turn down an invitation from Purves to show the boy something of Holland that month. 'Of course,' he wrote to Graham Robertson, 'travelling in August is always infernal, and we had to couch like the beasts of the field in temperance inns and such. But the weather was magnificent, and we were in the most beautiful country, even for the Highlands. The boy was simply drunk with it all, and grieved sorely to leave it.'

Alastair was now in his final year at prep school and both Elspeth and Kenneth were determined that he should have a public school education. In 1912 Kenneth had approached Q with enquiries about Winchester and Rugby: finally they settled on the latter, and Alastair was provisionally promised a place if he passed the entrance examination. This he contrived to do—though very near the bottom of the list—on 5 July 1914. The time for fantasy was over: for the first time in his life Alastair was going to be confronted with harsh and unimaginative realism. He had had a governess till he was ten; he was still immersed in a world of pirates and fairies, mixed with much precocious and aphoristic chat picked up from his parents. He was gruff-voiced, spotty, appallingly shy, and much given to waving his arms about in moments of excitement. Worst of all, there was that frightful squint, with its accompanying semi-blindness. It was not an auspicious endowment for public school life. Alastair was what his parents had made him; he had always struggled desperately to live up to their myth. But the private myth of *The Wind in the Willows* and the public myth of the English gentleman were hard for a thirteen-year-old boy to reconcile. Q foresaw trouble, and events proved him right.

XIII

ILLUSION AND TRAGEDY

1914–20

Alastair Grahame entered School House, Rugby, in September 1914, and was desperately unhappy there. His father later declared: 'I took great pains and trouble to assure myself that that was the best school he could go to,' perhaps he was unaware of Rugby's robust tradition. He went down to the school after a week or two, and saw Alastair's tutor, Roger Raven, who seems to have been a charming and enlightened man. At all events he sent the following note to his pupil:

> You know, your Father kindly came on Tuesday to see me and had a long talk with me; so that I more or less understand how things are. I said to him then what I repeat to you, now, that whenever you want somewhere to sit by yourself I hope you will come round here,—mornings, afternoons, &, if you like, after lock-up. I do all my work upstairs in the study, so that the dining-room below is always at your disposal. I know that invitations to 'drop in any time' are difficult to accept in practice, but I hope you will test this one at once; and you will find that you will be welcome and undisturbed. If you feel any delicacy in appearing to make free of someone else's rooms, you have only to put your head round the study door and say 'me voici' when you arrive; or if you find me unoccupied, you shall come in and talk to me as long as you like. There are some books here if you haven't enough of your own.—I have written this because I thought that if I came to your study and did not find you alone, it would be difficult to *say*. But in all cases believe me
>
> Your affec. tutor, R.A. RAVEN

Such delicacy and kindness might palliate Alastair's condition, but obviously could not cure it. 'So far as I could gather,' Grahame wrote to Austin Purves, 'the pace and the pressure were altogether too much for him, and I fancy that the new boys, with whom he naturally had to spend his time, happened to be a roughish lot. Anyhow though he stuck it out for six weeks, he got no better, and in the end I thought it right to take him away.' He then wrote to Q for advice, and got in in no uncertain terms:

> I had my doubts all along and for two reasons. (a) The Public School business has become such a silly specialized system that only the *larger* preparatory school really

> prepares the poor chap for what he has to undergo. ... The smaller private school (with better intentions) quite frequently doesn't. (b) Rugby is the place of all others where you get the system in full blast, with the least pity. Plenty of kindness on the part of X & Y but in the end no pity at all from the system. At Eton, Winchester, Wellington [!] a toad may dodge the harrow: they allow for 'eccentricities' (as they call 'em) and a certain understood adoration of the place often carries through a boy who is not of the run. He understands it (after a pathetic struggle often) and it first allows for and finally gets a particular liking for him—or may. But Rugby is ruthless. And it's all system.

Q was very anxious indeed about the boy, and said so. He then went on, tactfully, to suggest two possible alternatives. First, there was Clifton, which had the advantage of accepting day-boys as well as boarders. 'But,' he adds revealingly, 'you will not only have to live there; Mrs Grahame would have to make a vow to yield the boy over to the School whilst living under the same roof with him.' Perhaps sensing the improbability of Mrs Grahame ever doing anything of the sort, he next suggests a private tutor—'a thundering good fellow, massive, ex-Rugby Blue for Oxford'. Nevertheless, probably under pressure from Elspeth, Grahame got the boy into Eton, in January 1915. The war, it seems, made the usual long wait for a vacancy unnecessary.

Alastair lasted rather longer at Eton than he had at Rugby; over a year in fact. 'Scratch us,' he declared during this period, 'we are all barbarians but it happens that I prefer curios and they prefer cricket bats.' This kind of remark would probably find more tolerance at Eton than at most other schools; but even so his Dame was moved to admonish Alastair for not talking to his neighbours at table, which produced the reply: 'How can I talk to people whose powers of conversation lie only in their elbows?' This aloofness seems to have impressed the maid in his tutor's house, however; 'He was the only boy,' she declared, 'that I ever even *thought* of cutting the bread-and-butter thin for.' She also sent him a Christmas card signed 'Your faithful maid': this amused Grahame, who said it sounded like a pastoral poem.

Alastair was promoted to the Remove in the Michaelmas Term, 1915; and on 11 December Elspeth and Kenneth went down to see him and two hundred other boys confirmed by the Bishop of Oxford. Kenneth gave him a bicycle, and Elspeth wrote to her brother that 'he seems to have won very good opinions in the short time he has been at Eton'. But despite Elspeth's incurable optimism, within two months another emotional crisis had occurred, and in the middle of the Lent Term, 1916, Alastair was removed from Eton also. On 28 March Elspeth wrote about the whole affair to Courtauld, who was now in the Middle East with the Red Cross.

> ...We do not profess *ourselves* to understand exactly why a Public School life is so uncongenial to him for he is by nature the most spartan & the most uncomplaining creature possible. ... It is so great a disappointment to us that it makes me unhappy even to write about it. ... K. was really splendid in trying to do everything in his power to buck him up with plenty of pocket & subscription money & good clothes & orders on the shops & *anything* that cd hearten & help him—& attach him to the place & life

> there—but we *cd* do no more than we have done & it was not of *any* avail as things are.
> We hope after the Easter holydays [*sic*] he will go to a very good Tutor in Surrey.

Up to that critical point both she and Kenneth appear to have believed that they could bribe the boy into accepting a system which, quite patently, drove him nearly insane. Yet Elspeth wrote this letter in the firm belief that they had done all they possibly could to make Alastair happy. That they should have sacrified their own ambitions long before never seems to have occurred to her. Only physical collapse would force her to face the truth: Alastair must have had a really serious nervous breakdown.

How far Kenneth was influenced by her wishes over Alastair's education we have no means of telling. But he must have been either weak or blind; there is no other alternative. Q had warned him in the strongest possible terms; and any man of Grahame's intelligence must have seen the danger of plunging a nervous, taciturn, precocious, and physically handicapped boy into the rough-and-tumble of Rugby or Eton. Perhaps he wanted to get him away from Elspeth's smothering and eccentric influence: if so, he acted too late. 'I don't think he [Alastair] will care about the young human boy in the raw,' he prophesied before the Eton period, and added, 'Nor do I, for that matter.' It seems more likely that he was powerless to resist Elspeth's social demands for Alastair's career, and surrendered despite his own inner misgivings.

Q later blamed Elspeth bitterly for Alastair's sufferings: and it cannot be doubted that she tried to mould the boy into her own preconceived fantasy of what he ought to be. Till the age of ten she kept him in a world of sentimental fantasy; then, after an abrupt transition, she expected him to turn overnight into an athletic and social Apollo like Bevil Quiller-Couch. She had not the least notion of the havoc this kind of treament would wreak on a boy of Alastair's nervous temperament, and was puzzled and hurt when, in later adolescence, he drifted away from her emotionally.

This kind of fantasy-behaviour is most often rooted in a need for compensation: and we do not have to look far to find it in Elspeth's relationship with her son. The truth, I suspect, is that *au fond,* whether consciously or not, she was bitterly ashamed of Alastair; that she resented his squint, his semi-blindness, his acne, and his gaucheness; the fact that he was not particularly clever or good at games, that he had been born with a cataract and was distinctly odd in his behaviour. She stifled this resentment by over-lavish maternal attention, and by creating a mythical Alastair in whose actuality she firmly believed: brilliant, witty, accomplished, and, above all, *popular*. Over and over again she emphasizes how popular Alastair was: independent witnesses are considerably less enthusiastic. After Chalmers' book appeared the then Bishop of Oxford wrote, rather drily, to Elspeth, remarking that 'the account of Alastair is very different from my experience of him.' We may well believe it.

Meanwhile the war had come to Blewbury; seventy volunteered out of a total population of five hundred, among them the ex-sergeant of Marines who, with his wife, had been helping to run Boham's. 'For over six months,' Grahame wrote to Purves, 'we have rubbed along somehow with casual help from the village, rough and untrained, and though at last we have secured a couple, they only came two days ago; and meantime the garden of course had gone to pot, and the house was dirty and disordered.' (Kenneth and Elspeth themselves appear to have lacked domestic enthusiasm, for all their passion for the simple life.) Kenneth was on the Derby Committee, and, as Elspeth told her brother, 'we've also been extremely busy with our war work—making crutches and splits, leg & back rests for base & shop hospitals—in the shed generally used for repairing agricultural machines.'

On top of all this Grahame found himself (as an ex-Territorial) more actively concerned with military matters:

> The 'veterans' of Blewbury have started a Volunteer Defence Corps, and we drill in the evenings in a beautiful great framed thatched barn—like my own, only three times as big. The rats run in and out of the thatch along the rafters, and the barn cat, who ought to be attending to them, sits on wheatsacks and reviews us with great delight. He is having the time of his life, for he thinks that these drills are specially got up for him, to brighten the monotony of his dull evenings. The Corps have elected me their Commanding Officer—the cat concurring—because they said I was the most martial looking of the crowd—and there I agree with them; they were careful to add, however, that it wasn't for any other reason whatever, and that also I can fully understand.

Q was equally busy: he had been released from Cambridge for the term and was going round Cornwall on a recruiting drive ('with a visit now and then to fire off a lecture at the seat of learning'). It was all very new and strange and alien: yet Grahame, curiously, welcomed the change. To a correspondent in Washington he wrote: 'Yes, Latin is passing fast away, and many another thing with it; and a new world is being born, wherein they will tell other tales than those of tall Troy and Phaeacia. And one cannot grieve for the old, the new is all so wonderful.'

Despite his many other preoccupations, however, Grahame found time to complete a project which he had begun several years earlier—the *Cambridge Book of Poetry for Children.* The anthology was well under way in 1913: 'I have got my two little vols about three-quarters done', he told Graham Robertson on 4 December of that year, 'but am rather stuck for a little more matter, which I can't find to my liking, so I have been rather letting the thing slide; but I shall have to make a push and send the stuff in to Cambridge, somehow.' In June 1914 he was still rounding up material; on the 22nd John Masefield wrote to him: 'All the poems you mention are at your service, but I would prefer them to remain anonymous if you do not mind. ... [Grahame complied with these terms.] The boys will be lucky to be catered for by you.'

The 'two little vols' finally appeared early in 1916, and, on the whole, reviewers echoed Masefield's tribute. 'If Mr Grahame cannot compile a book of poetry for children,' the *Literary World* declared, then Lord Kitchener could not compile a book on Army organization!' However, it was an idiosyncratic collection which was criticized for containing poems which were too abstruse, American patriotic 'tosh', or which avoided death—an essential element of heroic poetry and common in childhood play.

Grahame may well have been oppressed in spirit by the thought of the fearful slaughter at that moment proceeding in France; but his distaste for death was more deeply rooted than that, went back further. He had never come to terms with any religious faith, in the end: and one characteristic of neo-pagans bred in the Yellow Decade, who depended on sensation of one sort or another for their well-being, was a progressively increasing distaste as they got older to face the fact of mortality. Grahame was no more immune from this weakness than any of his contemporaries. His ideals had rested on fragile and transient foundations: now everywhere the dream which had supported him was being attacked. He was cut off—in more than one sense—from the South. He had quarrelled with Roland over money matters in 1913, and now the brothers were not on speaking terms. He had long been estranged from Helen. His marriage was, at best, a compromise. Worst of all, his only child was physically malformed—perhaps the sport of hereditary disease—and desperately unhappy. He could no longer find the heart to write: the mainspring of his creative mind had failed. And day by day the hideous unromantic war ground on its muddy course. Where were the Hesperides now? 'Perhaps some day', he wrote wistfully to Cockerell, 'there will be Feasts again, and these present things will seem far away.'

In the summer of 1917 he and Elspeth took Alastair for a holiday at Blue Anchor in West Somerset—'no church, post, nor shops, in fact *nothing*'. There was, however, excellent swimming, which delighted Alastair: like many people handicapped for other sports, he took naturally to the water. Perhaps for the same reason he developed a passion for riding about this time, 'first getting lessons from a Trainer on the Downs & then at his Tutor's in Surrey. The Trainer told us', Elspeth characteristically adds 'that he "never saw anyone take so naturally to a horse".' Like his father—and with more obvious reason—Alastair clearly had a *penchant* for solitary pleasures.

At the same time, however, he joined the Volunteers, and, again, according to Elspeth, 'is only afraid that the war might end before he gets into the regular army'. But there was little doubt that he would be rejected for service through his grave defects of eyesight; and nothing more clearly shows Elspeth's capacity for self-delusion than her obvious fear that he might, in fact, see active service. 'Of course,' she wrote defensively to Courtauld that December, 'once a boy *is* overstrained or broken down he is of no use to himself or his country either.' There is no mention of his bad eye as an excuse. It was true, though, that Alastair had outgrown his strength—he already stood six foot two in his stockinged feet—and the Colonel of the OTC and Cadet Corps at Oxford had advised Kenneth that the boy should train for a commission with them. He would not, the Colonel said in explanation, be fit for A Class at the age of eighteen. For this reason it was arranged that he should go up to Christ Church earlier than had been intended, in the Lent Term of 1918, instead of having another term with his tutor. 'This is all unexpected to us,' Elspeth declared to her brother. It is difficult to see why until we remember the myth.

Alastair was no happier at Oxford than he had been at Eton: perhaps he found any kind of community life intolerable. Yet the University would not put the same kind of pressure on him; if he chose to remain solitary no one would stop him. It seems that his unhappiness had become endemic, and that his surroundings made little difference to him. Professor Sir Keith Feiling, who at the time was his tutor, recalls how he always seemed miserable during his time at Christ Church, sighing and groaning audibly. Apart from anything else his bad eyesight (which had apparently deteriorated) must have handicapped him considerably in his reading. He eventually took Mods (at the second attempt) by *viva voce* examination, and the Senior Examiner suggested that application be made for an amanuensis for future occasions, as was done in the case of blind candidates.

ALASTAIR GRAHAME
as an Oxford undergraduate.

Occasional well-meaning efforts were made to draw him out of his solitary gloom. Kenneth's agent, Curtis Brown, invited him up to London in 1918 for his daughter Beatrice's coming-out dance. Beatrice herself recalls how Elspeth sent him off with a little American flag as an identification-mark for those expecting him at the London terminus. She found him very reserved and sardonic, and still suffering badly from acne. He made no attempt to dance, but spent all the time talking 'interminable dullness' to her father. The expedition seems to have pleased Kenneth, however; when it was over he wrote to Curtis Brown:

> It was most awfully good of you to give the boy such a splendid time. He seems to have enjoyed every minute of it. Owing to the War he has been simply starved on the social side of him and this visit was just what he wanted and what was best for him. For he is a 'social animal' really. I dare say you discovered what a passion he has for abstract discussion and first principles as opposed to anything concrete. He would, for instance, sit up all night discussing the principles that went to the drawing up of the American Constitution, while being languidly indifferent to personal details concerning any President.

Was Grahame putting a brave social front on a hopeless case? It seems hard to believe. More probably he, no less than Elspeth, could not bring himself to face the bitter truth, and therefore managed to convince himself that the mythical Alastair represented his son's true condition. If this is so, he was to pay a bitter price for his unwillingness—or inability—to come to terms with reality.

The state of his mind in 1919 is curiously illuminated by a letter he wrote on 24 September to Professor G. T. Hill of London University, who had enquired (being a literal-minded man) how Mole's goldfish, and Mole End generally, had been looked after during his owner's prolonged absence. The letter is, obviously, a *jeu d'esprit*; but it is one that only a certain type of mind, adept at dodging unpleasant problems, could have thought up. After solving the question by producing a mythical 'charmouse', Grahame goes on:

> In support of his theory, I would ask you to observe that our author practises a sort of 'character economy' which has the appearance of being deliberate. The presence of certain characters may be indicated in or required by the story, but if the author has no immediate use for them, he simply ignores their existence. ... Toad Hall ... must have been simply crawling with idle servants eating their heads off. But the author doesn't happen to want them, so for him they simply don't exist. He doesn't say they are *not* there; he just leaves them alone.

It is clear that Grahame extended this principle to his dealings with life in general; indeed, his whole career, and everything he wrote, demonstrate his refusal to face unpalatable realities. At the first hint of trouble he took refuge in an ideal fantasy-world, and from this vantage-point satirized what he had rejected. The satire itself was tough, astringent, and very much to the point: but the satirist's personal position was fatally vulnerable. Sooner or later his account with the world of facts would have to be squared.

In February 1919 Bevil Quiller-Couch, after surviving four years in action, died of Spanish influenza within a month or two of returning home. It was a bitter blow to Q, and a dark presage of what was to come.

From the beginning of 1920 Alastair was working desperately for the Mods examination, and at the same time grappling with a personal religious crisis. He appears to have had little spiritual assurance from his father or his former tutor, A. W. Dall, to whom he had confessed his agnosticism.

We know very little about this side of Alastair's nature; but what evidence there is has a suggestive quality. Even as a young child he has been what his governess described as 'a bit of a mystic':

> On one of my early days with him [Miss Stott wrote in her memoir] he saw a picture of Our Lord in a Holland Street shop. Mouse pointed it out to me. 'That is my Friend,' he said, 'the Carpenter. When I was ill [during his attack of peritonitis in 1904] He came to see me and sometimes I go and talk to Him.' On another day he said to me, 'Death is promotion.'

We cannot rule out the possibility of Alastair's having had some kind of genuine mystical experience: and that would have made his later agnosticism all the harder to bear.

Alastair got through Mods on 19 March 1920: on Palm Sunday, a friend of his wrote: 'I hope you are enjoying a holiday, with the consciousness that the bogey of Pass Mods has been settled with for ever. Of course I was not surprised at the news, for we were both determined that nothing else should happen, were it only for the Toad's sake! But now you have satisfied yourself that "will" means "can" you will go on to success in the subject of your choice.' Elspeth's attitude to this examination can be gauged from a letter she wrote at this time to a young acquaintance of Kenneth's still at school: 'Now your foot *is* on the ladder do not take it off again but mount it steadily rung by rung. ... Your place in form should be just as zealously guarded and as keenly contested as any goal at footer. ... There is no doubt if you can forge-ahead sufficiently to do all you can ... *while* at school it gives you far more time to devote to getting an Honours Degree the only aim of the true Scholar. ...' It is not hard to imagine the effect of such constant exhortations on a nervous, depressed, and purblind boy.

By 4 May it seems as though Kenneth had made an attempt of a sort to help Alastair's religious difficulties: on that date a clerical friend of the family wrote to the boy:

> By your parents' desire, I am sending you 'Cruden's Concordance' which I hope you will find useful. I trust you have settled down comfortably in your new rooms and find everything as you wish. I am wondering what you have decided to go in for. Whatever it is, I wish you all success. In any case, you will have to work jolly hard. ... As in a way you are making a new start at Oxford, I hope you are arranging your life there on practical lines. You have much to do and time is short.

Time, indeed, was shorter than this well-meaning correspondent could have foreseen.

On the night of Friday, 7 May 1920, Alastair Grahame dined in Hall at Christ Church, and at the end of the meal asked for a glass of port—'which', a fellow-undergraduate afterwards testified, 'I had not known him do before'. After Hall—it could not yet have been dark—he went out for a solitary walk across Port Meadow, where his father as a boy had played cricket for St Edward's. This was the last time he was seen alive. Early in the morning some railway gangers found his body on the line at Port Meadow, lying across the rails, at some little distance from the level crossing. He had clearly been killed by a train; and in his pockets was a large number of religious tracts.

The inquest was held on Thursday 13 May and the Coroner's jury contained among its members several Christ Church dons. The Dean, Dr T. B. Strong, testified that Alastair was 'a very quiet and reserved man, and I never got to know him well.' The boy's family relations were described as excellent, and he had, it was stated, no financial difficulties. His blindness in one eye was confirmed, and the jury quickly reached a verdict of Accidental Death. It was assumed that he had crossed the tracks with his blind eye towards an oncoming train, and perhaps abstracted in a brown study; and had thus been struck down and killed.

Unhappily, there is considerable evidence which suggests that another and grimmer verdict—though it might have served no useful purpose—would have come nearer to the truth. Many people, including Q, suspected that Alastair had committed suicide, although Q went out of his way in his *Oxford Magazine* obituary notice to kill the rumour, which had already come to Grahame's notice. Q was chivalrously determined to spare his old friend the useless agony of mind which blunt honesty would have brought about. Alastair was dead, whatever the verdict; it was the living who needed comfort.

We do not have to rely on Alastair's personal or family history to support the case of suicide, though they corroborate it strongly; nor on the opinions of contemporary friends. We need, in fact, look very little further than the inquest itself. The body was found, not at the level-crossing, but some way further down. It was lying across the rails. Even taking Alastair's blind eye into account, are we to assume that he was also deaf? And if for some reason he had chosen to cross the lines away from the normal point, would he not have taken extra precautions? We cannot be sure at what time the accident occurred: but even in the dark a steam-driven locomotive is hard to miss.

But the most conclusive piece of evidence is that provided by the medical officer, Dr W. D. Sturrock, who examined the body:

> The cause of death was decapitation, and that was compatible with being run over by a train. The right arm was fractured below the shoulder, the left leg four inches above the ankle, and all the toes of the right foot. There were also numerous bruises on the body.
>
> *The Coroner:* Are these injuries compatible with being knocked down by a train and then run over?—I could not answer the first part of the question as to being knocked down, but certainly they are compatible with being run over.

Nothing could be clearer or less ambiguous. The nature of the injuries makes it almost certain that Alastair lay down across the track, in a slightly diagonal position, his neck and one shoulder resting on one rail, his right foot and left leg on the other. It is impossible to conceive any other way in which those particular injuries could have been inflicted. The 'numerous bruises' would be due to abrasure by projecting parts of the engine and train as they passed over him. No intelligent person who 'read the evidence carefully'—least of all Q—could have reached any other conclusion: and whether Grahame himself, in his heart of hearts, ever believed the alternative verdict seems extremely improbable.

There remains the question of motive: and here we have ample choice. Alastair's visual deficiency, coupled with his nervous disabilities, would alone have provided a sufficient cause. He was intensely shy, and cut off from much of the social gregariousness of his class and age. He felt himself, there can be little doubt, marked, peculiar, different, a misfit, and an outcast. His extraordinary upbringing left him cruelly defenceless when he was suddenly exposed to a harsh, unfriendly world that had no patience with oddness or precocity. The myth that Elspeth wove round him—and expected him to live up to—must have strained him almost beyond belief: apart from anything else, he was forced to fight against a terrible physical handicap in struggling to attain even an average academic standard. Lastly, there was the religious crisis, the loss of faith, which he experienced shortly before his death: this may have deepened his depression to the point where he totally despaired of the future. All things considered, it is a miracle that he survived as long as he did: Elspeth was right when she described him as 'a real Stoic, who never would complain, or plead his own cause in any way'. He suffered silently; there was no one to whom he could turn.

The funeral took place in Oxford, from Keith Feiling's house in Holywell, and Kenneth scattered lilies of the valley over his son's coffin. Perhaps, as he made that last gesture, he remembered with bitter irony those other obsequies he had celebrated so many years before: 'Achievement ever includes defeat: at best I should only have found myself where I am now—with a narrowing strip of sun and sward between me and the vast inevitable pit agape for us each and all. And the grapes are sour; and the hopes are dead; and the funeral is nearing its end.'

XIV

THE REEDS BY THE RIVER

1920–32

In August 1920, three months after Alastair's death, the Purves brothers returned for yet another visit to England; and Kenneth, despite his bereavement, undertook to show them round Oxford. He booked them rooms, came up from Blewbury for four or five days, and devoted the entire time to their enlightenment and entertainment. Every college and many other of the University buildings were explored in turn. 'I am not aware', Austin Purves writes, 'that Grahame liked or knew anything about music but he made it possible for us to have very special seating at organ recitals in Christ Church College. Some of us drew and painted and Grahame suggested various spots such as Iffley where we could sketch some truly romantic English things.'

Why did Grahame insist on discharging the duties of a cicerone at such a time? John C. Purves recalls that 'Grahame was too reserved, and his suffering must have been intense.' He suggests, very convincingly, just what it was that drove him to swallow his private grief and overcome his natural urge for solitude. 'We boys had never seen Mouse,' he explains, 'but Grahame believed that it was Mouse's earnest wish to show Oxford to us. Back of this was Grahame's deep love for a University and town of which he had never been a part as a student and which he attended vicariously through his son.'

This last sentence hints at a good deal more than its immediate context. Though neither of them would ever have admitted it, even to themselves, Alastair's death (once the initial shock was over, and a satisfactory 'accidental' cause established) must have lifted a great weight off his parents' shoulders. This—and the coroner's verdict—stifled any lingering sense of personal responsibility. Alastair's end was a tragic sport of Fate, fit theme for a Hardy novel. Furthermore, they had come more and more to live their lives, vicariously, as Mr. Purves says, through Alastair. In Alastair, Grahame at last entered the long-denied gates of Oxford; in Alastair Elspeth re-created her long-abandoned myth of high society. Their guilt and unhappiness was all the greater because their son would not, could not, play the part they had chosen for him. Now there was no longer any awkward living reality to confront the myth they had built up in their imagination. Alastair himself was forgotten: only his legendary *alter ego* remained, growing steadily more perfect and brilliant as the years went by. Unhappiness was smoothed away in blessed oblivion and once again Kenneth and Elspeth could exist as themselves, and not merely through their child. They said nothing; but their actions were eloquent.

The first thing they did after the Oxford episode was to sell a large number of their personal effects from Boham's—Dutch and Sheraton cupboards, French mirrors, sets of Wedgwood china, all their Bohemian glass-ware, a Weber player-piano, various dolls' services, their Welsh dresser 'with Nelson's head and motto on the handles', and all Kenneth's 'Sailor's Farewell' glass rolling-pins. They were not short of money; it was as though they were consciously abandoning everything that reminded them of their old life. Most significant of all, Elspeth disposed of all Alastair's clothes and possessions at a Blewbury jumble-sale: an action which, not surprisingly, disconcerted her neighbours, but only serves to confirm one's suspicions as to her state of mind at the time.

A month later Boham's was let for eighteen months to a Mr Davies. On Thursday, 28 October, Kenneth and Elspeth moved to London; and two days later they embarked on the ss *Orvieto* (with a personal introduction to the captain) and sailed from England. Their destination—at long last, and in a sense too late—was Kenneth's beloved Italy. In some curious way Alastair's death seemed to have reopened this door also. Kenneth and Elspeth were drawn closer by their loss—and the unconscious relief it brought them—than ever before in their marriage; and, for the first time perhaps, Kenneth was glad of companionship. He was never to travel alone again. In any case he was now over sixty; and though Ulysses at that age still nursed an incurable Hesperidean urge, Grahame was made of gentler stuff. He had returned to his Golden City; but now—supreme irony—it was as an ordinary cultured tourist, with the tourist's main preoccupations: architecture and food.

Of the two, architecture emphatically occupied the second place. It was the local cuisine that drew him irresistably: cheeses, *mortadella* sausage, roast chicken or *porchetta,* fresh anchovies, and every other Italian delicacy, together with their accompanying wines. It was the major consolation he had left; and the cathedrals, as he said, knew how to wait. The Grahames spent most of 1921 in Rome, and during that time Kenneth got to know every restaurant and *trattoria* the city contained. He also developed an inordinate passion for Italian ice-cream, which Elspeth (believing it was bad for his health) tried in vain to curb.

But his explorations had their more serious and cultural side. He became an expert on Roman topography, and learnt all he could from the English and American archaeologists resident in the city. Water had always had a dreamy hypnotic effect on him; and now he would sit for long hours by any of the innumerable fountains which abound in Rome, lulled by its quiet music.

Just as he had delighted, a year before, in showing off Oxford, so now he yearned to guide willing guests round this other city of his dreams. About Easter Grahame found accommodation in Rome for Dale and Edmund Purves and guided them around the city. Edmund Purves recalled that 'it was a wonderful experience. Mr Grahame seemed to know every nook and cranny.' He also—when Elspeth was

THE CAPITOL, ROME.
Kenneth Grahame often visited Rome and became an expert on its topography.

absent from these expeditions—made a habit of refreshing himself liberally and frequently in taverns along the route: a practice in which the Purves boys, who had been strictly brought up, did not join him.

Meanwhile an indignant letter had arrived from the Grahames' tenant, Mr Davies, complaining—not altogether surprisingly—that 'a good deal of litter and disorder' had been left behind. There were also those mouse-nests in the larder. Grahame replied denying the charges with the kind of self-explanatory heat which is normally engendered by embarrassment. Every farmhouse had mice, he declared; and then, changing his tack, added: 'Personally I have not myself seen a mouse inside Boham's for years, though, I am perfectly well aware that every time Mr Lay thrashes out a rick, some non-paying guests of this sort seek admission to the house, and my cat's face begins to wear a strained and haggard appearance suggestive of the need for a rest-cure. But nothing more is seen of the mice!' With this crumb of comfort poor Mr Davies had to be content.

During the same year there was another interesting sign of Grahame's 'release': he began to write again. The American Ambassador, Mr R. U. Johnson, asked him in February for a five-minute tribute to Keats, to celebrate the centenary of the poet's death on the 24th of that month. Grahame, surprisingly, agreed. The speech has not been preserved, but in it he remarked 'how easily John Keats might have heard his nightingales on the rural heights and twilit copses of the hamlet that, in those days, his native Hampstead remained.' The occasion was a striking success; and Sir Rennell Rodd, the British Ambassador, who was also present, promptly invited Grahame to lecture to the Keats-Shelley Association.

Once again Grahame accepted; and the talk he gave, entitled 'Ideals', was later reprinted in the *Fortnightly Review*. It forms an extended and revealing apologia for his main *credo*: and I have quoted from it extensively during the course of this book. It led up to a discussion of 'the dream-city, the City Celestial or the New Jerusalem'; and its climax may appropriately be reproduced at this point:

> What, then, is the conclusion of the whole matter? Is it not that we are all idealists, whether we would or no? And that we are all idealists, chiefly by virtue of our waking dreams, those very imaginings which we are so ashamed of, and so reluctant to speak about, which we sternly discourage in others, but which all the same we secretly cherish to the very end? For in these dreams we are always better than ourselves, and the world is always better than it is, and surely it is by seeing things as better than they are that one arrives at making them better.

It is the despairing claim of one of the last romantics, in a post-war age which laughed at such high ideals: and its concluding words supply an ironic gloss on the tragedy of the speaker's own life. He had indeed seen things as better than they were; but his optimistic self-delusion had brought only calamity.

In August the Grahames made a visit to Cortina d' Ampezzo in the Italian Dolomites, where Kenneth once again resumed his habit of long solitary walks in the mountains. Another holiday-maker there recalls that 'he was a remarkable-looking man, striding across hill and dale, his Inverness cape swirling around him, his hair all swept up by the wind. On and on he went, solitary, absorbed in his own thoughts, until he vanished in the distance. I think he was deeply grieved over the loss of his son and I hesitated to intrude on his self-imposed isolation.'

That autumn Curtis Brown wrote to him suggesting excerpts or an abridgment of *The Wind in the Willows* for use in schools: this proposal Grahame turned down without hesitation. 'I can't abridge satisfactorily without loss of quality,' he told his agent, 'and that's the long and short of it. I know that School Committees will only have books on their own terms, more or less, but that's not my fault.' But he raised no such objections when Q demanded two long extracts (including a large part of 'Wayfarers All') for the *Oxford Book of English Prose.* This settled, he and Elspeth left Rome and made their leisurely way north to Rapallo, which they reached in February 1922. They spent the spring on Lake Garda, and returned for a short visit to England in June. Mr Davies' tenancy had expired, and on 1 September Grahame wrote to A. A. Milne offering to let Boham's to him as soon as they returned to the Continent. The deal seems to have fallen through: the Milnes were looking for a permanent house.

Kenneth and Elspeth got back to Italy in time to witness Mussolini's march on Rome. As Elspeth later wrote to her brother 'we used to hear the Fascists cracking the skulls of the Socialists at street corners, with cannons at both ends of the bridges and snipers shooting over the high wall surrounding the courtyard of the GPO.' This did not appear to disturb Kenneth; he had found a new restaurant run by an exiled Russian princess, who wore diamond earrings while cooking omelettes. When the meal was served by an Archduke, the danger of being shot at by revolutionaries when you stepped out into the street seemed unimportant by comparison. After Christmas they migrated to Capri, where they stayed in the Pensione Faraglioni. Here Kenneth had another attack of bronchitis; but this did not prevent him gossiping 'with old women porters who would "remember back", to please the Englishman, to the very times of Tiberius'. The Grahames remained in Italy until the spring of 1924 when they returned to England.

Grahame had succeeded in selling Boham's: the house and the village had disagreeable memories for them, and they were probably anxious to move somewhere where the details of their private tragedy were not so intimately known. Blewbury, after all, had been Alastair's home for ten years. And Kenneth was beginning to yearn for a Thames-side home once more: the River claimed him, as it had always done. Now he made his last home at Pangbourne, in a pleasant house called Church Cottage; it had the old village lock-up for a tool-shed, a big ship's bell at the front door, and a garden that ended in an enchanting high-banked grass amphitheatre. Kenneth once said (with his perennial passion for circuses) that 'there ought to be Shetland ponies galloping round, ridden by monkeys.'

The new arrivals struck the inhabitants of Pangbourne as distinctly odd. Kenneth they found withdrawn but amiable: a tall, white-haired figure in black-and-white check scarf and consciously countrified red-brick Harris tweeds, who sat alone in his garden for hours on end and refused to have either servants or telephone permanently installed in the house. Elspeth was another matter. By now she was a pallid, haggard ghost, with an aureole of fuzzy grey hair and clothes that would have disgraced a jumble-sale. Her meanness, especially over food, was proverbial. The village would often be treated to the spectacle of Mr and Mrs Grahame taking lunch on the porch out of a paper bag; and Elspeth was quite

ELSPETH GRAHAME IN 1930.
By this time she had become a pallid, haggard ghost whose meanness was proverbial.

capable of haggling like a fish-wife over two ounces of ham in the local butcher's—much to Kenneth's embarrassment.

Despite all this she had lost none of her lady-of-the-manor forthrightness: she stumped round Pangbourne, a dragon anything but reluctant, and her bemused neighbours found themselves doing her endless favours without knowing quiet how they had been talked into it. As a last touch of eccentricity, it was quickly noticed that the Grahames might stint themselves on food (though Kenneth occasionally treated himself to a complicated curry of his own making) but that their consumption of champagne and port was remarkable.

Yet Elspeth, in her own curious way, could still be charming and considerate when she chose. Her fund of anecdotes about the great literary figures of her youth was fascinating and inexhaustible. Her interest in people (as Kenneth had remarked years before) remained intense: and they did not need to be notabilities. She cultivated friendships with care; her memory for domestic minutiae was phenomenal; and till her sight failed she was an indefatigable letter-writer. She could even, on occasions, be a good listener. In her old age she seems infinitely pathetic: a lonely, disappointed woman, still clinging to the tatters of her past, still playing the *grande dame* to an indifferent audience.

Grahame was now virtually a recluse. 'I very rarely go up to town nowadays,' he wrote to A. J. A. Symons in July 1925. However, he was lured out on occasion: sometimes to make a Prize Day speech at St Edward's, sometimes to address the Pangbourne Literary, Dramatic and Musical Guild. Mr Malcolm Elwin recalls him in the train to Paddington, talking City shop with an old friend, the late Sir Harold Hartley, 'sitting in his corner seat with his back to the engine, elegant in pepper-and-salt trousers, short black coat, and neat cuffs, a handsome and dignified figure of an elderly city man'. Mr Elwin also met him and Elspeth twice at the Hartley's house, and gives this telling portrait of them together:

> He was a biggish, broad-shouldered man, inclined to portliness as all of his generation over sixty tended to be, grey of hair and grey of face, his shoulders bent so that he stooped slightly, his general appearance giving the immediate impression that he suffered from ill-health. I suspect that he also suffered from the wearing personality of his wife, ... [who] talked stridently and interminably, laying down the law about her preferences in literature and art, and never taking much heed of what anybody else had to say. I gathered that Mr Grahame had long since learned that it was a waste of time and energy to attempt to express any opinion in his wife's company.

Nevertheless, Grahame continued to write a little. In 1925 he produced his most substantial piece since *The Wind in the Willows*: a long and vigorous Introduction to 'Lord' George Sanger's memoirs, *Seventy Years a Showman*. This is full of rich reminiscence of circus-life and the magic spell of caravans: nostalgic, witty, and wistful. On the other hand he reveals in it a new avenue of escape-fantasy he has recently discovered—the cinema. 'We like it,' he wrote (and here he had the vast majority of the population on his side), 'because it is not exactly the sort of life we daily lead; and as we stroll homeward across the starlit common towards our farmhouse, vicarage, or simple thatched cottage, we think "I wish—oh, *how* I wish—I had married an Indian half-breed".' Perhaps that was no more than the truth.

And year after year the obsessional, restless travelling went on. It was as though Kenneth still nursed the dwindling hope of somewhere, some day, finding his New Jerusalem. *An easy matter,* he had written, long ago; but now the irony had a bitter flavour. Venice, Perugia, Genoa, Taormina; the Northern Lakes and the Dolomites, he saw them all. They never returned to any place more than once, with the exception of Rome, Florence, and Venice. They looked on at vintage festivals (like Rat in the harvest-field), struggled across the lava-fields of Etna, and in Palermo attended the re-trial of a notorious brigand who was appealing against a sentence of a hundred years' imprisonment. (The charges included thirteen proven murders.)

In 1926, Curtis Brown, probably encouraged by these signs of renewed literary activity, wrote to him suggesting that he might care to embark on his autobiography. Grahame replied, on 29 April: 'My chief trouble is that I have kept no diaries or memoranda at all (this was not true, though he may have destroyed his diary himself) and since the War my memory seems to have gone all to pot. I doubt much if I could ever get as much as a book together; but I will, as I said, consider if I can get out an article or two on a line of my own, which should be reminiscent in character.' He did, in fact, start making notes about his schooldays, and these have survived; out of them he produced the posthumously published piece, 'Oxford through a Boy's Eyes', and on a combination of the two I have largely based my own account of this period of his life. But that Grahame could be expected to write a full autobiography with any real degree of honesty was clearly out of the question. His memory may well have failed conveniently; at all events, two years went by without his making any attempt to provide Curtis Brown with what he wanted.

In November 1928 Curtis Brown tried again, tempting Grahame with the proposition of a 4-5000 word article on his experiences at the Bank of England. 'Of course,' he added, 'there is deep craft and guile in this scheme, for I figured it out that if you were to do the article you would find it so interesting that you could be tempted to do another later on, and then another, until the first you knew there would be most of that volume of Memoirs I have been yearning for.' But Grahame was not to be drawn. 'Many thanks for your would-be provocative letter,' he replied on the 11th. 'But Nothin Doin' about B. of E. Much too dull a subject.' Dull? Or unpleasant? It was 1931 before Grahame capitulated, and promised to try and rough out his reminiscences; but by then it was too late.

Grahame was not, however, so out of touch and unwordly that he failed to keep a very sharp eye on his business affairs. He remained the Scots businessman to the end, especially where royalties were concerned. He queried Curtis Brown's commission on his foreign rights and in reply to Curtis Brown's justification of his charges he sent the following letter on 21 January 1929. The letter is highly entertaining, but its waggishness conceals a shrewd insistence on his financial dues:

My dear C.B. Before I received your kind letter of the 18th, I had frankly suspected—& no doubt you suspected that I had suspected—that the account that had so shocked me had been a piece of quite laudable if mistaken departmental over-zeal, which had somehow escaped the eye of the Capitoline Jove. But when I read your classic periods, so firm yet so tender, I wilted, I sagged, I crumpled. I shed bitter tears. I finally collapsed on the floor, a sodden heap of misery. As I lay there, however, I found myself murmuring something, but very soft and low, so that it should not reach your ears. Something like this: 'Alas, yes, how true it is, and how well I knew it, that there are publishers who claim 50% on Foreign rights, and others who ask 100, and many who will demand 150, & then ask for a little bit more for "all their trouble";

but—

but—

(here I became almost inaudible)

since when—(I was now only whispering)—

since when have——Ltd. based their practice on the tenents of Messrs. B-r-bb-s & Co.?'.

Then I shed a few more tears.

Then I rose to my feet & washed and had some light refreshment—the first for days.

So now that is all over, & I will try and be good, and I will try and not do it any more. And I am ever so glad that you couldn't have heard a word of those awful sentiments I murmured to myself as I lay crying on the floor. But...

(No, I won't begin again. I have sworn it.) All the same...

No; the end of the page is in sight, and I am not going to get on to a new one. At least I *will* turn over a new leaf, of course, for I have said it already. But not a new leaf of this letter.

~~BECAUSE IF I DID~~—O this unruly typewriter! It all comes of using a Blick. Common little beasts, Blicks. I ought to get something high-class and toney and expensive. ~~'But how can you if'~~ ... There he goes again. He must be stopped.

Yours finally and very truly,

KENNETH GRAHAME

In October 1929 Roland died. He and Kenneth had not been in communication since their bitter quarrel seventeen years before; and it was Helen, now retired to a house at the Lizard, who sent Kenneth and Elspeth details of his funeral, which of course they had not attended. Another link was snapped; the children had come a long, bitter, disillusioning journey from that sunlit orchard in Cookham Dene. *Et in Arcadia ego*: Death too, had come to Arcadia, indifferent to the decree of banishment that Kenneth had pronounced over him. The shadows were lengthening over the lawn, and soon it would be night.

E. H. Shepard, who (with some misgivings) had agreed to illustrate a new edition of *The Wind in the Willows*, visited Grahame at Church Cottage in 1930, and recorded the following details of his interview:

Not sure about this new illustrator of his book, he listened patiently while I told him what I hoped to do. Then he said 'I love these little people, be kind to them'. Just that; but sitting forward in his chair, resting upon the arms, his fine handsome head turned aside, looking like some ancient Viking, warming, he told me of the river near by, of the meadows where Mole broke ground that spring morning, of the banks where Rat had his house, of the pools where Otter hid, and of Wild Wood way up on the hill above the river. ... He would like, he said, to go with me to show me the river bank that he knew so well, '... but now I cannot walk so far and you must find your way alone'.

THE WIND IN THE WILLOWS.
E. H. Shepard felt that *The Wind in the Willows* was one of those books which should not be illustrated and 'perhaps if it had not already been done, I should not have given way to the desire to do it myself'. But he met Kenneth Grahame and showed him his drawings. Though critical, Grahame seemed pleased and, chuckling, said 'I'm glad you've made them real.'

He was delighted (as countless children and adults have been) by the drawings Mr Shepard produced; but it is curious to note that by now the scene of *The Wind in the Willows* had been transferred in his mind to the country and riverside surrounding his new home. So potent, in fact, have the Shepard illustrations been that many people remain convinced to this day not only that Rat and Mole lived near Pangbourne, but that *The Wind in the Willows* was actually written there.

Then, in 1930, came *Toad of Toad Hall,* which introduced the River-Bankers to a yet wider audience. Curtis Brown had for some years unsuccessfully tried to interest theatrical managers in *The Wind in the Willows*; but they had invariably turned it down on the grounds that it was 'too whimsical, and the characters quite impossible to represent in believable costumes'. It is easy to see their point, which has considerable force; but Grahame was bitterly disappointed. Then it was suggested to A. A. Milne that he might like to try his hand at an adaptation. Milne and Grahame had never met, though they had corresponded sporadically ever since Milne had sent the author of *The Wind in the Willows* a congratulatory letter on the book in February 1918. Milne, delighted, agreed: 'I think it should be a children's play', he wrote, 'with a little incidental music'. He set about it at once, and Harold Fraser Simson composed a delightful score.

LYRIC THEATRE
SHAFTESBURY AVENUE, W.1.

Licensee: A. C. BELSEY
Lessee and Manager: GILBERT MILLER

BASIL FOSTER and TOM MILLER beg to announce that on Wednesday, December 17th at 8.0 p.m., they will present

TOAD OF TOAD HALL
by
A. A. MILNE
From KENNETH GRAHAME'S
THE WIND IN THE WILLOWS

Music by H. FRASER-SIMSON

Should you desire to be present on this occasion I shall be obliged if you will let me have your application for seats for this or subsequent performances as soon as possible.

Yours faithfully,
Edgar Eyles.

LYRIC THEA
Licensee—A. C. Belsey. Lessee and Ma
Shaftesbury Avenue, London,

TWICE DAILY: Matinees 2.30,

BASIL FOSTER and TOM M
present

TOAD OF TOAD H

by
A. A. MILNE
From Kenneth Grahame's book "The Wind in the Willows
Music by
H. FRASER-SIMSON.

Characters in the order of their appearance:

Marigold	Wendy Toy
Nurse	Mona Jenkins
Mole	Richard Goolden
Water Rat	Ivor Barnard
Mr. Badger	Eric Stanley
Toad	Frederick Burtwell
Alfred	Peter Mather
The Back Legs of Alfred	Halliday Mason
Chief Ferret	Alfred Fairhurst
Chief Weasel	Ronald Alpe
Chief Stoat	William McGuigan
First Field-Mouse	Gordon Tucker
Second Field-Mouse	Robert Sinclair
Policeman	Alban Blakelock
Gaoler	Alfred Fairhurst
Usher	Humphrey Morton
Judge	Alfred Clark
Turkey	Gordon Tucker
Duck	Robert Sinclair
Phoebe	Joan Harker
Washerwoman	Dorothy Fane
The White Rabbit	Marian Wilson
Mama Rabbit	Phyllis Coulthard
Lucy Rabbit	Daphne Allen
Harold Rabbitt	Marcus Haig

Jim Soloman
rances Waring
ylvia Gartside
Jill Clayton

by the Willows

The River Bank

wo Minutes only between Acts 1 and 2

ACT II.

	The Wild Wood
	Mr. Badger's House
3.	The Same (Some weeks later)

ACT III.

SCENE 1.	The Court House
SCENE 2.	The Dungeon
SCENE 3.	The Canal Bank

ACT IV.

SCENE 1.	Rats House by the River
SCENE 2.	The Underground Passage
SCENE 3.	The Banqueting-room at Toad Hall
EPILOGUE	The Wind in the Willows

The ORCHESTRA under the direction of I. A. de ORELLANA

Scenery and Dresses designed by
Miss MURIEL STERLING (by permission of Sir Barry Jackson)

The Children are Pupils of Miss EUPHAN MACLAREN.

TOAD OF TOAD HALL.
The first performance of A. A. Milne's adaptation of *The Wind in the Willows* was announced in 1930. Richard Goolden, who has since become synonymous with Mole, played in that first performance.

Now a good deal of criticism was levelled at Milne, both at the time and later, complaining that he had reduced his original to mere sentimental cosiness. *Punch* declared that he 'perhaps has had his eye too exclusively fixed upon the children and averted from the less important grown-ups. ... Mr Milne has jettisoned, perhaps perforce or for policy's sake, all that makes the enchantment of *The Wind in the Willows* for the mature mind.' This is perfectly true; and the result has been that many who come to Grahame's masterpiece by way of *Toad of Toad Hall* were considerably discouraged. Nevertheless, Milne knew exactly what he was about: and if he put his own sentimental stamp on the adaptation, he did it for perfectly intelligible motives.

He saw, more clearly, than most people, the difficulty of pinning down these fluid, shifting characters for a stage presentation. 'Once we put Mole and his friends on the boards,' he wrote in his preface, 'we have to be definite about them. What do they look like?' It was an impossible question to answer. 'Of course,' Milne admitted, 'I have left out all the best parts of the book; and for that, if he has any knowledge of the theatre, Mr Grahame will thank me. With a Rat and a Mole from the Green Room Club, a Baby Otter from Conti, a Pan from Clarkson's and a wind (off) whispering in the reeds of Harker, we are not going to add any fresh thrill to the thrill which the loveliness of "The Piper at the Gates of Dawn" has already given its readers.' One can only, while agreeing with every word of this, wish that Milne's final version had not been quite so intolerably mawkish: it is hard to shake off its influence when one turns back to the book.

The end was now very near. Dr Bourdillon, Grahame's medical adviser, cut down both his diet and his long country walks: by the beginning of 1932 he was suffering from high blood pressure, advanced arteriosclerosis, and fatty degeneration of the heart. The walks he could forego; good food was harder. '*Do* let me have something to eat, Bourdillon!' was his constant cry at every visit, and he still slipped out unrepentantly (eluding Elspeth) to eat ice-creams whenever he could get them. Despite ill-health, he still held himself erect and spoke firmly and clearly, like a man half his age: and on 25 June he went up to London for the Lewis Carroll centenary at Bumpus's bookshop. He still wrote occasional letters in that square, careful handwriting that hardly changed throughout his life.

On Tuesday 5 July 1932 there was no sign of trouble. He did *The Times* crossword in the morning, and complained that it did not last long enough; he spent most of the afternoon by the river. At dinner he performed his traditional ritual of mixing the salad. Constance Smedley described this with some percipience in a letter to Elspeth: 'Beneath the delight in the earth and the fruits thereof, was a great reverence. When he dressed a salad, the oil meant the olive-trees of Italy and France; the herbs—chervil from the sun-baked sand, tarragon from watered soil—were creatures of the elements; the lettuce was the green leaf, wet with dew and strong with rain and sun—the occasion a lovely intimate ceremony.' Now the ceremony, with all its associative meanings, was performed for the last time: an unconscious valediction to the things which Kenneth had loved so well. When dinner was over he and Elspeth went for a short stroll, and soon afterwards he retired to bed with Walter Scott's *The Talisman.*

About one in the morning Elspeth heard a noise from his room. She went in immediately to find the light still on and the book lying on the floor. Kenneth was in a deep coma. He had had a cerebral haemorrhage, and died, without regaining consciousness, shortly before 6 am.

The funeral took place on Saturday 9 July 1932, at the church of St James the Less, Pangbourne: and among the other mourners was Annie Grahame. Curtis Brown's secretary, Miss Barnes, has left this description of the scene:

> The church was a marvellous sight—a blaze of glorious colour and sunshine—with masses and masses of flowers, delphiniums and roses (and willows gathered from the river that very morning) and all the things that grow in a cottage garden. And perhaps the most touching thing of all were the flowers sent by children from all over the country, with cards attached in a childish scrawl, saying how much they loved him. The grave was lined with thousands of sweet peas and the scent was unforgettable.

Later Kenneth's body was transferred to a permanent resting-place in Holywell Churchyard, in his beloved Oxford: he had come home at last. Over the grave was carved an inscription composed by Anthony Hope: 'To the beautiful memory of Kenneth Grahame, husband of Elspeth and father of Alastair, who passed the River on the 6 July 1932, leaving childhood and literature through him the more blest for all time.' It would be hard to think of a more just epitaph.

Critics of literature have paid scant attention to the author of *The Wind in the Willows*: he has not even been considered worthy of a place in the *Cambridge Bibliography*. A minor writer? Perhaps. Yet the world he created will be remembered and cherished in years to come by countless readers ignorant of the sources from which it was born. The vision of *The Wind in the Willows* will entrance thousands of children and adults in the future as it has done in the past: how many of them will guess the personal tragedy it represents? And that, after all, is as it should be. A myth has no history; a classic—and by any criterion *The Wind in the Willows* deserves that honourable title—can stand alone. Posterity may well judge that, in the end, Kenneth Grahame found his Golden City without knowing it.

BIBLIOGRAPHY

This bibliography of Kenneth Grahame's writings is based, with minor modifications and additions, on the bibliography published by Mr Roger Lancelyn Green in *The Times Literary Supplement,* 9 June 1945, and I am deeply indebted to him for permission to use it here. Following his example I have printed the items in chronological order, and placed an asterisk against those originally published anonymously. A citation in brackets after an item indicates where the item was subsequently published in book form. (PP = *Pagan Papers,* GA = *The Golden Age,* DD = *Dream Days*).

1. 'The Good and Bad Effects of Rivalry', *St Edward's School Chronicle,* No. 5, Oct. 1873.
2. *'By a Northern Furrow', *St James's Gazette,* 26 Dec. 1888.
3. *'A Bohemian in Exile', *St James's Gazette,* 27 Sept. 1890 (PP).
4. *'Of Smoking', *Scots Observer,* 18 Oct. 1890 (PP).
5. *'A Parable (Overheard and Communicated by our own Cat)': *St James's Gazette,* 19 Nov. 1890.
6. *'Loafing', *National Observer,* 24 Jan. 1891 (PP).
7. *'The Romance of the Road', *National Observer*, 14 Feb. 1891 (PP).
8. *'Non Libri Sed Liberi', *National Observer*, 28 Feb. 1891 (PP).
9. *'Cheap Knowledge', *National Observer*, 11 April 1891 (PP).
10. *'The Rural Pan', *National Observer*, 25 April 1891 (PP).
11. 'As You Like It' (poem), *National Observer*, 30 May 1891.
12. *'The Romance of the Rail', *National Observer,* 8 Aug. 1891 (PP).
13. *'The White Poppy', *National Observer,* 5 Sept. 1891 (PP).
14. *'The Olympians', *National Observer,* 19 Sept. 1891 (PP; GA).
15. 'Quis Desiderio?' (poem), *National Observer*, 19 Sept. 1891.
16. *'Justifiable Homicide', *National Observer*, 10 Oct. 1891 (PP).
17. *'The Fairy Wicket', *National Observer*, 20 Feb. 1892 (PP).
18. 'Love's Reveille' (poem), *National Observer*, 27 Feb. 1892.
19. *'Marginalia', *National Observer*, 26 March 1892 (PP).
20. *'The Eternal Whither', *National Observer*, 9 July 1892 (PP).
21. *'Aboard the Galley', *National Observer,* 3 Sept. 1892 (PP).
22. *'Deus Terminus', *National Observer*, 1 Oct. 1892 (PP).
23. 'Cradle Song', *National Observer*, 8 Oct. 1892.
24. *'Concerning Ghosts', *National Observer*, 5 Nov. 1892.
25. *'Orion', *National Observer*, 12 Nov. 1892 (PP).
26. *'The Lost Centaur', *National Observer*, 26 Nov. 1892 (PP).
27. *'An Autumn Encounter', *National Observer*, 11 Feb. 1893 (PP).
28. *'A Whitewashed Uncle', *National Observer*, 25 March 1893 (PP; GA).
29. 'The Finding of the Princess', *National Observer*, 20 May 1893 (PP; GA).

30. 'Young Adam Cupid', *National Observer*, 20 May 1893 (PP; GA).
31. 'The Burglars', *National Observer,* 24 June 1893 (PP; GA).
32. 'Snowbound', *National Observer*, 23 Sept. 1893 (PP; GA).
33. *'The Barn Door', *National Observer*, 28 Oct. 1893.
34. *Pagan Papers* (London: Elkin Mathews & John Lane). Published Oct. 1893, but dated 1894 on the fly-leaf.
35. 'What They Talked About', *National Observer*, 16 Dec. 1893 (GA).
36. *'The Triton's Conch', *National Observer*, 23 Dec. 1893.
37. 'A Harvesting', *National Observer*, 13 Jan. 1894 (GA).
38. 'Alarums and Excursions', *National Observer*, 10 Feb. 1894 (GA).
39. *'Pastels', *National Observer,* 17 Feb. 1894.
40. 'The Argonauts', *National Observer,* 10 March 1894 (GA).
41. *'An Old Master', *National Observer,* 24 March 1894.
42. 'Exit Tyrannus', *National Observer,* 28 April 1894 (GA).
43. 'The Roman Road', *The Yellow Book,* July 1894, pp. 211-26 (GA).
44. 'Sawdust and Sin', *National Observer,* 25 Aug. 1894 (GA).
45. 'The Headswoman', *The Yellow Book,* Oct. 1894, pp. 25-47 (Published in book form 1898).
46. 'The Blue Room', *Phil May's Illustrated Winter Annual,* Dec. 1894 (GA).
47. 'A Falling Out', *The Yellow Book*, Jan. 1895, pp. 195-201 (GA).
48. 'The Secret Drawer', *The Chapbook* (Chicago), 15 Jan. 1895 (GA).
49. 'A Holiday', *New Review,* Vol. 12, no. 70 (March 1895), pp. 225-31 (GA).
50. 'Lusisti Satis', *New Review,* Vol. 12, no. 70 (March 1895), pp. 231-5 (GA).
'A Holiday' and 'Lusisti Satis' were originally published under the common title 'In Arcady'. 'Lusisti Satis' was then called 'Satis Diu Lusisti', and ends at 'rot and humbug, and only fit for kids!', thus lacking the two final paragraphs which appear in *The Golden Age.*
51. *The Golden Age* (London: John Lane). Published Feb./March 1895.
52. 'The Inner Ear', *The Yellow Book,* April 1895, pp. 73-6.
53. 'Long Odds', *The Yellow Book,* July 1895, pp. 78-86.
54. 'The Iniquity of Oblivion', *The Yellow Book,* Oct. 1895, pp. 192-202.
55. 'The Twenty-first of October', *New Review,* Vol. 13, no. 77 (Oct. 1895), pp. 359-66 (DD).
56. 'Dies Irae', *The Yellow Book,* Jan. 1896, pp. 101-14 (DD).
57. 'Saturnia Regna', *New Review,* Vol. 14, no. 82 (March 1895), pp. 248-52.
58. 'Mutabile Semper', *New Review,* Vol. 14, no. 83 (April 1896), pp. 436-444 (DD).
59. 'The Magic Ring', *Scribner's Magazine,* Dec. 1896 (DD).
60. 'To Rollo, Untimely Taken' (poem), *The Yellow Book,* Jan. 1897, pp. 165-6.
61. 'Its Walls were as of Jasper', *Scribner's Magazine,* Aug. 1897 (DD).
62. 'The Invention of Fairyland' (review of Evelyn Sharp's *All the Way to Fairyland),* *Academy,* 18 Dec. 1897, p. 542.
63. *The Headswoman* (London: John Lane), Bodley Booklets, No. 5.
64. 'A Saga of the Seas', *Scribner's Magazine,* Aug. 1898 (DD).
65. Preface to Eugene Field's *Lullaby-Land*, pp. 713 (London: John Lane), 1898.
66. *Dream Days* (London: John Lane, The Bodley Head). Published Dec. 1898. Date on fly-leaf 1899.

67. 'The Reluctant Dragon', first published in DD (66).
68. 'A Departure', first published in DD (66).
69. Introduction to P. J. Billinghurst's *A Hundred Fables of Æsop* (translated by Sir Roger l'Estrange), pp. i-xv (London: John Lane, 1899).
70. 'The Fabric of the Fairy Tale' (review of children's books), *Daily Mail,* 16 Dec. 1899, p. 4.
71. 'The Mountain Stream' (poem), *Hull Weekly News,* 15 April 1905.
72. *The Wind in the Willows* (London: Methuen & Co.). Published Sept. 1908.
73. 'The Fellow That Goes Alone', *St Edward's School Chronicle,* Vol. 12, no. 321 (July 1913), pp. 270-1.
74. Preface to *The Cambridge Book of Poetry for Children* (1916), pp. xiii-xv (Cambridge U.P.).
75. 'Ideals' (lecture), *The Fortnightly Review,* Dec. 1922.
76. Preface ('Sanger and his Times') to 'Lord' George Sanger's *Seventy Years a Showman* (1926), pp. 5-29 (Dent).
77. 'Oxford through a Boy's Eyes', *Country Life,* 3 Dec. 1932.
78. 'A Dark Star' (lecture), *The Cornhill,* Vol. 74 (June 1933), pp. 649-67.

Undated and Miscellaneous Items

79. 'A Funeral', set up in proof for the *National Observer,* but never published. Probably *c.* 1890, printed by Chalmers, pp. 28-31.
80. 'Bertie's Escapade', written *c.* April 1907, and first printed by Chalmers, pp. 154-60.
81. 'Christmas' (poem), published by Chalmers pp. 165-6.
82. 'Lizard Lights' (poem), printed by Chalmers, p. 182.
83. 'Plate-Smashing and the Conjuror', published from MS by Chalmers pp. 209-10. The transcription contains numerous errors and omissions.
84. Letters to his Son: written in 1907, published in FW (1944), pp. 48-89, with photostat.
85. Letters to Austin Purves, 1908-15: published by Chalmers, with omissions, pp. 219-48.

Fragments still in MS and the extracts from the 'ledger-diary' which Chalmers cites, are not included in this Bibliography.

ACKNOWLEDGEMENTS

AUTHOR'S ACKNOWLEDGEMENTS
From the original edition of his biography

This book could never have been written without the most generous co-operation given me by the Executors of the late Lord Courtauld-Thomson. Elspeth Grahame, Kenneth's wife, was Lord Courtauld-Thomson's sister. When she died, shortly after the end of the last war, she left a vast mass of letters and documents, both her own and Kenneth's, which Lord Courtauld-Thomson preserved and sorted. This collection is stored at Dorneywood, the house he left to the nation. I wish here to express my gratitude to Mr John Fletcher and Mr John Wiltshire, who not only allowed me to remove original documents and examine them at my leisure, but also gave me every kind of practical advice and help in my search. This book is primarily based on the Courtauld-Thomson Collection, and I am deeply indebted to the Executors, both for permission to reproduce evidence from this source, and for allowing me free access to it in the first place. And I am grateful to the Secretary of the University Chest Office, Oxford, for permission to print hitherto unpublished Kenneth Grahame writings.

Many others have generously come to my assistance in various ways. To Mr John Grey Murray, I am indebted for the use of a room in Albemarle Street where I could research at leisure, and constant support and encouragement at every stage of my work. To Mr Roger Lancelyn Green I owe an especial debt: though he had long cherished the idea of writing about Grahame himself, he most generously put all his knowledge at my disposal when I asked for his help, and has allowed me to reproduce (with minor additions and modifications) the bibliography of Grahame's work which he originally published in *The Times Literary Supplement* on 9 June 1945.

I am also profoundly grateful to Mr Austin Purves, Jr, Mr Dale Purves, Mr Edmund R. Purves, Mr John C. Purves, and Mr Pierre M. Purves in America, all of whom wrote to me at great length and in most meticulous detail of their family friendship with the Grahames. To Mr Pierre M. Purves I am further indebted for most generously sending me photostats of Grahame's correspondence with his father, Austin Purves, which revealed passages omitted by Chalmers in his biography.

The late Mr L. A. G. Strong most generously allowed me to make use of his privately printed *Memoir* of Lord Courtauld-Thomson.

To Mrs Margery Newnham Davis I owe a special debt of gratitude: her voluntary help in secretarial matters has gone far beyond even the demands of literary *pietas*. Besides typing by far the larger part of my MS, she has helped me throughout with information, advice, encouragement, and occasional most welcome criticism.

I am grateful to all those who have allowed me to reproduce letters in their possession: Mr Charles E. Feinberg, Mr Richard G. Hubbard, the Rev. K. H. Jocelyn, Mr Alan W. Lidderdale (who also took me on a delightful expedition to Cookham Dene), Mr Kerrison Preston (the late Graham Robertson's literary executor), Mr Pierre M. Purves, and Miss Foy Quiller-Couch. For this, and much other help they have given me during my researches, I wish to express my thanks here.

I wish to thank, also, those many correspondents and witnesses who, by answering my queries, allowing themselves to be interviewed, and sending me unsolicited material, helped to piece together the mosaic of Kenneth Grahame's life, work, and background. These include the following: Lady Arundel; Dr Geoffrey Best, of Trinity Hall, Cambridge; Mr E. E. Bissell; Mrs Esther Boumphrey; Mr Spencer Curtis Brown; Mr Cyril Caddy; Mr John Connell; Miss J. L. G. Crookston; Mr A. W. Dascombe, the present Secretary of the Bank of England; Mrs Anna Debenham; Miss Kay Dick; Mrs Ellershaw; Mr Malcolm Elwin; Dr Anthony Feiling; Professor Sir Keith Feiling; Mr Lawrence Forbes; Mr Iain Fletcher, of the Faculty of Arts, Reading University; Dr Philip Gosse; Miss Hilda K. Grahame; Mr John K. Grahame; The Hon. C. Hope-Morley, the present owner of The Mount, Cookham Dene; Mrs Beatrice Horton; Mrs Florence Image; Mrs Kay Ingles; Miss Marjorie Ingles; the Keeper of Western MSS, Bodleian Library, Oxford; Miss Pamela Hansford Johnson; Mrs Ruth Lichtensteiger; Sir Compton and Lady Mackenzie; The Rev. J. A. B. Mercier; Miss Enid Mitchell; Mr A. E. Morgan, Warden of Toynbee Hall; The Hon. Hugh Fletcher Moulton; Mr Frederick Muller; Lt-Col. Arthur Newland; Mr Maxfield Parrish; Mrs Elsie Ricardo; Lady Rose; Mr Ernest H. Shepard; Mr H. A. Siepmann; Mr and Mrs L. Smith, who devoted so much time and ingenuity to obtaining such excellent photographs for me; Miss E. A. Soper; Mr Frank Swinnerton; Miss Barbara Euphan Todd; Miss A. S. Watts; Mrs Kathleen R. West; Mrs M. Hesketh Williams; Mr J. Alan White, Managing Director of Messrs Methuen & Co., Ltd; Mrs A. Vere Woodman; and Mrs Delia Wysard, who, besides giving me most valuable information, also entertained me most charmingly during my visit to Pangbourne.

For permission to quote copyright material I am greatly indebted to many authors, publishers, and executors, all of whom acceded to my requests with most courteous generosity. Quotations from Kenneth Grahame's *The Wind in the Willows* are made by kind permission of the Oxford University Chest and Messrs. Methuen & Co. Ltd, to whom I am further indebted for authority to quote from Patrick R. Chalmers' *Kenneth Grahame: Life, Letters and Unpublished Work,* Maurice Hewlett's *Letters,* A. A. Milne's Introduction to *Toad of Toad Hall,* and Elspeth Grahame's *First Whispers of 'The Wind in the Willows'.* For permission to quote both from Mrs Grahame's book and from her unpublished papers, my thanks are also due to her Executors (Lord Knollys, Mr John Fletcher, and Mr Gerald Russell) and the Dorneywood Trust: to them I owe a further debt of thanks for allowing me to quote from the late L. A. G. Strong's privately printed *Memoir* of Lord Courtauld-Thomson. Grahame's unpublished papers are reproduced by kind permission of Messrs Curtis Brown Ltd; to them, and to The Bodley Head, I am doubly grateful for permission to quote from all Grahame's published work with the exception of *The Wind in the Willows* and 'The Fellow That Goes Alone': the former is acknowledged above, and for the latter I am indebted to the Editor of the *St Edward's School Chronicle.*

For permission to quote from other copyright material my grateful thanks go to the following: The Bodley Head, for Oscar Burdett's *The Beardsley Period* and Evelyn Sharp's *Unfinished Adventure;* Dr David Daiches and New Directions, for Dr Daiches' R. L. Stevenson (copyright 1947 by New Directions. Reprinted by permission of New Directions); Mr J. E. Buckley and Princeton University Press, for Mr Buckley's *W. E. Henley;* Mr E. D. H. Johnson and Princeton University Press, for Mr Johnson's *The*

Alien Vision of Victorian Poetry; The Cambridge University Press, for Kenneth Grahame's Preface to *Poetry for Children,* and F. J. H. Darton's *Children's Books;* Messrs Jonathan Cape Ltd, for two quotations from A. E. Housman's poems; Messrs Constable & Co. Ltd, for J. L. Lowes' *The Road to Xanadu;* Mr Spencer Curtis Brown, for his father's, A Curtis Brown's, autobiography, *Contacts;* Mr Frank Duncaster, Editor of *The Old Lady,* for two articles by W. M. Acres and W. B. Hillkirk, originally published in that periodical; Mr Angus Davidson and Messrs John Murray (Publishers) Ltd, for Mr Davidson's *Edward Lear;* Mrs C. Day Lewis and Messrs Jonathan Cape Ltd, for extracts from Mr Day Lewis's sonnet-sequence *O Dreams, O Destinations*; Mr T. S. Eliot, O.M., Mr Louis MacNeice, and Messrs Faber & Faber Ltd., for extracts from Mr MacNeice's 'Eclogue for Christmas' and Mr Eliot's 'Burnt Norton' and 'The Waste Lane'; James Nisbet & Co. Ltd, for the Hon. Hugh Fletcher Moulton's *Life of Lord Moulton;* Messrs William Heinemann, Ltd, for Jane E. Courtney's *Recollected in Tranquillity;* Messrs Gerald Duckworth & Co. Ltd, for Constance Smedley's *Crusaders*; Mr Graham Hough and Messrs Duckworth, for Mr Hough's *The Last Romantics;* Messrs Macmillan & Co. Ltd, for W. B. Yeats' *Autobiographies* and *Collected Poems*; Mr John Marlowe and The Cresset Press, for Mr Marlowe's *The Puritan Tradition in English Life;* Mr Frank O'Connor and Messrs Hamish Hamilton Ltd, for Mr O'Connor's *The Mirror in the Roadway* and *Domestic Relations;* Mr Kerrison Preston and Messrs Hamish Hamilton Ltd, for Graham Robertson's *Letters;* The Oxford University Press, for R. C. K. Ensor's *England, 1870-1914,* R. G. Collingwood's *The New Leviathan,* and the first stanza of Gerard Manley Hopkins' 'Duns Scotus' Oxford', published in *Poems of Gerard Manley Hopkins;* Mr Alan Pryce-Jones, for his article 'Kenneth Grahame', published in *The London Mercury,* and in his capacity as Editor of *The Times Literary Supplement,* for permission to reproduce Mr Roger Lancelyn Green's bibliography of Grahame; Messrs Routledge & Kegan Paul Ltd, for Esmé Wingfield-Stratford's *Victorian Sunset* and *Victorian Aftermath;* Mr R. S. Thomas and Messrs Rupert Hart-Davis Ltd, for Mr Thomas's 'The Last of the Peasantry', published in *Song at the Year's Turning;* and Professor Lionel Trilling and Columbia University Press, for Professor Trilling's *Matthew Arnold.*

Chapter VI of the present work, 'The Rural Pan', first appeared, in a modified form, in *The Cornhill,* and I am grateful to the Editor for permission to reproduce it here.

This book was written, and much of the secondary research leading up to it conducted, in the Reading Room of the British Museum and, latterly, the Cambridge University Library. I would like to thank the staff of both those admirable institutions (who all too seldom receive the credit they so richly deserve) for their consistent courtesy and helpfulness. Without the facilities offered by these two great libraries, and—hardly less important—the Newspaper and Periodical Library at Colindale, this book could hardly have been begun, let alone brought to completion.

Lastly, I owe more than I can well express to my wife, who from the very beginning has encouraged and supported this project, and to whose kindly yet penetrating criticisms any virtues it may have are largely due.

PICTURE CREDITS

Signatures Limited have made every reasonable endeavour to trace the owners of copyright material used in *Beyond the Wild Wood.* Anyone who feels that they have a copyright claim should contact Signatures Limited, 24A Gandy Street, Exeter, Devon EX4 3LS.

The publishers wish to acknowledge the following:

Line illustrations by E.H. Shepard from *The Wind in the Willows*, copyright under the Berne Convention, reproduced by permission of Curtis Brown Ltd, London: 44, 55, 56, 107 bottom, 159, 162, 170, 171, 173, 211, back of jacket.
Illustrations by Maxfield Parrish and E.H. Shepard from *The Golden Age* and *Dream Days*, reproduced by permission of The Bodley Head Ltd, London: 18, 20, 105, 115, 116.
Colour plates by Arthur Rackham from *The Wind in the Willows*, reproduced by permission of The Heritage Press, Norwalk, Connecticut, USA: 26, 147, 148.

Portraits of John Lane and Henry Harland from *John Lane and the Nineties* by J. Lewis May, reproduced by permission of The Bodley Head Ltd, London: 98 top left and top right.

The publishers also wish to thank the following for supplying illustrations:

J & E Atkinson Ltd: 128 bottom; Berkshire County Libraries, Local History Collection: 172; British Newspaper Library: 111, 157; John Frost Historical Newspaper Service: 110; Dennis Hardley: 12, 13; The Raymond Mander and Joe Mitchenson Theatre Collection: 212; The Mansell Collection: 42, 60, 84 top left and top right, 144; National Portrait Gallery, London: 54; Noah's Ark Museum, Fowey: 125, 165; Oxfordshire County Libraries: 22, 35, 36, 37, 39 top and bottom, 63 89 top and bottom, 142, 186; Popperfoto: 73, 107, 205; Royal Institution of Cornwall, Truro: 71, 123, 128, 163; Signatures Ltd: endpapers, 63 top.

INDEX

Page numbers in *italics* refer to relevant illustrations.
All works listed are by Kenneth Grahame unless otherwise indicated.